Care Activism

Migrant Domestic Workers, Movement-Building, and Communities of Care

ETHEL TUNGOHAN

UNIVERSITY OF ILLINOIS PRESS
Urbana, Chicago, and Springfield

Library of Congress Cataloging-in-Publication Data
Names: Tungohan, Ethel, author.
Title: Care activism : migrant domestic workers, movement-
    building, and communities of care / Ethel Tungohan.
Identifiers: LCCN 2022061285 (print) | LCCN 2022061286
    (ebook) | ISBN 9780252045264 (cloth) | ISBN 9780252087400
    (paperback) | ISBN 9780252054785 (ebook)
Subjects: LCSH: Migrant labor--Canada. | Caregivers—
    Canada. | Foreign workers, Filipino—Canada.
Classification: LCC HD5856.C2 T86 2023 (print) | LCC HD5856.C2
    (ebook) | DDC 331.13/70440971—dc23/eng/20230221
LC record available at https://lccn.loc.gov/2022061285
LC ebook record available at https://lccn.loc.gov/2022061286

Care Activism

NATIONAL WOMEN'S STUDIES ASSOCIATION /
UNIVERSITY OF ILLINOIS PRESS FIRST BOOK PRIZE

A list of books in the series appears at the end of this book.

*I dedicate this book to the memory
of Petronila Cleto and Coco Diaz,
tireless migrant advocates whose spirit lives on
among the communities of migrant activists
that they built and nurtured.*

*I also dedicate this book to the memory
of my lola, Josefina Piguing Samonte.*

Contents

Acknowledgments

Acknowledging the community of care that surrounded me as I wrote this book is a daunting task. I have been tremendously lucky to have so many people who were rooting for me and this project, even when finishing it seemed impossible.

Thank you to the jury of the 2014 National Women's Studies Association (NWSA) Best Dissertation / First Book Prize. Thank you for your enthusiastic support for the project. Thank you to my University of Illinois Press editors, Dawn Durante and Dominique Moore, for championing the book. Dawn, I truly appreciate your encouragement from the very beginning of the project and your patient and thoughtful advice. Dominique, thank you for helping me see this project through. I am also very grateful to Dr. Salina Abji, who rescued this book project and provided incisive expert commentary. Salina, I am forever in your debt.

Parts of this book were presented at several academic conferences, including the annual conferences for the National Women's Studies Association, the American Political Science Association, the Canadian Political Science Association, and the Western Political Science Association. Thank you to all of the colleagues who commented on draft chapters. I also presented part of this book in plenary panels at the International Federation of Women's History and invited talks at the Global Labour Research Centre at York University, at the Department of Political Science at the University of Alberta, at the Department of Women, Gender and Sexuality Studies at Washington University in St. Louis, and at the Bell Chair Lecture Series at the Department of Political Science at Carleton University. Thank you to Mark Thomas, Siobhan Byrne, Rachel H. Brown, Eileen Boris, and Jonathan Malloy for giving me a space to engage with your respective communities about my work.

I am grateful for the generous and kind supervision of Joseph H. Carens and the advice given to me by Phil Triadafilopoulos and Audrey Macklin. Daiva Stasiulis and Abigail Bakan also provided wonderful insights. I also discussed parts of this project with my frequent collaborator, the always brilliant Yasmeen Abu-Laban.

I also benefited tremendously from the capable research assistance provided by Leny Rose Simbre and Beatrice Seardon. Thank you both so much for your work!

Care Activism is ultimately about dissident friendship. Had it not been for my feminist group chats (shout-out to Shaista Patel, Krittika Ghosh, Nisha Nath, and Mariam Georgis), which have been on the receiving end of many a complaint and ranting sessions—including rants about the interminable nature of book writing—my days would have been lonelier. Thank you to Andy Paras, Kara Santokie, Laura Kwak, Amelie Barras, Debra Thompson, Kelly Gordon, Suzanne Hindmarch, Jenny Wustenburg, and Stephanie Silverman for keeping me company during our writing retreats. Thank you to Louise from Thirteen Moons and Regina from the Moffat House for hosting many of these retreats.

The most inspiring memories I have in academia invariably involve my friends who are part of the Critical Filipinx Studies community. So many years have passed since we formed the Kritikal Kolektibo in 2008 and the Palimpsests conference in San Diego in 2017. Whenever I think back to those nascent conversations that led to Filipinos in Canada and other initiatives—including 2022's FilipiNext—I get inspired all over again. *Maraming salamat* to John Paul Catungal, Roland Coloma, Bonnie McElhinney, Conely de Leon, Von Totanes, Fritz Pino, Ilyan Ferrer, Monica Batac, Casey Mecija, Marissa Largo, May Ferrales, Maureen Mendoza, Valerie Francisco-Menchavez, Robyn Rodriguez, Gina Velasco, Nerissa Balce, Nora Angeles, and others for being incredibly inspiring.

My community of *kasamas* and *kaibigans*, comrades and friends, inspired me to write this book. Thank you to the women of Gabriela-Ontario: Tita Pet, Cynthia Palmaria, Conely de Leon, Mithi Esguerra, Jessica Ticar, Pinky Paglingayen, Jesusa Santos, Claire Provido, Roumela Soribello, Ate Ruth Dadivas, and others. Thank you to my Migrante-Alberta comrades: Marco Luciano, Mauriene

Tolentino, Clarizze Truscott, Mila Bongco, Poushali Mitra, Whitney Haynes, Vangie Cayanan, Novie Sambat, and Danilo De Leon.

A huge debt of gratitude goes from me to the powerful women who always speak truth to power, even when it is difficult: Tita Pura Velasco; Tita Erie Maestro; Tita Beth Dollaga; Ate Jayne Ordinario; Tita Tess Cusipag; Nanay Evelyn Calugay; Cecilia Diocson; Ate Maru Mesa; Ate Vilma Pagaduan; Tita Terry Olayta; Tita Martha Ocampo; the brilliant Kwentong Bayan Collective, Althea Balmes and JoSi Malaya Ocampo; Joms Salvador; Aimee Beboso; and many others. I stand in awe of your bravery.

And now, a thank you to family. Thank you to my little brother, Johann Tungohan, for your great sense of humor and for taking care of Cornelius. Thank you to Tita Grace Romero, Tito Buddy Romero, and Tintin and Medel Minoza for the love you showed my kids when I was in the Philippines and in Vancouver for research and had to leave the kids under your care! A special thanks to Tita G and Tito B for hosting me during fieldwork.

Thank you to my daughters, Winifred Tungohan-Chu and Georgina Tungohan-Chu. You accompanied me to countless meetings and gatherings and to protests and to conferences across Canada and in different countries. You were patient with your mama when I just had to take "one more minute" to finish what I was working on. To my rock, my best friend, my one true love, Wayne Chu, who first heard about the project when we were still graduate school friends and cheered me on over the years as I endeavored to finish the book. Thank you also for taking care of the children when I was researching and writing the book. Care work is work, and I know how challenging it sometimes was for you to be a solo parent so I could write.

The final and most important note of gratitude that I want to give, however, is to my parents, Leonides Fulgueras Tungohan and Arlene Samonte Tungohan. Our journey to Hong Kong and then to Canada was at times challenging. The moments I captured in this book sometimes reflect the moments that our family also went through. Settling in a new country is never easy, but both of you persisted. You built a beautiful life for me and Johann. Your unreserved and unconditional love saw me and Johann through so many challenges. Thank you.

Care Activism

Introduction

Care Activism and Communities of Care

On a blustery mid-September afternoon in 2017, fifty Filipina migrant caregivers gathered in front of Immigration, Refugees and Citizenship Canada (IRCC) offices in Toronto to protest ongoing family trauma caused by Canadian immigration policy. Holding placards decrying Canada's caregiver programs, the women who gathered were united in their anger and sadness over being kept apart from their children. While passersby observed, the caregivers chanted:

Canada, Canada, you're no good
Treat your workers like you should!

What do we want?
Our families reunited!
When do we want it?
Now!

In between chanting, migrant women gave speeches on how hard it was to be kept apart from their families. Caregiver activist Jocelyn Goderoy talked about how her daughter was ten years old when Goderoy first left the Philippines to work as a domestic worker in Hong Kong. At the time of the rally, her daughter was twenty-three. At that point, Goderoy had been waiting seven years for the Canadian government to process her citizenship application, which, if successful, would reunite her with her daughter. Following Goderoy, Shayne

Hontiveros, a community organizer whose mother was a caregiver, recounted how sad she was when her mother missed major milestones such as school graduations. In fact, to make her mother proud, Hontiveros worked hard in school to win academic medals, which she hoped would compel her mother to come home. When they finally reunited in Canada, her mother and her siblings took awhile to adjust to living together.

At the conclusion of their testimonies, the organizers invited everyone to a nearby coffee shop. Everyone shared a sense of accomplishment: not only did they take up space through their protests and make visible their otherwise hidden moments of grief, but it was also cathartic for everyone to listen to each other. When experienced in isolation, the everyday realities of family separation were painful. But when shared with a community of fellow caregivers, they became more bearable.

A key issue at stake for the caregivers was how to fight against the seemingly insurmountable challenges that they faced. Coming to Canada was initially appealing: Canada, unlike other countries, had a policy that allowed caregivers to apply for Canadian citizenship after completing their two-year live-in work contracts. However, the reality did not live up to their expectations. Among the many challenges they faced, the power of employers over their lives was a central issue. Unlike other nonimmigrant workers, employers' power over caregivers is magnified by a mandatory live-in requirement under the Live-In Caregiver Program (LCP, in place from 1992 until 2013), which at the time required that caregivers live in their employers' households. Moreover, caregivers' ability to eventually qualify for Canadian citizenship depended on their continued employment, a reality that many employers knew and used to their advantage. Ever-shifting policies set by the Canadian government meant that it was becoming increasingly hard to qualify for Canadian citizenship. The backlogs caregivers' citizenship applications faced, coupled with increasingly punitive interpretations of policies that led to their applications being rejected, contributed to their stress. These conditions worsened in 2020 and in 2021, during COVID-19, when many caregivers found themselves trapped at home with their employers and when pathways to acquire Canadian citizenship contracted. Underlying all of these challenges of acquiring citizenship were the structural realities that led rich countries like Canada to recruit care and domestic workers from developing countries like the Philippines.

It is therefore not surprising that the fifty caregivers who gathered that day in 2017 to protest the Canadian government's policies chanted "Canada, Canada, you're no good, treat your workers like you should!" In this book, I focus on the activism of migrant caregivers, as seen in the 2017 protest.[1] I call this type of activism "care activism," and I argue that it is an important yet overlooked form of activism among migrant justice movements. I define care activism as the distinct ways that migrant care workers care for themselves, for each other, for fellow migrant care workers in their immediate circles, and for the larger, transnational community of migrant care workers (and migrant workers). As a framework, care activism challenges stereotypical perceptions of abject, downtrodden, and long-suffering migrant care workers (Manalansan 2008).

The care activism that I showcase in this book also extends beyond political forms of organizing often favored in academic analysis. In contrast to other forms of worker organizing or migrant organizing, which focus on gaining political recognition of the needs of workers and migrants, care activism is fundamentally based on "communities of care" (Francisco-Menchavez 2018). Such communities of care extend beyond the local or even the present day to entrench relationships of care and accountability toward the migrant care workers who preceded them and those who come after.

The best example of how migrant care worker activists see each other not just as fellow activists but as part of a larger, affective support network is to consider how they refer to each other. Within Filipino migrant care worker organizations, a common way of addressing each other is to call each other *kasama*. While the English activist counterpart of kasama is "comrade," being a comrade denotes membership in the same organization; being a kasama, however, denotes something deeper. A kasama—loosely translated as "someone who is with you"—bears witness to your struggles and your successes, helps you meet your challenges, and is someone who is there in ways that even your family members cannot and should not be. Given the arduous realities of domestic work and life abroad, many migrant care workers do not wish to have their family members experience vicarious trauma when hearing about their struggles; only fellow migrant care workers, as kasamas, can relate and give support. Kasamas form close ties with each other, so much so that events organized by migrant care worker organizations can include personal celebrations such as birthday parties and gatherings for Christmas and Mother's Day. More than a comrade, kasamas create communities of care built on affective ties.

In what follows, I begin by outlining the framework of care activism that came out of the extensive ethnographic research I conducted between 2009 and 2021 in Canada and internationally. I then situate this framework within two important bodies of scholarship: research on migrant domestic workers' activism and more recent scholarship on "caring citizenship" and communities of care. In doing so, I show how the framework of care activism extends what we currently know about social movement organizing by emphasizing the important role of caregivers in leading and transforming the communities in which we live and work. The introduction ends with an overview of my methodology and an outline of the chapters in this book.

Care Activism as a Framework
for Social Movement Organizing

In this book, I argue that care activism challenges conventional understandings of social movement organizing by showing that migrant care worker activists desire more than just material improvements in their lives through policy changes and through overturning (and perhaps even abolishing) unjust power structures. Care activism involves creating communities of care that can help them and their families survive and even thrive despite arduous working and living conditions, prolonged family separation, and acrimonious experiences with family reunification. Hence, the goal of this book is not only to make visible migrant care workers' activism but also to illustrate the myriad ways that migrant care workers are involved in affective acts of caring that, at the heart of it, create new ways of knowing and of being.

The care activism that I study in this book is an extension of caregiving work and acts as a unifying force for care workers. The migrant care workers featured here had different approaches when reacting to migration challenges. At times, they were even at odds ideologically with each other. Yet what unified them was their engagement with care activism, which acted as an extension of the care work that they do daily. Rather than accepting, without question, societal devaluation of care and domestic work, the migrant care workers I spoke to all uniformly saw care work as being essential and believed that they—and their work—are important. In fact, from the time I first started working with the migrant care workers' movement in 2010 until the present moment of COVID-19 in 2021, which has laid bare just how essential care work is to society, I noticed how their care activism remained constant. Political contexts and policy environments may differ, and socioeconomic conditions may shift drastically, yet care workers' demands in different spaces and in different historical junctures remained the same: that care work be accorded the respect it deserves, that they and their families be treated with dignity, and that they be cared for in much the same way as they care for other people.

Paying attention to care activism requires that one recognize the power and agency of migrant caregivers. Indeed, despite lacking formal citizenship in Canada, migrant care workers did not let this stop them from seeking policy and structural changes. The chapters in this book describe many moments of caregiver power, describing the multiple ways that caregivers themselves resist their circumstances. They do so through small acts of microrebellions in their everyday lives and through their participation and leadership in the migrant caregivers' movement in Canada. By examining migrant care workers' participation in the politics of the everyday and the grassroots politics "from below" of movement activism, this book showcases the significance of migrant caregivers being at the forefront of migrant justice movements. My analysis in this book thus runs contrary to popular and academic depictions of caregivers as being abject and unknowing, which stem in part from long-standing colonial stereotypes of Global South women as downtrodden and oppressed (see, e.g., Mohanty 1991). My analysis is opposed to "damage-centered frameworks," which see migrant care workers being uniformly harmed. I use instead what Eve Tuck (2009) calls a "desire-based framework," which recognizes migrant care workers' humanity, including the oftentimes contradictory emotions that characterize their activism.

Unlike other actors whose participation in social movements may be driven, say, by a sense of moral obligation, feelings of solidarity, and shared interest, migrant care workers have the embodied and experiential knowledges of the inequities of global economic structures and care migration policies that then prompt within them a desire for change. Migrant care worker activists, for example, demanded changes that were in line with other migrant, feminist, and labor movements and often worked in solidarity with these movements. Nevertheless, the migrant care worker organizations that I worked with prioritized centering the needs of migrant care workers themselves. This book highlights how migrant caregiver activists use their embodied knowledge of oppressive structures and institutions to disrupt the status quo.

The framework of care activism that I develop in this book also draws attention to covert sites of resistance. Indeed, a primary intervention that I make in this book is to showcase sites of resistance that are oftentimes sidelined in academic analyses in favor of research on public protest actions that are driven by the need to change policies and shift discourses. Migrant domestic workers' activism encompasses conventional modes of protest and artistic endeavors, such as the use of art and beauty pageants as forms of protest, and religious interventions, such as the creation of a migrants' "stations of the cross." Equally important, it also involves everyday resistances, such as microrebellions in the workplace, the creation of community networks, and practices of transnational mothering. The formation of these affective care networks as seen through the creation of spaces of care, support, and spectacle (i.e., beauty pageants) is not, as some social movement scholars might assume, a "distraction" from the larger fight. By turning its analytical gaze onto these diverse sites of protest, this book provides a nuanced understanding of migrant caregivers' agency within and against oppressive power structures and state institutions.

Extending Research on
Migrant Domestic Workers' Activism

There have been, of course, a number of important texts that document migrant domestic workers' activism in different spaces, from the national to the transnational. Premilla Nadasen's (2016) compelling text, *Household Workers Unite: The Untold Story of African American Women Who Built a Movement*, presents a rich and vivid picture of how Black women in the United States created a movement representing domestic workers through the use of storytelling, thereby creating bonds of solidarity among different domestic workers. Such bonds of solidarity led to the creation of organizations such as the National Committee on Household Employment, which sought labor protections for domestic workers. Kim England (2017), Sheila Bapat (2014), and Nancy Perez (2017) have also provided detailed examinations of how migrant domestic workers organized themselves as a political force in the United States, leading to activist successes such as stronger labor protections, as seen through the domestic workers' bill of rights. Yet other researchers have discussed the formation of migrant care and domestic worker organizations in other national contexts, all leading to substantial labor-related victories (see, e.g., Bridget Anderson [2010] and Zhe Jiang and Marek Korczynski [2016] on migrant domestic worker organizing in England; Kudakwashe Vanyoro [2021] on migrant domestic workers' fight for labor rights in South Africa; and Eva-Maria Hochreuther [2019] on migrant domestic workers' political activism in Lebanon).

Researchers have also examined migrant domestic worker activism in regional and transnational forums. Helen Schwenken (2005) assesses migrant domestic worker activism within the European Union, looking at the debates among migrant domestic worker activists on whether to frame their demands through the rubric of "domestic slavery" or through "workers' rights." Domestic workers' efforts to secure international legal recognition for their labor rights within the International Labour Organization were vividly documented in three groundbreaking texts: Jennifer N. Fish's *Domestic Workers of the World Unite! A Global Movement for Dignity and Human Rights* (2017), which uses participatory research spanning six years to show how migrant domestic worker activists organized themselves and ultimately secured the passage of the Domestic Workers Convention (Convention 189; see International Labour Organization

2011); Adelle Blackett's *Everyday Transgressions: Domestic Workers' Transnational Challenge to International Labor Law* (2019), which juxtaposes accounts of domestic worker activism with Blackett's legal assessment, as the chief legal architect of Convention 189, of how the convention itself transgresses the "law of the household workplace" to create an international legal document enshrining the labor rights of domestic workers; and Eileen Boris's *Making the Woman Worker: Precarious Labor and the Fight for Global Standards, 1919–2019* (2019), which documents the creation of global labor standards in relation to women's work, including Convention 189 and the centrality of domestic workers in helping pass this convention.

There are, in addition, researchers who compare different sites of migrant care worker activism, seeing this as evidence of "globalization from below." Nicola Piper (2005, 2006) explains the complications that emerge when migrant care worker organizing becomes a cause assumed by both migrant organizations and trade unions, both of which have overlapping but ultimately divergent end goals. While migrant organizations are not limited to traditional modes of union organizing and are arguably better equipped to deal with the issues faced by migrant care workers, they are also "limited-member organizations" without access to a permanent funding base, unlike unions (Piper 2005, 108). She argues that despite these differences, "transnationalism from below" can best represent the needs of migrant care workers if migrant organizations and labor unions work together. Such cooperation is especially needed in light of states' indifference when tasked with creating national legislation that would protect migrant care workers. The ability of these two types of organizations to work together at the transnational level can, at the very least, shame states into compliance.

Similarly, Ligaya Lindio-McGovern (2007) shows how migrant domestic worker advocacy organizations challenge existing power structures. She traces how "circuits of resistance" operate in response to "interlocking power structures" into which migrant care workers' lives are "enmeshed" by interviewing migrant activists representing organizations in Hong Kong, Taipei, Rome, Vancouver, Chicago, and Manila (19). Lindio-McGovern discovered that such circuits of resistance target other "centers of power" that "may include employment agencies or traders . . . state bureaucracies . . . [and] the IMF and the WTO" (17). She argues that while "neo-liberalism divides and isolates workers as a tool to disempower them," workers respond in turn through "public, collective resistance" (19).

Piper and Lindio-McGovern show that there is globalization from above, which facilitates the migration of women from developing countries into developed countries to assume precarious work. Then there is globalization from below, which illustrates how migrant women's reactions to these economic imperatives lead them to form movements that allow them to fight for their rights and to influence public policies.

What these assorted works capture powerfully are the manifold tactics used by migrant care workers to ensure labor protections and to critique the inequalities wrought by the state and by neoliberal institutions. The authors above detail the efforts that migrant domestic workers put into ensuring that their voices get heard, even when the odds of them being heard were minimal. This was especially clear, for instance, in Fish's (2017) account of how migrant domestic workers strategized to ensure that the creation of a convention on domestic work was placed on the agenda of the International Labour Organization conference. In this book, I address similar tactics when I examine how migrant care worker activists sought political recognition in Canada and in other countries, in transnational spaces such as the ILO and the International Migrants Alliance (IMA), and even within their places of employment.

This book is an extension of these works in that it provides further support for the argument that migrant care workers' activism is crucial in enshrining legislative victories. However, this book also departs from these works by looking at how care itself—and not only the need for material improvements—is at the heart of care activism. Although it is true that migrant care workers mobilize to ensure that their labor rights are recognized and that their claims to legal citizenship are acknowledged, to see care activism as being the sum total of these claims for recognition is to miss a crucial part of the story. By creating "communities of care" for themselves and their families (Francisco-Menchavez 2018) both within and between state borders, migrant care worker activists go beyond making political demands. As kasamas, they are not necessarily "sisters," a term that does not resonate in this context because of the forced imposition of kinship relations that hides power imbalances and that universalizes gender struggles as the crucial site of solidarity (Qi 2010, 329). Instead, the networks of care and support that they form is more aptly described as an example of "dissident friendships."

The migrant care worker activists in this research are not just comrades in solidarity with each other but also dissident friends. I am inspired by Elora Halim Chowdhury and Liz Philipose's (2016) reflections on the subversive potential of dissident friendships. Dissident friendship is different from sisterhood, a concept that antiracist, postcolonial, and transnational feminists have long critiqued as being a colonial construction that imposes "rescue" narratives. Instead, dissident friendships are fundamentally grounded in subversion.

8

As Chowdhury and Philipose note, "Friendship is an important impulse that counters fear and speaks truth to power in a unique way by embodying and experiencing human and heart-centered connections.... [I]n friendship, then, is our resistance to the divisive and fragmenting lies of structural power; the seeds of global compassion, generosity, empathy, and love; and the foundation of a world that works on behalf of life" (2016, 4, emphasis added).

Dissident friendships are rooted in practices of affirmation, support, and witnessing; in "being there" and showing up for each other; and on collective forms of resistance. Friendship, particularly in a context where forming relationships with each other is difficult and can in fact be deemed threatening to the status quo, becomes a political act when it is formed and persists. Michael P. Brown's (1997) discussion of queer friendships formed during the HIV/AIDS crisis and the revolutionary potential of "being there" for each other is a similar example of how dissident friendships are political.

The migrant care workers in this book who lead migrant movements were not only in solidarity with each other. In collectively striving for a more just world, they created communities of care where they provided support and dissident friendships for each other in ways that sending states, receiving states, and other activist organizations could not or would not. In what follows, I engage with more recent scholarship on caring citizenship to help situate communities of care as a key component of care activism.

"Caring Citizenship" and Communities of Care

In centering practices of care, migrant care worker activists grounded their work in forms of "caring citizenship" (Mingol 2013). As a feminist approach to citizenship that values relationality, caring citizenship has its roots in a relational ethics of care approach where normative questions of justice are interpreted not from an individualist framework but from an approach that sees human beings as being interconnected with each other (Mingol 2013; Tronto 2013; Nedelsky 2011). Contrasted frequently with an ethics of justice approach that has at its core the autonomous, "rights-seeking" individual, ethics of care sees human beings as being embedded in communities and as thus always being in relationship with each other (Gilligan 1982). Rather than seeing human beings as individuals with distinct and oftentimes adversarial interests, ethics of care theorists see human beings as all having caring needs. As Joan Tronto (2013) has long asserted, all human beings at different points in their lives need care. Valuing care more than, say, profit is a way to create a more humane society—a more "caring democracy" (Tronto 2013).

Valuing care rather than profit means that the importance of reproductive forms of labor (as opposed to productive or market and profit-based forms of labor) becomes clearer. Doing so draws attention to gendered forms of paid and unpaid care work that are routinely invisibilized and devalued in society, showing that society cannot actually function without care work and care workers. Thus, "implicit in the moral maturity of the 'ethics of care' is a more committed, responsible, and interconnected citizenship," that is, a caring citizenship (Mingol 2013, 409).

As a concept, caring citizenship puts together an ethics of care approach that illuminates the essential role care and care workers play with discussions on active citizenship (Sevenhuijsen 2003). "Caring citizenship" creates space for those who have conventionally played the role of caregivers (i.e., women) to participate in public deliberations about policy priorities and societal values without being seen as having a "fixed caring identity," adding depth and nuance to these discussions by bringing in the perspectives of those who see relationality as central to human life (Sevenhuijsen 2003, 15). A frequent critique of the ethics of care is that it reinforces essentialist notions of gender identity, where "carers" (i.e., women) are seen as being more consensus driven and thus able to facilitate more harmonious deliberations. In contrast, "caring citizenship" acknowledges that centering care and its related values of "attentiveness, responsibility, competence, responsiveness, trust and asymmetrical reciprocity" (Sevenhuijsen 2003, 179) can benefit everyone by ensuring that social policies are evaluated from this standpoint. The context of the global health pandemic makes clear, in fact, that more robust notions of "caring citizenship" are warranted, given how entire countries' healthcare infrastructures have been unable to accommodate an increased demand in healthcare services after decades of neoliberal austerity that led to increased defunding of the public sector and to cuts. If care becomes the central value animating policy decisions, one wonders what, then, the world would look like (Fine and Tronto 2020; Allen, Jenkins, and Howard 2020).

In fact, "caring citizenship" widens the ambit of democratic participation to encourage human beings to be more collectively engaged with civic life, encouraging a more active form of democracy (Tronto 2013; Mingol 2013). Practices of "caring citizenship" abound, from various peace-building movements led by women globally such as the Argentine Mothers and Grandmothers of the Plaza de Mayo, the National Coordination of Widows of Guatemala, and the Committee of Mothers of the Disappeared in El Salvador to transnational consortiums such as the Women's International League for Peace and Freedom. Caring citizenship thus envisions a world where care is centered (Mingol 2013).

In advancing a care activism framework, I argue that the contemporary migrant care workers' movement exemplifies "caring citizenship." Led by migrant care workers who are embedded in multiple relationships of care domestically and transnationally, migrant care worker activists make advocacy decisions not only from an individual standpoint but also while taking into account the standpoints of others in their community. For example, evaluating changes in immigration policies is seen not only from the perspective of individual migrants but also from the standpoint of how these consequences will create a ripple effect and affect the lives of individual migrants' families and communities. In addition, ethos of relationality are practiced in organizational proceedings. Decisions are not imposed from the top down; instead, they emerge collectively, accounting for everyone's insights.

As I show in the book, practices of caring citizenship extend beyond organizational practices. Within these organizations, migrant care workers create communities of care by being each other's kasamas. When understanding migrant care workers' formation of communities of care, Valerie Francisco-Menchavez's (2018) work is key to unpacking these dynamics. Her discussion of the communities of care she witnessed among Filipina domestic workers' organizations shows how acts of care take place not only between domestic workers but also between transnational family members and within the larger community of domestic workers. Communities of care are "a form of reorganizing care, from migrants to other migrants informed by their transnational familial context. . . . [T]his horizontal care among migrants is configured socially rather than biologically, [relying] on the subjectivities produced by the liminality of migrancy, undocumentation and precariousness as the social sphere in which they care for one another" (Francisco-Menchavez 2018, 97). Francisco-Menchavez's ethnography of Filipina domestic worker organizations in New York consequently shows how affective acts of care extend to each other, as seen when fellow domestic workers bear witness to each other's life journeys and frequently replicate family dynamics by using familial terms of respect such as *ate* (older sister) and *tita* (auntie). Such acts of care also extend to each other's families, as seen when fellow domestic workers become "other mothers" for their kasamas and even for other migrant domestic workers whom they do not personally know, as seen when they fundraised to send money to the relatives of a deceased Filipina domestic worker (Francisco-Menchavez 2018).

Care activism expands current notions of caring citizenship. I explore this activism in two major ways: first, by showing how migrant care worker activists' creation of communities of care extends beyond the nation-state to encompass a transnational community of fellow migrant care workers; and second, by showing how activists' caring citizenship extends even beyond the current temporal moment to include previous and future migrant care workers and their families. Care activism therefore extends toward one's "imagined community" (Anderson 1983) of present-day fellow care workers, encompassing migrant care workers and their families who have experienced and will experience the same challenges in the future. "Why am I active in these organizations?" Adela, a migrant care worker whose narrative forms part of this book, once mused. "Well, because I want to continue doing the work that previous generations of care workers did for us. I want to fight for me and my family and for caregivers today. I am also trying to fight for future caregivers and their families. I hope that what I go through won't be what they go through."

In seeing the lineage of past, current, and future migrant care worker activists as being connected by similar struggles, these activists show that one's imagined community of care is not limited to the present day. Seen this way, care activism is a praxis of caring for and being accountable to migrant care workers and their families historically, now, and in the future.

Methodological Approach

The book uses feminist interpretivist methodology. It places at the center migrant care workers' own interpretations of their narratives and their understanding of key events in their advocacy engagements (Schwartz-Shea and Yanow 2011). The data gathered for this book span from 2009, when I first chose to examine migrant domestic worker movements in Canada as part of my doctoral work, until the early part of 2022, during a time of heightened attention to care and migration under the COVID-19 pandemic.[2] Over this period, I used a mix of different methods to gather data, from archival research at the Canadian National Archives and the Canadian Women's Movement Archives in Ottawa and policy and documentary analysis of government documents (including but not limited to ministerial briefing notes, policy papers, and ministerial speeches) to critical ethnography.

I define "critical ethnography" as a mode of immersion into communities where I saw myself not as a detached observer but as an observant participant (Moeran 2009). As part of my ethnography, I conducted one-on-one interviews with migrant care worker activists and their allies, interviewing a total of 136 activists in the Canadian cities of Vancouver, Toronto, and Montreal (103 in total); in Geneva during the International Labour Organization meetings concerning the creation of a convention on domestic work; in Manila during the 2010 International Migrants Alliance meetings; and in fieldwork in Singapore,

Hong Kong, and the Philippines in 2010 and in 2017 (33 in total).[3] The vast majority of the women whose narratives formed the basis for this book are Filipina (122 in total), a proportion that is reflective of how Filipina migrants constitute 90 percent of all migrant care workers in Canada.

When interviewing, I used Lee Ann Fujii's (2018) approach to relational interviewing, which sees interviews as ongoing conversations. Such an approach does not see the purpose of interviews as extracting information from respondents but rather as understanding "how [respondents] make sense of the world by engaging them in dialogue" (Fujii 2018, 8). The data then come from "this intersection rather than interrogation" (8). Some of these interviews spanned one meeting, while others spanned a formal interview and then subsequent "catch-up" conversations.

As a critical ethnographer and as a socially engaged researcher, I was clear to the migrant care worker activists whom I spoke to and the leaders whom I worked with that my political commitments involved migrant justice. This meant that whenever organizations needed my help, whether through booking classrooms for their meetings, leading workshops to explain to domestic workers and other migrant workers how policy changes impacted them, and testifying in Canada's House of Commons to discuss the potential repercussions of said policy changes, I stepped in, always careful to be self-reflexive when doing so. In keeping with critical ethnographic ethos, I attended numerous consultations, meetings, rallies, caregiver beauty pageants, theatrical productions featuring migrant domestic workers, potlucks, parties, and other events organized by migrant domestic workers. I went to spaces in these cities where domestic workers gathered even when there were no organized events.

My purpose when conducting fieldwork in Geneva and in Manila during International Labour Organization and International Migrants Alliance meetings was to see how the migrant care workers whom I knew and followed in Canada became active in calling attention to their concerns in transnational forums. I was less interested in the transnational dynamics that informed these deliberations. I went to Geneva, Switzerland, in June 2010 and in 2011 during the discussions on the creation of a Convention of Domestic Work at the annual International Labour Conference. I examined how the same migrant organizations that were present in Geneva participated in grassroots transnational migrant justice assemblies. Consequently, in 2011 I attended the International League of Peoples' Struggles (ILPS) conference in Manila, the Philippines. Because the ILPS is a broad umbrella of different social justice organizations, I opted to attend the IMA meetings, which some of the same organizations that were present in Geneva also attended.

When I was in Hong Kong, Singapore, and the Philippines, I spent time in the offices of migrant organizations and visited a shelter for abused migrant workers. I also hung out and spoke with migrant domestic workers during their days off, spending time in sites where migrant domestic workers gathered, such as Lucky Plaza in Singapore and Victoria Park and Central in Hong Kong. In the Philippines, I visited Migrante-International and Gabriela-International's headquarters in Quezon City, conversing with migrant activists about their work, including those who recently returned from stints as migrant domestic workers.

The question of positionality now emerges. I take to heart Roland Coloma's advocacy of a "constitutive approach to subject formation" that "refuses to present subjects as essences, resists the separation and hierarchy of positions, and develops new spaces for more complex, contingent, and contextualized positions" (2008, 21). Hence, I discuss issues of positionality to highlight the complications of insider/outsider status and to clarify how my standpoints may have influenced the arguments I am making.

As a Filipina scholar who lived in Hong Kong and who later immigrated to Canada, I know firsthand that Filipinas were associated with migrant domestic workers. Growing up in Hong Kong, I experienced nearly daily acts of discrimination because I was visibly Filipina. I also understood that class privilege insulated me from the harsh policies facing domestic workers in Hong Kong. Since my mother was, at that time, the executive director of the Bayanihan Trust, which is an organization that provided services for Filipina domestic workers, I spent many Sundays at the Bayanihan Centre, where I hung out with and spoke to Filipina domestic workers. I came of age in this community of women, who shared food and stories. I heard about their families back home and saw pictures of their children, nieces, and nephews whom they were sending to school. It is difficult for me to truly capture the collective strength derived through community felt by the women I knew in Hong Kong and those whom I later encountered in my research. I appreciated being able to bear witness to these women's moments of strength even when they faced arduous living and working conditions and underwent horrific personal struggles.

Upon moving to Canada, where my family and I immigrated in 1999, I noticed that migrant care work was also present here. But care work in Canada was strangely rendered both hypervisible and invisible: hypervisible in the sense that there were occasionally panicked mainstream media articles about Filipina nannies and their distress and invisible in that the essential labor that migrant care workers undertook remained largely unacknowledged, a point that my coeditors and I unpack in *Filipinos in Canada: Disturbing Invisibility* (Coloma et al., 2012). Hence, my research on migrant caregiver resistance was born out of these personal experiences and out of a desire to capture the microacts of resistance and grassroots organizing that I kept observing. I had to navigate being both a community insider who is conversant in Tagalog and who understands the dynamics of migrant care work through decades of conversations with migrant care workers and an outsider who is not herself a migrant care worker.

Ultimately, I am not "neutral" when writing about migrant care worker activism. I see migrant care workers' activism as being rooted in individuals', families', and communities' assorted attempts to rectify long-standing structural, workplace, and community-level inequities. More importantly, their activism is born out of their conviction of the centrality of care in their work: these women believe that subversive and revolutionary care is manifested by being there for each other and for the larger community of migrant care worker activists surrounding them. It is a conviction that I share.

Book Overview and Chapter Previews

Care is woven into every facet of migrant care workers' lives. They are paid to be direct care workers who are intimately involved in the everyday lives of their employers by helping them with acts of daily living (i.e., eating, bathing, and taking medication; these workers may also supervise the schoolwork of employers' children and clean employers' homes), help that often frees employers' family members to find paid employment outside the home. Indeed, "we work so they can work," is a common observation that migrant care workers shared with me. They are also caregivers across borders for their families and their community members back home and for a labor brokerage state that exports workers to different global regions (Rodriguez 2010). Despite living several time zones away, many continue to be involved in their families' daily lives not only by sending remittances to support household expenses and educational and career goals but also by supervising household tasks and giving advice from afar. They additionally care for fellow migrant care workers. By forming dissident friendships, they care for each other by providing support when needed and by celebrating and mourning different life events. Such care, of course, is also witnessed in their advocacy work. Campaigns for policy change and for the abolition of interlocking structures of power that lead to the export of labor are, at the heart of it, grounded in the need to care for migrant care workers and their families in the present and in the future.

This book takes readers on a journey that critically examines various moments of care activism. It shows how care workers center affect and relationality, where their ambit of care extends toward each other and toward previous, current-day, and future care workers and their families. Rather than simply participating in an activist organization because of the political conviction that migrant care workers need to be treated fairly, the care workers in this book see their leadership and participation in these groups as the ultimate act of caring for the larger community of care workers. They see themselves as being tied together by shared life experiences and recognize each other as human beings with individual needs and desires. The stakes are therefore much higher, given their own lived experiences as care workers: care activism is ultimately grounded in the creation of bonds of solidarity that are rooted in care because migrant care workers recognize all too well the challenges that migrant care workers and their families face and how important it is to be there emotionally. The strength of affective ties being established is why, in many spaces, fictive kinship becomes the norm in migrant care activist circles, with migrant care workers calling each other *ate* (older sister), *nanay* (mother), or *kapatid* (sibling). Care activism is thus distinct from other forms of activism because of the intimacy wrought by a shared understanding between migrant care worker activists of what precisely migrant care work entails and of what migrant care workers and their families need.

Care is the unifying thread that cuts across different moments of care activism. This book accordingly traces Canadian-based migrant care worker organizations' advocacy efforts in Canada (chapters 1 and 2) and in transnational spaces (chapter 3). It then analyzes migrant care worker activism in other countries to see how different national contexts might affect the type of activist engagements that migrant care workers pursue (chapter 4). Finally, it looks at everyday manifestations of migrant care activism, examining how individual migrant care worker activists practice care activism in their daily lives (chapter 5).

Chapter 1, "Contextualizing Care Activism," assesses the history of migrant care worker organizing in Canada, weaving together an overview of key policies on migrant care work alongside migrant care worker organizations' responses. Within this analysis, one can see that every single instance of policy change that is grounded in improving migrant care workers' lives in Canada came in part because of care activism. Migrant care activists saw care for each other and for their imagined community of past, present, and future migrant care workers as being central in their work. Migrant care worker activists saw the deep injustices woven into their own experiences with abusive employers and recruiters, their invisibilization in the policy landscape, and their separation from their families. This chapter, of course, makes clear that there are deep-seated ideological divisions between migrant care worker organizations. In other words, the migrant care workers' movement is far from being unified. Despite these differences, however, their demands for change is fundamentally rooted in their care for their fellow migrant care workers.

Chapter 2, "Care Activism within Migrant Advocacy Organizations," delves into the specific tactics and goals of key organizations, analyzing their histories, their activities, and their normative visions. It analyzes the interviews I undertook with leaders and members of key organizations, most of whom provided oral life histories that prompted them to get involved in organizing work. It also discusses the tactics used by different groups to get their voices heard. It draws a contrast between organizations that deliberately take a more militant approach where marching in rallies and being vocal in condemning the Canadian government and other stakeholders are commonplace; those that see negotiating with the government in a less confrontational manner as being more effective; and those that specifically call themselves "nonpolitical" by choosing deliberately to disengage from more visible spaces of advocacy such as marching in the streets or considering the impacts of specific policy changes. I show how these organizations, while prioritizing care for migrant care workers as the crux of their advocacy work, nevertheless have different definitions of what such care looks like, and these definitions in turn shape their organizing strategies.

Chapter 3, "Scaling Up Care Activism in Transnational Spaces," discusses transnational organizing by two migrant caregiver organizations in Canada. It focuses specifically on their participation in the deliberations in 2010 and in 2011 leading up to the creation of the Convention on Domestic Work and the 2011 International Migrants Alliance. It addresses the dynamics that these organizations encountered in transnational spaces and highlights the various negotiations representatives of these organizations had to make when considering what care and care activism should look like when scaled up.

Chapter 4, "Care Activism in the Philippines, Hong Kong, and Singapore," scrutinizes how migrant care worker organizations care for migrant care workers within different policy contexts. It shows how migrant care workers care for each other when they are seen primarily as remittance senders and not as human agents (as in the case of the Philippines, as a migrant-sending state) when facing policy environments where there are ample openings for civic involvement but where permanent residency rights remain elusive (as in the case of Hong Kong) and when there are draconian restrictions against migrant mobility and migrant organizing (as in the case of Singapore).

Chapter 5, "Everyday Care Activism," shifts away from the organization-level focus of previous chapters by examining migrant care workers' everyday engagements with care activism in their individual lives. By looking at individual migrant care workers' everyday forms of activism, the chapter uses a "desire-based" framework (Tuck 2009) to show that migrant care workers' ambitions, hopes, dreams, and desires for themselves and for their families motivate their attempts to subvert stereotypes regarding the inevitably "tragic" circumstances of their lives (Manalansan 2008). It looks at how migrant care workers navigate live-in care work, their relationships with their children and their partners, and their daily encounters with other figures such as immigration officials. It assesses, too, the diverse (and at times contradictory) ways that migrant care workers deliberately and strategically uphold care work not only as being empowering and therefore worthy of pride but also as only constituting a small part of who they are. They shift discourses surrounding migrant care work by participating in covert acts of workplace rebellion, participating in beauty pageants, and even making jokes with each other about their existing realities. They do these with fellow care workers as a way to form community, where they bond with each other as a result of shared experiences. Through these everyday engagements with care activism, what is clear is that migrant care workers are continuously thinking of how their interventions can impact other migrant care workers.

The conclusion, "Toward a Politics of Critical Hope and Care," considers the future of care activism. Can there be a politics of critical hope in light of the persistence of global inequalities and structural disparities between Global North and Global South countries? The conclusion lays the foundation for arguing in favor of placing care and critical hope at the center not only of migrant care worker organizing but also of other progressive social movements.

At the heart of migrant care workers' advocacy agendas is their conviction that they should care for each other and for an imagined community of previous, present, and future care workers. In an environment where migrant care workers are always seen as serving others, including sending and receiving states and their employers' families and their families, centering care for themselves and for their fellow migrant care workers becomes a subversive and political act. The migrant care workers whose narratives and whose experiences form the core of this book showed in manifold and at times contradictory ways how they embodied care activism.

Chapter 1

Contextualizing Care Activism

COCO DIAZ: We decided that it was insufficient to only meet [migrant care workers] once they faced problems. We needed to do something, so what we did was, we lobbied for the support of all levels of the government, from the federal to the provincial to the municipal. The federal and the provincial went hand in hand; workers work in provinces, so the province has to protect their labor rights, but the federal government is also in charge of the program. So doing joint campaigns at these levels of government became a key part of Intercede's work.

PURA VELASCO: We wrote letters, which we sent to different government officials. We would picket the Liberal Party headquarters. We would picket in front of Immigration Canada offices. We were always there. At that time, too, there was a regular monthly meeting that Intercede would do at the Cecil Community Center. And the membership at that time of Intercede was three thousand. And no less than a thousand would attend meetings monthly. Can you imagine? We did not invite other people to make our marches, our pickets bigger, because we could do it and sustain it on our own. We were big enough and visible enough.

PETRONILA CLETO: If you don't claim your rights, nobody claims it for you. The government gives you the law, but no one will enforce the law for you, no one will claim your rights for you.

Care activism for migrant care worker activists involved winning policy victories that would improve the lives of migrant care workers and their families. Given that migrant care workers know, through their own experiences, how restrictive these policies can be, seeking policy improvements was vital. Migrant care worker activists have been at the forefront of lobbying Canadian policymakers to improve policies on migrant care work. In the interview excerpts above, Filipina activists Coco Diaz, Pura Velasco, and Petronila Cleto describe the work of Intercede, an organization that was founded in 1979 by feminist academics and lawyers to lobby for justice for migrant domestic workers, who at that time did not have the right to settle in Canada permanently. As longtime activists in the movement who came to Canada as migrant care workers, Diaz and Velasco were strategic when lobbying the Canadian government for policy changes, alternating between protesting in front of government offices one day and writing letters and holding one-on-one meetings with government officials the next. With the support of thousands of migrant domestic workers and their allies, organizations such as Intercede fought vigorously on behalf of migrant domestic workers, eventually leading to policy victories.

Among the most important of these victories was winning migrant domestic workers the right to apply for Canadian citizenship in 1982 following the establishment of the Foreign Domestics Movement (FDM). Accessing Canadian citizenship was important for migrant domestic workers because they could make plans to be in Canada with their families in the long term, which also signified greater economic security, especially when considering rampant economic inequities in their home countries. Winning a concession from the Canadian state by acquiring the automatic right to apply for Canadian citizenship was therefore a huge win against the state. Yet securing pathways to permanent residency in Canada was, for migrant care workers, not grounds to stop with their activist work. In fact, from the time migrant care workers first arrived in Canada until the present day, their organizing has been part of Canada's activist landscape. In part because of ever-increasing permanent residency requirements that curtailed their ability to apply for permanent residency, migrant care workers have continued to organize for change.

This chapter weaves together an overview of care activism among migrant care workers in Canada alongside developments in Canada's migrant care worker policies. While I recognize that migrant domestic workers arrived in Canada prior to the 1900s, my archival research revealed recorded instances of migrant organizing starting in 1913. When examining migrant care workers' activist interventions from 1913 until 2021, I could see that policy changes that were grounded in improving migrant care workers' lives all came in part because migrant care workers mobilized. Migrant care worker activists like Coco Diaz and Pura Velasco all saw the deep injustices woven into their own experiences with abusive employers and recruiters, their invisibilization in the policy landscape, and their separation from their families. Yet there were also deep-seated ideological divisions between Intercede and other migrant care worker organizations. Despite these differences, however, care activism remained a unifying framework for understanding activists' political organizing.

Although organizations that support migrant care workers have existed for as long as Canada has recruited domestic workers from abroad, there have been periods when migrant care worker activism is heightened. Namely, "transformative events" (McAdam and Sewell 2001) catalyze movement organizing, functioning as key moments in present-day migrant care worker activists' construction of the genealogy of the movement. In particular, the migrant care workers' movement in Canada considers as a transformative event the campaign led by the seven Jamaican mothers, which later inspired workers to create the slogan "good enough to work, good enough to stay." Likewise, the Juana Tejada law, which drew attention to the bodily harm and health concerns facing migrant care workers, is often considered a transformative event. I discuss both below.

A key theme in this chapter is the important legacy of care activism. There is a symbiotic, circular relationship between the Canadian state and migrant movements. Every time the Canadian government passes policies in relation to migrant domestic work, migrant domestic workers mobilize in response; in turn, the Canadian government is susceptible to the pressures exerted by migrant care worker activists. Alongside policy victories, the role that key movement leaders have played in ushering communities of care for today's migrant care workers has been a source of inspiration for migrant care activists in later decades, with many of them seeing their roles as building on this robust legacy of care activism. Migrant care workers who were movement leaders in previous historical periods and those who were active in the contemporary period all saw care for each other and for their imagined community of past, present, and future migrant care workers as being central in their work. While there were divisions among migrant caregiver organizations on the basis of strategies and "appropriate" action, the question of abolition versus reform, and activist scope, a fundamental belief in "shared fate" and the necessity of caring for each other occasionally helped overcome deep-seated ideological divisions, leading to short-term coalitions across various activist organizations.

Empire Settlement and the
Caribbean Domestics Movement, 1900–1981

In Canada, migrant care workers have historically been relied upon to provide care work. A racial hierarchy from most to least desirable has long existed, with Europeans on top and Asian and Caribbean women at the bottom (Bakan and Stasiulis 1997).

European women, primarily from England, Ireland, and Finland, came to Canada as nannies, nursemaids, and governesses from the eighteenth to the early twentieth century (Macklin 1992; Sharpe 2001).[1] Their value primarily lay in the role they played in Canada's settler-colonial project, which hinged on the dispossession of Indigenous territories (Green 2017). European domestics were initially recruited as domestic workers and then later became the wives of white settlers, enabling, in particular, the rapid settlement of western provinces; as one newspaper editorial published in a British Columbia newspaper put it, "Good servants make excellent wives to poor men" (as quoted in Perry 1997, 513).

In the middle of the twentieth century, the Canadian government widened its reach and recruited migrant care workers from other parts of Europe, giving them permanent residency status automatically. As a settler colony, however, Canada nevertheless subscribed to a belief that there were certain "races" of women who were more desirable. Women from different European countries were ranked: western European women ranked above central and eastern European women, Spanish women, and Greek women. British women were seen as ideal nation-builders, whereas central, eastern, and southern European women were deemed less desirable. As I discuss in the next section, non-European women (i.e., women from the Caribbean and, later, Asian countries) were at the bottom of this racial hierarchy and were initially seen as not deserving of the right to get Canadian citizenship upon arrival. Canada permitted domestic workers' entry into Canada under the Empire Settlement Plan (Iacovetta 1992; Barber 1991). The placement of migrant care workers in this hierarchy affected the way they were treated. For example, eastern European migrant domestic workers were given lower wages compared to their British counterparts (Barber 1991, 16).

Similar to today, the conditions surrounding care work were oftentimes exploitative, with migrant care workers complaining about abysmal labor standards that led them to be paid poorly and irregularly and that also ensured that they lacked privacy. These experiences led numerous European care workers to take part in covert actions to express agency, or what I call "microrebellions."

Workers were aware of the limitations of their circumstances and strategically ensured that their interests within the workplace were met by finding oftentimes surreptitious ways for their employers to respect their rights. For example, Franca Iacovetta's description of Italian domestics having relatively more mobility showed just how much more power these women had in comparison to migrant care workers who came in later migrant care worker streams: "What most irritated employers and officers alike were the acts of defiance committed by domestics who complained about their job placements, demanded job transfers, or abandoned their posts for more appealing prospects. Their apparently cavalier approach offended the sensibilities of Canadian employers and officials who had expected young Italian women to act submissively" (1992, 43). In the same way, Finnish migrant care workers' ability to organize on behalf of their interests through microrebellions and through their decision to join organizations such as the Socialist Party—which in some cases had its membership rosters consisting primarily of Finnish migrant women—showed the extent to which migrant care workers were able to represent themselves (Lindström-Best 1988).

European migrant care workers were also driven to establish organizations to represent their interests. Research conducted at the Canadian National Archives revealed two such organizations. The first was the formation in 1913 in British Columbia of the Home and Domestic Employees Union, which called for a nine-hour workday limit, a minimum wage (Epstein 1980, 7), and "recognition as a body of industrial workers—they hoped eventually to establish a union hiring hall where employers would directly contract workers . . . [and] to someday lease a building for a co-operative rooming house where they could live in healthy surroundings and enjoy a social life" (Rosenthal 1979, 50). (The women's dream to have a space of their own where they could form their own communities reflects, in fact, the ambitions of other organizations, as I discuss in chapter 2.) The second was the Domestic Workers Union Local 91, again in British Columbia, which made the same demands (Epstein 1980, 7). Meeting minutes reveal that organizers were driven by a conviction that they needed to care for fellow domestic workers, whose work would otherwise remain unrecognized. More crucially, both unions saw that organizing on the basis of shared class interests was important (Rosenthal 1979, 52). Both organizations dissolved years after they were founded due in part to the difficulty of organizing domestic workers who were isolated in their employers' households, faced long working hours, and worked for various employers and thus could not directly bargain for better working condition with a single supervisor. Nevertheless, these organizations set the stage for later attempts at organizing.

European migrant care workers engaged in protest actions periodically in the early to mid-1900s to draw attention to their substandard working conditions. Specifically, they protested against "grueling tasks, poor working conditions, lack of privacy, non-specific job descriptions, and sexual harassment" (Sealy 1991, 2). It is important to note, however, that these women were already Canadian permanent residents and were not tied to their employers in the same way as the Caribbean and Filipina migrant care workers who would follow under subsequent programs. This residency status likely gave the women more latitude to dissent.

Compared to European domestic workers, Caribbean migrant domestic workers, who came to dominate domestic service after European women, were subjected to greater labor restrictions.[2] Domestic service was one of the few industries open to Caribbean women (Calliste 1989; Henry 1998). The 1910s saw Caribbean women coming to Canada as care workers. Some employers, in fact, saw them as being better workers compared to European migrant care workers and even local workers, who were supposedly not as docile and compliant.[3] Yet the federal government subsequently barred Caribbean domestic workers' entry into Canada for "physical and moral reasons," preferring instead to recruit European women (Barber 1991, 14).

It was only in the middle of the twentieth century that the Canadian government revisited its stance. Since Caribbean workers were considered "reserve laborers," Canadian immigration authorities loosened immigration criteria for them to come into Canada during the two World Wars, when Canada was facing a labor shortage. The Canadian government allowed Caribbean workers entry into Canada on a temporary "trial" basis (Henry 1998, 71).[4] The entry of more Canadian women into the workforce from 1945 to 1955 led to a care gap. This care gap, coupled with the perception among some Canadian employers that European domestic workers were being too disruptive on account of their participation in protest actions, led employers to lobby the Canadian government to permit the entry of more Caribbean domestic workers (Sealy 1991, 2). These employers saw Caribbean women as "more desirable" because they were perceived as being easier to control. As Abigail Bakan and Daiva Stasiulis (2005) note, whenever migrant care workers from specific racial communities became marked as "protestors," employers tended to recruit workers from other racial communities whom they perceived as being more docile.

Nevertheless, while Canadian employers saw Caribbean women as being suited to domestic service, the perception that they were not fit for permanent entry into Canada because they remained reserve laborers affected their access to permanent settlement. Unlike immigration recruitment schemes for

European migrant care workers, who came to the country as immigrants, Caribbean women were only allowed into Canada under the Caribbean Domestics Scheme (CDS), which was established in 1955 as a bilateral trade agreement between Canada, Barbados, and Jamaica. Canada gave "financial aid" to these countries in the form of the remittances that Caribbean domestics sent back to their countries. In exchange, Canadians benefited from Caribbean domestics' labor (CADIW 1977, 3). Caribbean countries saw the economic benefits of exporting labor and viewed remittances as being tied to a development strategy.[5]

Other factors motivated the establishment of the CDS. During this time period, Caribbean government officials expressed their unhappiness over the Canadian government's exclusionary policies toward Caribbean citizens, prompting Canadian trade commissioners based in the Caribbean to push for a "more tolerant immigration policy . . . that would permit the entry of a restricted number of people from the Caribbean without regard to their ethnic origins" (Calliste 1992, 90). Canadian officials feared losing access to the region if they did not adopt such a policy, perceiving it as crucial to Canada's economic interests. Programs such as the CDS that allowed Caribbean nationals limited access to Canada appeased Caribbean government officials and helped Canada to continue trading and investing in the region (90).

Under the CDS, Caribbean women were given Canadian permanent residency with the requirement that they worked one year in domestic service (Henry 1968, 83). They were monitored regularly, subjected to frequent pregnancy tests, and paid less compared to their European counterparts. Significantly, this scheme asked prospective applicants to fulfill criteria that European women were not asked to meet. This problematic practice was noted by Caribbean domestic workers at the time. For example, Antonia Sealy (1991) from the Barbados Association of Canada came to Canada from Barbados under this scheme. Later, she contacted fellow domestic workers recruited under this program to get more information on their experiences. While all domestic workers faced harsh working conditions, she observed that the way Caribbean women were "bound by contract" made them more vulnerable:

> Any of the concerns expressed here [about domestic work] would apply to women and particularly to poor mainstream, Native, Black, and other visible minority women working under similar conditions but these women were not bound by contract or by legal situations. And, of course, people born in a country have an edge, though a very thin one, on those immigrating into a country. Many Caribbean women have never accepted the fact that Domestic Schemes were not designed in their favour or in their Government's favour

but rather to profit the Government and the employers of the host country Canada and its capitalistic economy. (Sealy 1991, 1)

Sealy further added that Caribbean domestics' specific experiences during the mid-1900s have effectively been erased from history, leading her to dub this cohort the "forgotten women" (1991, 1). The onerous requirements Caribbean women were subjected to under the Caribbean Domestics Scheme—in contrast to European women, who faced greater mobility rights and who additionally were given the protections of Canadian citizenship—led Sealy to conclude that having Caribbean women assimilate into Canadian society was never a policy priority for the Canadian government. If anything, Caribbean domestics were seen as providing labor as servants and not much else.

Frances Henry's interviews with Caribbean domestic workers affirm these findings, with many women sharing with her that they were socially isolated and experienced "downward social mobility," which carried over even after they finished the program, with many employers reluctant to hire "maids" (1968, 88). They even experienced stigma among the Caribbean community in Canada, with some organizations (e.g., the Jamaican association) reluctant to be associated with domestic workers "because they never associate with domestic workers back home" (89). Other domestic workers nevertheless formed and found refuge in diasporic organizations, with the Trinidad and Tobago Association and the St. Vincent and St. Lucia Association providing support for domestic workers (89). The presence of these organizations somewhat insulated migrant domestic workers from the racism that they faced regularly.

It is thus clear from such analysis that arguments pertaining to individuals' ability to assimilate into Canadian society have affected the way migrant care workers from different racial groups were perceived. Indeed, the argument by immigration activists that "race and ethnicity have played a very important part, over about gender and class, in shaping the status and conditions of domestic workers" rings true in this case (Arat-Koc 1997, 78). Migrants' racial attributes and countries of origin determine the type of work they are seen as doing, subsequently explaining why European women were more likely to be seen by members of the Canadian public and Canadian policymakers as nursemaids and women of color as servants.

There were attempts in the 1960s and the 1970s to eliminate such racial and cultural criteria. The persistence of discriminatory immigration criteria led Canadian and international critics to decry Canadian racism, which in turn led to the move to the "skills-based admissions system" in 1962 (Triadafilopoulos 2010, 182). Prime Minister Lester B. Pearson's white paper on immigration, published in 1966, indicted racial and cultural discrimination and endorsed an immigration system that allowed individuals without "discrimination by reason of race, colour and religion" (Canada Manpower and Immigration 1966, 6). At the same time, however, Pearson also saw immigration as a way to bolster the Canadian economy. Skilled migrants were preferred to unskilled migrants because the former were seen as crucial to bolstering the Canadian economy (Canada Manpower and Immigration 1966). Canadian immigration policy has since been structured according to the twin goals of attracting a diverse populace and improving Canada's economic standing, though it is clear that because of the way migrants are classified on the basis of "skill," the latter is prioritized. In short, economics was ultimately the most crucial consideration, which critics such as Lisa Marie Jacubowski (2003) and Nandita Sharma (2006) hold has been reinforced by pervasive racial and cultural preferences. According to these scholars, the contradictions inherent in having a racially and culturally blind immigration policy that simultaneously saw the need to attract immigrants with the best economic prospects masked the way economic suitability was also racially and culturally coded. However, they hold that because immigration criteria were now couched in the language of economics, it is initially difficult to understand how racial bias continues despite such economic "neutrality."

The points system—founded in 1967 and formally enshrined in 1976— ranked migrants using "objective" criteria that prioritized migrants who were deemed to have high potential in bolstering the Canadian economy. Formulated under the leadership of Deputy Minister of Manpower and Immigration Tom Kent, the points system was devised to respond to critics of the white paper, who questioned how "criteria relative to education and skills could be applied to without a clearly defined set of standards" (Triadafilopoulos 2010, 183). This ultimately led to an immigration system that government officials felt balanced the importance of Canada being able to regulate immigration flows while also heeding the need for nondiscriminatory and universal immigration criteria.

That said, while the points system permitted the entry of multitudes of skilled migrants, it was unable to meet Canada's care-giving needs. Rather than considering potential migrant care work contributions as a permanent and ongoing need, Canadian officials deemed such labor unskilled because of the low status care work has been accorded traditionally. As Audrey Macklin explains in support of her suggestion that the points system be challenged through section 15 of the Canadian Charter of Rights and Freedoms, the points system "systematically devalues the skills required for domestic work because of its status as 'women's work.' . . . [T]he skills deployed in 'women's work' are disregarded, discounted, or denied because they are treated as inherent to women and therefore not acquired abilities deserving of recognition, much less compensation" (1992, 741–42). Macklin further argues that the points system's focus on skill, as opposed to other factors such as occupational demand, the applicant's aptitude and experience, and even the availability of concrete job offers at the time of the application, prohibits migrant care workers from coming to Canada as landed immigrants (743).

Technically, the Temporary Employment Authorization Program, founded in 1973, allowed migrant domestics entering Canada under this scheme to apply for permanent residency. They were, however, "effectively barred" from doing so because the low wages they were paid as domestic workers made it difficult for them to meet the points system's criteria of showing "economic self-sufficiency" (Khan 2009, 26). Magnifying the scheme's restrictiveness were regulations that migrant care workers seeking to change employers had to do so with permission from Canadian immigration officials (Barber 1991, 24; Ramirez 1982, 90). The absence of any regulatory body ensuring that migrant care workers' labor rights were protected added to the abuse migrant care workers faced (Barber 1991, 24). Figures from this time period show that migrant care workers stayed for an average of three years and were then sent home (Ramirez 1982, 90).

Abuse against migrant care workers became so endemic that members of the Canadian public began to take notice. Numerous migrant caregiver organizations emerged at this time. These included Women Working with Immigrant Women, founded in Toronto in 1975; the Association pour la défense des droits du personnel domestique de Montreal, founded in Montreal in 1975 and later renamed the Association des aides familiales du Québec (AAFQ) in 1998; the Labour Advocacy and Research Association (LARA), founded in Vancouver in 1977 and which became the first organization to campaign for the inclusion of care and domestic work in the Labour Act; the Ad-Hoc Committee on Domestic Workers' Rights, founded in Toronto in 1977 and which was part of the Filipino advocacy organization Kababayan Community Centre (KCC); Intercede; and the British Columbia Domestics Association, founded in Vancouver in 1979.

The creation of these organizations was crucial in instilling political awareness among migrant care workers. Discussing how migrant domestic workers felt after one of LARA's meetings, Rachel Epstein observed: "For the first time, people were describing the often horrendous stories of their treatment in Canada and there was the exhilaration of finding other people with similar anecdotes and experiences. People were also starting to learn about the few rights they have and in some instances started to deal individually with their exploitation" (1980, 8). In some cases, these awareness-raising sessions inspired some women to launch formal complaints to Canadian immigration officials, find better employment, and be active in campaigning for policy changes.

Raising migrant care workers' political consciousness was crucial in compelling migrant domestic workers to take action against unjust policies. Because there was rising awareness of the injustices facing migrant domestic workers and a political climate that saw the visibility of feminist and antiracist organizing, the belief that migrant caregiver programs were exploitative and needed to be changed hardened. For instance, the Ad-Hoc Committee on Domestic Workers' Rights began agitating on behalf of migrant care workers. It campaigned for permanent residency for all migrant care workers, "inclusion in the Employment Standards Act and Ontario Human Rights Code, full coverage under the Workers' Compensation Act, and the Right to Organize under the Labour Relations Act" (Root 2008, 50–51). To make their demands public, its members, which included migrant caregiver activists Fely Villasin and Ging Hernandez, disseminated leaflets to the Canadian public outlining their concerns, wrote press releases, marched in the streets, and lobbied policymakers for these changes. The committee also sought to publicize cases that illustrated the circumstances facing migrant care workers.

One such case involved Elizabeth Lodge, Carmen Hyde, Eliza Cox, Elaine Peart, Rubena Whyte, Gloria Lawrence, and Lola Anderson. In a highly publicized case in 1978, the seven women faced a deportation order after Canadian immigration officials charged them with misrepresenting their marital status and the number of children they had in order to gain entry into Canada as migrant domestic workers under the Caribbean Domestics Scheme (Lawson 2013). Rather than accepting their deportation orders, the seven women, who were dubbed the "seven Jamaican mothers," resisted the "gendered racialization of their labour in Canada" (Lawson 2013, 149) and their disposability. As Elaine Peart observed, "We were brought here to clean rich folks' homes and now we're not cleaning rich folks' home, you want to throw us out" (Peart quoted on 140).

The experiences of these women soon captured the interests of the Black community in Canada. During this time period, there was a growing awareness of the pervasiveness of anti-Black racism, especially following the Toronto police's killing of a twenty-four-year-old Black man named Andrew Evans in 1978 (Lawson 2013, 50). The case of the seven Jamaican mothers, when looked at alongside Evans's case, catalyzed the Black community. In addition, fellow migrant domestic workers were also inspired by the women. For them, what made the seven Jamaican mothers' case especially unjust was the fact that the

Jamaican government and the Canadian government tacitly encouraged such misrepresentation (142).

As word of the plight of these seven Jamaican mothers spread, migrant worker activists in Vancouver, Ottawa, and Montreal spearheaded their own campaigns to give the women landed status and to change the terms of the Temporary Employment Authorization Program. A new organization called the Committee Against the Deportation of Immigrant Women (CADIW), consisting of members of the Black community in Canada, migrant care workers, and feminist allies, was formed in 1977 in Toronto (CADIW 1978). Not only did CADIW organize a fundraising drive to support the seven Jamaican mothers' legal costs, it also organized rallies, held press conferences where members spoke about the plight of the seven Jamaican mothers and emphasized that their situations were commonplace among migrant care workers, lobbied government officials directly, and disseminated position papers. In one such position paper, CADIW (1978) made it clear that the raids that led to the Jamaican mothers being apprehended had become a common occurrence because immigrants were being blamed for the economic crisis taking place at that time. CADIW also emphasized the gendered nature of these raids, stressing that its members had personally experienced being physically and sexually harassed by immigration officials into disclosing information that would lead to the arrests of so-called illegal immigrants (1977, 1). In the end, the public pressure campaign worked. Six out of the seven Jamaican mothers were eventually allowed to stay in Canada through minister's permits, showing how activist mobilization was successful.

Mobilization efforts undertaken on behalf of the seven Jamaican mothers were the first documented evidence of migrant domestic workers coming together in support of fellow migrant domestic workers and widespread social mobilization on their behalf. While it is true that prior to this time period, individuals and even organizations were formed to support migrant domestic workers, these microrebellions did not "scale up" and lead to a mass movement (Pero and Solomos 2010). In contrast, the collective efforts that were undertaken on behalf of the seven Jamaican mothers were decisive in entrenching the idea that migrant domestic workers have specific interests and subsequently have a "movement" representing them. This was a transformative event that defined the migrant care workers movement in Canada, oftentimes being seen as the origin story of the movement.

The Foreign Domestics Movement, 1981–1991

The seven Jamaican mothers campaign galvanized other migrant care workers who were not happy with how the mothers received Canadian permanent residency as an exception to the long-standing rule forbidding migrant care workers from settling in Canada permanently. The refusal of the government to shift policies in this regard served as further ammunition for migrant care workers to continue to organize for policy changes. It was during this time that migrant care workers first conceived of the slogan "good enough to work, good enough to stay." Brandishing this slogan, migrant caregiver organizations, Filipino and Caribbean community members, and even sympathetic members of the Canadian public waged numerous protests.

The first protest included a demonstration in front of Canadian immigration offices in Toronto (Ramirez 1982, 89). Another one was held in front of a "high-class" Toronto restaurant where Liberal Party leaders had gathered, during which activists cornered immigration minister Lloyd Axworthy and gave him "thousands of protest letters" denouncing migrant care workers' hardships (90). Yet another protest was held in one of Toronto's public parks. It drew two hundred migrant care workers, most of whom were Filipino, but also protesters from countries as varied as Jamaica, the United Kingdom, and Ireland (Cusipag and Buenafe 1993, 152).

These demonstrations were not without controversy. Counterprotests were organized by the politically and socially conservative group Filipino Homemakers Association. During this protest, its members decried the activities of migrant caregiver activists by arguing that these activists would "rock the boat" and lead the Canadian government to abolish its migrant caregiver programs (Cusipag and Buenafe 1993, 152). Such sentiments, as I show later in this chapter, reflect the beliefs of conservative migrant caregiver organizations in the importance of maintaining a "good" relationship with the Canadian government.

Aside from rallies across Canadian cities, migrant care worker organizations continuously lobbied policymakers. Members of Intercede, for example, contacted organizations that they deemed sympathetic to their cause and urged them to return a form letter written by Intercede indicating their support for Intercede's policy suggestions. In this letter, Intercede emphasized three demands: (1) it wanted migrant care workers to be given the ability to apply for landed immigrant status, (2) it wanted work contracts signed by the federal government and migrant care workers' employers to be "legal and binding," and (3) it wanted the provincial government of Ontario to include migrant care workers in minimum wage legislation.[6] Intercede also demanded that "domestic workers," "baby-sitters," and "elderly companions" be placed under the same job category, arguing that the exemption of the latter two occupations from the Employment Standards Act was egregious when all three entailed the same responsibilities.[7]

The activists at Intercede wanted to care for current migrant care workers who withstood abysmal labor conditions in order to care for their families at home by sending remittances. Intercede organizers were also trying to care for future care workers so they would have an easier time in Canada. According to Intercede's executive meeting minutes on May 14, 1980, this letter campaign was extremely successful and yielded substantial donations from various feminist, labor, and religious organizations.[8]

Other organizations joined Intercede in lobbying the government. For the Filipino community, activists who fled the Philippines in opposition to the dictator, Ferdinand Marcos, founded organizations that supported prodemocracy movements in the Philippines. Because of their prodemocracy and social justice orientation, this work then evolved into migrant advocacy. In Vancouver, the anti-Marcos organization, the International Association of Filipino Patriots, formed a subcommittee called the Committee for the Advancement of the Rights of Domestic Workers (CARDWO), which not only provided services for migrant domestic workers by giving them immigration and labor advice and holding social events but also lobbied the Canadian government for landed status (Epstein 1980, 12). One of CARDWO's mandates was to ensure that migrant domestic workers themselves participated in these lobbying efforts, so a substantial portion of its activities involved leadership training for migrant care workers to "chair meetings, write articles and speeches, and speak publicly" (12).

Another organization, initially called the International Committee Against Racism (INCAR) and later called the Domestic Worker's Union (DWU), was also formed in Vancouver in 1980 (Epstein 1980, 12). The goal of the organization, which consisted of migrant domestic workers from different ethnic groups, was to form a union, which meant that its organizational structure resembled a trade union. Nevertheless, its efforts to form a union were unsuccessful, and in its brief existence, the DWU lent its support to CARDWO's campaign for landed immigrant status (12).

Rather than working separately, these organizations coordinated their efforts. Referring again to Intercede's meeting minutes on June 9, 1980, it is clear that members of Intercede were in close contact with other allied groups to discuss the steps they needed to take to launch a national campaign. These organizations gathered in Ottawa in May 1980 during the first ever conference of migrant caregiver organizations in Canada, where they networked and coordinated their lobbying activities.[9] Those who attended the conference also met then Minister of Immigration Lloyd Axworthy to discuss their concerns, during which they emphasized the importance of giving migrant domestic workers permanent residency (Ramirez 1982, 90). The concerns they raised were then integrated into the 1980 report written by the Canadian government's Task Force on Immigration Practices (Bakan and Stasiulis 1997).

These mass mobilization efforts eventually culminated in the creation of the Foreign Domestics Movement (FDM) in 1981. Not only was the movement able to galvanize support from migrant care workers, it was also able to win over members of the Canadian public on its side. Intercede's Coco Diaz, who at that time was a migrant caregiver, reflected on the key events that led to the creation of the FDM: "It was a great moment. We all came together—all of us from different organizations—and fought hard to get recognized. Even though there were some who were scared that we were asking for 'too much,' we never wavered in our call. We wanted citizenship and we got it."[10] Indeed, the pervasive, positive coverage of migrant caregiver organizations' campaigns in national, local, and ethnic presses helped in this regard.[11]

While the creation of the FDM was a major victory for the Canadian migrant care workers' movement, for Diaz and her fellow migrant care workers, it was not enough. Although government officials later lauded these changes as evidence that they were responsive to migrant care workers' needs, migrant care workers were disappointed that the changes did not fully give them what they sought and in fact hampered their security, as outlined below.

The migrant care worker activists whom I interviewed were unified in their understanding of the FDM's shortcomings. The Canadian government acknowledged that migrant domestic workers were made vulnerable by their temporary status and that they also made important labor contributions to Canada. Yet, due to ongoing stigma against racialized groups, the government wanted to maintain control over the entry of "suitable" groups. Consequently, the government has ensured that migrant care workers did not get permanent status automatically. They could only apply for permanent residency after twenty-four months of continuous live-in employment in the same household, which was then followed by a "post-entry" evaluation that assessed migrants' "suitability" and "self-sufficiency" (Daenzar 1997). The FDM's restriction of migrant care workers' mobility rights by tying them to one employer was a further cause of concern for activists, who saw the mandatory live-in requirement as making migrant care workers more vulnerable to employer abuse. Activists were especially vocal about their opposition to federal immigration requirements asking migrant care workers to provide letters of reference from their employers when applying for permanent residency, because they saw this as heightening opportunities for employers to blackmail migrant care workers. They were also wary of the immense power the FDM gave to federal immigration officials, who ultimately judged whether migrant care workers' applications for permanent residency were valid. Because the application process commonly involved interviews with a federal immigration official, activists were concerned about the arbitrariness of the decision-making process.

For Intercede, the reality that the FDM enabled the continued abuse of migrant domestic workers by heightening the power employers had over domestic workers meant that it needed to move away from being a grassroots organization to one that has a set funding base. To do so, Intercede applied and received a grant from the Canadian government—an "imprimatur of legitimacy," claimed former Intercede member Judy Fudge (1997)—and widened its membership roster to include more migrant care workers. Upon receiving funding, Intercede was able to hire full-time staff, including counselors who gave migrant care workers pro-bono advice. According to Diaz, "From 1981 to 1984, domestic workers just went wherever; we met them at churches and in random meetings. Only then did we hear about their problems."

Following consultations with migrant care workers, Intercede developed new campaigns for the improvement of the FDM. Calling the FDM "a first step, rather than a final solution," Intercede sent then Ontario Labour Minister Russell Ramsey policy recommendations seeking the inclusion of all migrant care workers into standard minimum wage regulations, a limit to the amount of money employers were allowed to deduct from migrant care workers' wages for room and board, and set days off.[12]

Intercede also had national campaigns, such as its call to professionalize migrant care work. According to Diaz, members of Intercede saw the importance of professionalizing the program in order to recognize that migrant care workers were not "merely" housekeepers but rather undertook care work for children, disabled children and adults, and seniors: "This is a caregiving job. [Using the terms] 'housekeepers' or 'domestics' or 'nannies' don't show that there is significant human involvement—that human care is a significant part of the job."

Intercede also called for the abolition of the mandatory live-in requirement and asked that migrant care workers under the FDM be given permanent residency upon arrival.

During the 1980s Intercede became the voice of migrant care workers. Intercede was adamant in prioritizing migrant care workers in all of its activities. However, because of its visibility, Intercede had numerous detractors. Owners of employment agencies were especially scathing about its work. One such agent described Intercede's activities as follows:

> Intercede is basically like a union, and they want to protect domestic worker's rights. What they want to do is fine but they don't do it the right way.

They'll tell you all kinds of horror stories and you don't get the other side of the story. There have been employers' agencies and employers who want to help but they'll shun them. Intercede is mostly Filipino girls. But it's just radicals who are behind it. They have workshops that are completely negative. They'll do chants and things they make up. It's really just like a union. (quoted in Bakan and Stasiulis 1995, 327)

The Canadian Coalition for In-Home Child and Domestic Care (since renamed the Canadian Coalition for In-Home Care), formed in 1987 to oppose the strides being made by migrant care worker organizations such as Intercede, actively opposed the activities of migrant activists and campaigned in favor of making requirements more onerous for prospective migrant care workers to come to Canada. For example, it lobbied the government to increase educational requirements for migrant care workers to become eligible to come into Canada and asked that migrant care workers complete a training course first (Bakan and Stasiulis 1995, 328). Consisting primarily of employment agencies, this coalition therefore acted as a counterweight to migrant care worker activists' lobbying pursuits and made its own demands, which shifted policy. There were instances when its advocacy demands, along with groups such as the Association for Caregiver and Nanny Agencies (ACNA), directly contravened migrant domestic workers' interests.

The hardships migrant care workers suffered also inspired the formation of three key organizations: the West Coast Domestic Workers Association (WCDWA) in 1986, the Philippine Women's Centre (PWC) in 1989, the Vancouver Committee for Domestic Workers' and Caregivers' Rights in 1992, and Pinay in 1988 (although it only became known as Pinay in 1991).[13] The first three organizations were established in Vancouver, while Pinay was established in Montreal. All groups spent the first few years of their existence finding out more information about migrant care workers' experiences under the FDM and providing help for these women. Upon amassing more and more information about the exploitative conditions facing migrant care workers, the organizations initiated lobbying efforts and demanded that the Canadian government pay attention to the plight of migrant care workers. Like Intercede, they saw their work as a way to care for a group of workers whose interests were perpetually forgotten.

As a result of the lobbying efforts of these groups, federal immigration policymakers subsequently responded to these requests by conducting a wide-scale assessment of whether migrant care workers were able to perform their duties under the FDM in 1988. There was nowhere near the same level of mass mobilization compared to the late 1970s during the seven Jamaican mothers campaigns or even when compared to the early 1980s, when groups mobilized to obtain permanent residency for migrant care workers. Nevertheless, enough migrant care worker organizations had alerted the Canadian government of the FDM's deficiencies. Following this assessment, policymakers initiated a comprehensive policy review of the FDM, resulting in the creation of the Live-In Caregiver Program (LCP) in 1992.

The Live-In Caregiver Program, 1992–2014

Between 1992 and 2004 there were several key changes under the LCP. Unlike the FDM, the LCP no longer required potential applicants to show their self-sufficiency and ability to integrate into Canada. It raised the requirements for people to qualify for entry. In principle, it required applicants to have at least the equivalent of a Canadian grade 12 education and "six months of full time formal training in a field or occupation related to the job sought in Canada as a live-in caregiver" (Bakan and Stasiulis 1994, 15). In practice, it prioritized the entry of professionals with university degrees, as the activists whom I interviewed argued. The Canadian government's desire to "upgrade the quality of childcare" inspired this change (15).

A few of the activists whom I interviewed were at first cautiously supportive of certain measures. The elimination of the requirement mandating that potential permanent residents show proof of their self-sufficiency and their willingness to integrate into Canadian society by doing volunteer work or taking classes seemed positive because it took away what many activists saw as an unfair and unnecessary requirement in migrant care workers' applications for permanent residency. Of course, it should be noted that other activists observed how these voluntary and/or educational requirements at least forced migrant care workers not to be socially isolated and to interact with other people, thereby enhancing their integration in Canadian society. Terry Olayta, a longtime migrant care worker activist and the former chairperson of the First Ontario Alliance of Caregivers in Canada (FOACC), reflected on how taking classes while she was a migrant care worker not only helped her form social networks but also encouraged her to first become a migrant care worker activist.

These minor disagreements aside, these activists saw the explicit recognition of "care work," as opposed to "domestic work," as an important step when the LCP was first created, because this theoretically ensured that the care work they engaged in was considered a central component of their occupations. The seemingly semantic difference between being called a "domestic worker," which activists argued was mostly equated with menial labor, compared to being seen as a "caregiver" felt like an important movement toward occupational respect. When these measures were announced, these activists hoped that with greater recognition would come better treatment.

However, the reality was that the LCP did not live up to its promise of better treatment of domestic workers. Intercede's Carol Salmon's prediction that the LCP "will create more barriers for women of color and reinforce systematic racism in Canada's immigration policies" (as quoted in Larmour 1993) was prescient for the migrant domestic workers I interviewed. In the early years of the LCP, Caribbean and Filipina women's applications were rejected in favor of European women. The stipulation that prospective migrant domestic workers had to have six months' full-time training in caregiving was used as a way to prioritize the entry of women from European countries, which at that point were the only places that had schools training care workers (Serafico 1993). No such school in the Philippines was equipped to provide a training program (Larmour 1993).

The difficulty of sustaining this policy, however, led to a reversal of these numbers after 1992. Canadian federal immigration officials soon realized the difficulties of recruiting English and other European women and persuading them to stay in care work after they completed the program. This meant that these officials focused once again on recruiting women from the Philippines, which soon led Filipinas to be dominant in the program. In 1999 Filipinas comprised 87 percent of all live-in domestic workers, as opposed to 42 percent under the FDM in 1990 (Goli 2009, 3).

As migrant caregiver activists gathered more data on migrant domestic workers' experiences under the LCP, they began to see changes to the LCP as evidence of a policy failure on the part of Canadian government officials. Activists believed that if the Canadian government's original intention in professionalizing the LCP was to facilitate the eventual settlement of a "better class" of individuals, the absence of attention the government paid to policies and societal norms that presented barriers to migrant care workers from making this transition showed a lack of foresight. For the LCP, several issues were at stake.

First, migrant domestic workers felt that the changes made it appear as though care work was fleeting, transient, and undervalued. Imposing a probationary period for migrant care workers before they could qualify to live out of their employers' households and to apply for Canadian permanent residency made migrant domestic workers feel trapped and unappreciated. Adela, who came to Toronto under the LCP, argued: "Without us, Canada won't be able to care for children, disabled individuals, and elderly folks. Some of us actually like doing care work and think it is just as important to society than banking or medicine or teaching. We're doing important work. So why does it feel as though we're being punished for it?" Second, migrant domestic workers felt that the Canadian government's insistence on professionalizing the program while maintaining harsh restrictions on migrant care workers was contradictory. If migrant domestic workers under the LCP were meant to be more professional and better qualified to provide care work than those under the FDM, then why did their labor conditions and their salaries not improve? The LCP instead fostered feelings of depro-fessionalization and deskilling. Migrant domestic workers felt that they were expected to provide professional care work while being paid menial wages and while living and working in substandard conditions. As Petronilla Cleto from Gabriela-Ontario observed, virtually all of the women who entered the LCP had more than just a grade 12 high school diploma. According to Cleto, the majority hold university degrees and have professional work experience, with numerous migrant care workers previously working as registered nurses in hospitals.

Unfortunately, the recruitment of professionals into the LCP did not result in better treatment. Instead, the shift from the FDM to the LCP led only to a change in terminology. The responsibilities held by migrant care workers, the vulnerabilities they faced at home and at work, and the negative perceptions of their work remained constant. As the Philippine Women's Centre's Cecilia Diocson argued:

> Professionalizing the program doesn't mean that there is no exploitation or oppression. Also, why is it professionalizing the program? You don't need to have a college degree. In the LCP, the requirement is grade 12. For whom is the program getting professionalized? You need to ask this. It's a very critical question. [Federal immigration officials] said it is positive because it is pro-fessionalizing the program, but for whom? Who is benefiting from this? This happened because there was a strong lobby coming from the middle- and the upper-class families who want their domestic workers to speak English properly—that they know already how to use appliances, which is why they need to take a six-month course.

Third, the LCP did not solve the problems of getting jobs faced by domes-tic workers after the program in part because their foreign credentials remain unrecognized. A four-year university degree from the Philippines, for example, only counted as a two-year university degree in Canada. Canadian employers' preference for hiring individuals with Canadian work experience and the additional stigma associated with care work made it hard for domestic workers to get jobs.

Fourth, the fact that the LCP retained regulations stipulating that migrant care workers had to successfully complete the mandatory twenty-four-month live-in requirement before being able to apply for permanent residency felt like a betrayal. It had been the biggest change the activists had wanted. As Cleto argued, it was a "slap in the face." Cleto was especially frustrated because the FDM left open the possibility that future iterations of the program would make the live-in requirement optional; naming the new program the *live-in* caregiver program seemed to her to preclude this change from ever occurring:

> You are asking the government to stop the mandatory live-in requirement and now the Canadian government decided to enshrine the live-in requirement. . . . It forced the live-in requirement, and because there was still no monitoring of what the real conditions were, and how the contract was carried out, and who really observes the terms of the contract, nothing happened. Although it is placed in the law that there should be a monitoring body, nothing has been done to ensure this [years later]. All we can say to live-in domestic workers is that they should report these abuses. It is all they can do. It still happens today. Absolutely!

Evelyn Calugay from Pinay, based in Montreal, echoed Cleto's anger toward the federal government for establishing a program that enshrines the parts of the FDM that activists found most damaging to migrant domestic workers. She observed that in the years since the LCP was passed, migrant care workers' rights were trampled further, thereby leading her to conclude that the move to the LCP was a "step back" for migrant care workers.

Fifth, the institutionalization of bureaucratic procedures frustrated activists. Calugay argued that this was especially the case for those who were living and working in Quebec, where migrant domestic workers faced additional layers of bureaucracy when processing assorted paperwork: "In Quebec, it is harder because you have to answer to two governments, to two levels of government. Two levels of government processed immigration papers. Actually, there were three bureaucratic processes that you had to go through: HRSDC, Quebec Immigration, and Citizenship and Immigration Canada (CIC). In other provinces, one month is all it takes to obtain your work permit if you change your employer; here, it takes four to six months because of the bureaucracies. It became more restrictive." Diocson echoed Calugay's observations, indicating the additional layers of bureaucracy that made it difficult for migrant domestic workers seeking redress for their vulnerabilities at work and at home, which she also felt emboldened employment agencies to be more abusive. By creating a program where immigration is a federal mandate, whereas labor is a provincial prerogative, it was difficult to ascertain which body was responsible for migrant domestic workers' welfare. Diocson portrayed the impasse between federal immigration and provincial labor officials as follows:

> Immigration people are not interested in labour conditions and say, "We are not responsible for this. We are only responsible for their visas. We are only concerned about whether everything is completed and whether they can come into the country. It's your own problem now in the province." They pass the buck to the province on issues concerning contracts and employment standards, though there are no employment standard regulations in place. And they're not included. Really, domestic workers' presence here is not seen as being worthy of protection because they are not protected under labor laws.

According to Diocson, following the LCP's establishment, these cases of workers falling through the cracks of different governments became commonplace: "Coming from the community, you hear more stories of women who can't resolve their problems because of the issues presented by the LCP, and you want changes, but then you keep hitting the wall because you encounter insurmountable bureaucracy." Diocson and other activists had to be more strategic when forming partnerships in order to overcome these bureaucratic hurdles. Diocson, for example, spoke of having to collaborate with immigration and labor lawyers separately in order to understand the types of policy changes needed for each of these policy areas.

The bureaucratization of the LCP also meant that the flexibility that migrant domestic workers enjoyed under the FDM was reduced. Tess Tessalona, who came to Canada as a migrant caregiver under the FDM and became a prominent migrant activist through her work with the Immigrant Workers' Centre and with Pinay, noted that the government's management of the FDM, compared to the LCP, was less rigid. Government officials then did not seem to be as punitive when it came to adjudicating whether domestic workers were deserving of Canadian citizenship. At that point, perceptions of immigration as being primarily a "human resource" program, with its value lying primarily in its ability to attract individuals who could stimulate Canadian economic growth (Abu-Laban and Gabriel 2002), had not yet taken hold as it did in later years. The institutionalization of requirements for entry under the LCP—which became stricter in later years under new "caregiver streams"—meant that federal officials became more invested in ensuring that applicants met the criteria. Tessalona's points about the growing rigidity of immigration decision-making reflected the dominance of "new public management" arrangements in Canada, which prioritized making government bureaucracies more efficient and business-like, starting to influence government institutions in the 1990s (Howlett 2000). Hence, the professionalization of the LCP led to more punitive policies.

The problems faced by women under the LCP led even those who were initially supportive of the LCP when it was first announced to recant their support. These activists were united in decrying how the professionalization of the LCP led to the passage of more restrictive policies that only served to entrench migrant care workers under the Canadian state's regulatory framework.

While migrant activists were unanimous in their understanding of each of these problems, the question of how exactly to address them became contentious. At stake was identifying what exactly was the crux of the issue. In contrast to the activist politics leading up to the establishment of the FDM, activist politics after the LCP were confused and fragmented: activists did not have a unifying message on which they could agree. Whereas they agreed on a simple message when campaigning for what would eventually be the FDM ("Landed status now!"), they disagreed on their understanding of the problems and the solutions to the LCP. Migrant caregiver organizations believed either that the individual concerns facing migrant care workers should be the sole focus or that larger, structural issues pertaining to endemic economic inequities should also be addressed. They also disagreed on the question of whether and how to engage with policymakers.

On the one hand, organizations such as Intercede, Pinay, AAFQ, and WCDWA saw the importance of instituting policy reforms to the LCP. Intercede, for instance, called for "changes to admissions criteria" by eliminating the educational requirement, reversing the mandatory live-in requirement, and giving migrant care workers permanent residency upon arrival, all of which Pura Velasco requested in a letter written to Minister of Immigration Bernard Valcourt.[14] When it became clear that the Canadian government was not listening to its suggested changes, Intercede then shifted gears subtly. It maintained its calls to abolish the mandatory live-in requirement but muted its calls to abolish the educational requirement because it was clear that it was not getting any traction in that regard. It also slightly modified its calls to give migrant care workers permanent residency upon arrival by instead publicizing the need to "recognize the value of domestic work in the immigration points system"

(Intercede 1999, 2). This was a subtle but significant discursive shift that alluded to how giving migrant care workers permanent residency upon arrival could be implemented in other preexisting immigration streams.

Intercede, Pinay, the AAFQ, and the WCDWA sought landed status on arrival for migrant domestic workers, the removal of the live-in requirement, and the provision of open work permits that did not tie domestic workers to their employers. They were adamant, though, that the LCP should remain. Abolishing the LCP was first suggested by former Immigration Minister Sergio Marchi in 1994. Merchi stated that "those admitted in the program do not adjust well. In addition, the cost benefit of the program does not favour its continuance" (as quoted in Intercede 1994, 2). In response, Intercede condemned Marchi's comments, stating that these "contradict Canada's reputation as a progressive force on immigration and women's issues" (4) and called for "equality for domestic workers, not more barriers" (2). Intercede emphasized that the abolition of the program should only take place when migrant care workers were admitted as independent immigrants under the points system. It also criticized Marchi for assuming that migrant domestic workers were not adjusting to life in Canada because they were deficient and unwilling to integrate, conveniently ignoring that discriminatory government policies, such as foreign credential nonrecognition, were to blame (2).

The Philippine Women's Centre (PWC), in contrast to these organizations, was adamant that the LCP needed to be abolished because it was a sexist, racist program that led to the continuous entry of docile women from the Third World into Canada. Its famous mantra, "scrap, scrap the LCP; antiwoman, antiworker, racist policy!" was first conceptualized during a workshop with migrant domestic workers that Diocson facilitated in 1994, during which the racist and misogynous attributes were widely discussed. It was during this workshop that the PWC's progressive abolitionist stance was established. For Diocson, "scrap the LCP" was a deliberately provocative slogan. It was designed to make everyone who heard it, from policymakers to other activists to migrant care workers, feel defensive. In most cases, according to Diocson, this compels people to approach the PWC directly to ask about the rationale behind the slogan. This opening then allows the PWC to explain the troubling demographic characteristics of the LCP. As Diocson asserted, "Ninety-seven percent of the people who are part of the LCP are women from the Philippines. We are targeted for this program. Like black women before who became called Aunt Jemimas! Look at the domestic workers and nannies in the US! They are racialized women! Why are we targeted? Is this the only thing good for us? Is it because we are seen as only being capable of domestic work or live-in care work? We are not useful in any other ways. We no longer have the skills or the knowledge? How come?" The participants in this workshop therefore decided that scrapping the LCP was the only viable response to the many abuses wreaked by the program. Not only migrant care workers but also their families were affected. The larger Filipino community was also stigmatized in Canada because of the widespread association of the LCP with Filipinos. During this workshop, participants also agreed to support a call for a national childcare program and for the provision of permanent residency upon arrival for all migrant domestic workers. The PWC's policy campaigns against the LCP, which had at its core its abolitionist mandate, were arguably more upfront compared to other organizations that endorsed reform. As Diocson and Sayo said, while PWC engaged policymakers by speaking to them and writing to them directly about the harms facing migrant care workers under the LCP, it also frequently participated in activities such as rallies and marches against the Canadian government, making clear that the welfare of migrant care workers—which the PWC saw as being guaranteed only through the abolition of the LCP—cannot be compromised.

The seeds of discord between different organizations eventually hardened into divisions on the basis of organizations' stances on reform versus abolition. Organizations were divided on the question of whether the problems facing migrant domestic workers can be traced primarily to specific policies or whether these can be attributed to structural issues that highlight power imbalances between states. They were also divided on what, normatively, to do with the program. From the 1990s until the early 2000s, calls for reform were endorsed by Intercede, the KCC, the WCDWA, Pinay, and, to a certain extent, the AAFQ, which normatively sought the abolition of the LCP from the standpoint of migrants' rights and women's rights but believed from a pragmatic standpoint that activists needed to call for the reform and not the abolition of the LCP.[15] Opposed to these groups were the PWC and its affiliated organizations.

In the early 2000s Diaz informed me that Intercede, which until now had been publicly seen as the face of migrant caregiver activism in Canada, began to face financial difficulties, leading to a reduced public presence and its eventual dissolution in 2009. Yet Intercede's slow dissolution did not lead to a contraction in migrant caregiver activism. From 2004 to 2014 multiple migrant caregiver organizations were founded in response to several cataclysmic events that galvanized the Filipino and migrant caregiver communities. Rather than focusing only on desired policy changes, these organizations drew attention to the physical harms and even deaths facing migrant care workers. The case in Singapore of Flor Contemplacion, who was placed on death row after being convicted for allegedly killing another Filipina care worker, Delia Maga, and the child under Maga's care, reverberated among communities of migrant care workers in Canada. They saw in Contemplacion's case evidence of sending states like the Philippines and receiving states like Singapore abandoning the interest of migrant care workers, who not only have to work and live in challenging conditions but also have to face bodily harm. Thus, they sought to make visible how migrant care work can be sites of violence (Ong 2009, 2011). For them, to care for migrant care workers involves understanding the bodily harm that migrant care workers face.

There were two cases in particular that became the focus of migrant care worker activists who formed coalitions despite the ideological differences outlined above. Both cases functioned as another transformative event in the history of migrant care work organizing.[16] Similar to the seven Jamaican mothers campaign, these campaigns galvanized migrant care workers, leading them to form their own advocacy organizations. The women at the center of these campaigns, like the seven Jamaican mothers whose campaign led domestic workers to have the right to permanent residency, became seen as symbols of caregiver resilience.

Jocelyn Dulnuan was a Filipina caregiver whose brutal murder in October 2007 galvanized the Filipino community. Gratuitous information about the case was a common feature in Toronto newspapers. Vivid portrayals of Dulnuan as a "pretty young newcomer" who "landed a job as a maid and wound up living in a multimillion dollar mansion" were juxtaposed with gruesome descriptions of her death (City News 2007). For migrant care workers, Dulnuan's case was triggering. Not only did they relate to Dulnuan's decision to leave the Philippines in order to support her husband and her son, but the loneliness she faced while living in an isolated suburb also resonated all too well with migrant domestic workers.

Dulnuan's case highlighted the urgency of creating organizations representing migrant domestic workers. The death of a migrant caregiver starkly illustrated the bodily risks that workers faced, as well as the depths of their sacrifice when they left their families behind. Dulnuan's case was a wake-up call for many migrant domestic workers, creating feelings of catharsis that were similar to what they felt about Contemplacion's death.

Pura Velasco, who was formerly part of Intercede, mentioned Dulnuan's case as one of the reasons for why she decided to establish the Caregivers Action Centre (CAC) in 2007. Chris Sorio, a longtime Filipino community activist and anti-Marcos student leader, also saw Dulnuan's case as illustrating the absence of robust organizations that represented Filipino migrants in Canada. Dulnuan's case therefore helped inspire the formation of Migrante-Canada in 2007. Similarly, former migrant care worker and community activist Terry Olayta was also inspired by the Dulnuan case to form the Caregiver Resource Centre (CRC) in Toronto in 2007, which later expanded into different organizations and became part of the FOACC. Josephine Eric founded the Migrant Workers Family Resource Centre (MWFRC) in Hamilton, Ontario, in 1991 because the migrant care workers she interviewed for her master's thesis encouraged her to do so. Importantly, Eric mentioned during my conversation with her that Dulnuan's death proved to her the urgency of establishing an organization for migrant care workers in Hamilton, which at that point lacked such groups for migrant care workers.

Juana Tejada's case similarly catalyzed migrant domestic workers and other Filipino community members. Tejada came to Canada in 2003 under the LCP, leaving behind her son and husband. In 2006 she finished all her requirements and applied for Canadian permanent residency. However, upon taking the second medical test, which was mandatory for all live-in domestic workers before they could apply for Canadian permanent residency, she discovered that she had colon cancer. Canadian Immigration then ruled that Tejada was medically inadmissible, rejected her application for permanent residency, and asked Tejada to leave Canada. Because of her loss in status, she was no longer permitted to access health insurance, after which her access to provincial health insurance immediately ended (Fabregas 2010).

Many migrant caregivers and members of the Filipino community argued that Tejada's rejection was unfair. They pointed out that live-in domestic workers agree to be part of the LCP with the understanding that they would be granted permanent residency on the basis of their successful completion of the live-in work requirement. They argued that there was an implicit understanding between live-in domestic workers and the Canadian government that live-in domestic workers had "done their time" and completed this requirement. In other words, workers proved through their labor contributions that they were valid members of Canada. As Rafael Fabregas, who was Tejada's lawyer, argued, "We believe—I still believe—that it's manifestly unfair to kick someone out of Canada years after they've worked here because they get sick, because they're just hit with bad luck and got cancer and they're dying and it's time to kick them out. That was totally unfair, very un-Canadian, very inhumane." Marco Luciano, who organized with Migrante-Ontario but currently organizes with Migrante-Alberta, echoed this belief: "The most offensive thing about the Juana Tejada case is that her mistreatment does not come from an employer but from the very government that set up the program which now, in her time of need, rejects her. This is bureaucracy at its most cruel" (Migrante-Ontario 2008, 2). According to Fabregas, Tejada was willing to act as a spokesperson because she understood that her case had the potential to change existing LCP policies. After failing two appeals to rescind the CIC's decision, her legal options became virtually nonexistent (*Philippine Reporter* 2009). Her refusal letters indicated that because she was not granted permanent residency on the grounds of medical inadmissibility, she was being deported (*Philippine Reporter* 2009). Though she could apply for permanent residency on humanitarian and compassionate grounds, these applications sometimes took up to three years, which she did not have, because her disease was terminal.

In light of these limitations, Tejada decided that her best option was to mount a civil society campaign. She liaised with different migrant caregiver organizations, including those with divergent political beliefs. She also reached out to migrant domestic workers who were unaffiliated with an organization. In particular, she reached out to domestic workers who were members of churches, including the Our Lady of Assumption Church in midtown Toronto. That church later opened the Juana Tejada Drop-In Centre, which provided a gathering space for domestic workers. Tejada was able to get the support of different organizations and migrant domestic workers with divergent political beliefs because, as Fabregas argued, "There is no way that everyone can agree on one thing. And I think what happened in the Juana Tejada case was that everybody agreed that it was unfair. Finally, for all of these different activists working on the LCP, after many years of campaigning for changes to the live-in caregiver program, we all agreed on one thing. We all agreed that deporting Juana at this point was unfair and we weren't going to stand for it" (2010).

Tejada's situation inspired Filipino community activists to come together despite their political differences. Although Fabregas noted that there were some differences among people on approach and strategy, eventually, they were able to overcome these disagreements. Churches, which tended to maintain networks distinct from migrant advocacy organizations, also got involved. Migrant workers who were members of Our Lady of Assumption Parish, in particular, became heavily involved in the Tejada case. Each of these activists used their personal networks to get support for Tejada. They circulated a petition asking that Tejada be granted permanent residency, which Fabregas observed got over two thousand signatures in the span of a week. They organized a massive rally in front of the CIC offices in Toronto and participated in a media campaign that was featured prominently in mainstream media publications such as the *Toronto Star* and in ethnic presses such as the *Philippine Reporter*, which gave Tejada more support. Through these efforts, Tejada was able to get the support of other organizations, such as No One Is Illegal and the United Steelworkers Union, which community activist Connio Sorio claimed encouraged all 218,000 of its members to support Tejada by either signing the petition or contacting their government representatives about Tejada's case. Government members of Parliament such as the National Democratic Party's Peggy Nash also became aware of Tejada's situation and lobbied on her behalf. Tejada also decided to establish the Association of Filipino Women Workers (IWworkers). IWworkers' affiliation with the United Steelworkers and with Migrante-Canada allowed it to expand its reach by getting support from both union members and migrant activists.

Initially, Tejada was granted an extension to her visa, which Tejada and her supporters felt was insufficient. They intensified their activist pursuits. Eventually, Tejada's application for permanent residency was granted in 2008, two years after her first application for permanent residency was rejected. She passed away less than a year after her permanent residency application was granted, in 2009.

Inspired by Tejada's situation, different activists cooperated with each other in support of the Juana Tejada Campaign, which sought the elimination of the second medical exam that live-in domestic workers were required to take through an amendment of the Immigration and Refugee Act (Fabregas 2010). Tejada's case, in fact, prompted other live-in domestic workers facing similar circumstances to come forward (Astorga-Garcia 2007). Together, these cases prompted serious consideration of the question of Canada's obligations to live-in domestic workers who otherwise fulfilled the LCP's requirements but were deemed medically inadmissible.

Because of Tejada's case, other domestic workers with terminal illnesses came forward to discuss their struggles. These efforts resulted in the Juana Tejada law, which removed the regulation that domestic workers had to pass a medical test after completing their two-year live-in work requirement and before applying for Canadian permanent residency.

The Juana Tejada law was a decisive campaign victory for all the migrant care worker activists whom I interviewed. It led to renewed interest in working in coalition to support caregiver justice. For example, the Grassroots Hub, which consisted of different community and religious groups and which was helmed by migrant care worker activists such as Pura Velasco, was formed in response to the Juana Tejada campaign (Astorga-Garcia 2007). While this coalition was short-lived, it led members of various organizations to discuss other issues facing live-in domestic workers that merited further attention, such as better working conditions and a more streamlined immigration program. The Grassroots

Hub also submitted a report to the CIC outlining live-in domestic workers' situations under the LCP and the Grassroots Hub's policy recommendations.

Against the backdrop of the Tejada case and the Dulnuan murder, Petronila Cleto and Cynthia Palmaria founded Gabriela-Ontario in Toronto in 2008. Convinced that these events signaled the necessity for a Filipina feminist organization, Cleto and Palmaria started recruiting members to be part of Gabriela-Ontario and were soon able to establish a vibrant organization consisting of Filipina women, most of whom were part of the LCP. Gabriela-Ontario soon became active in lobbying for policy changes to the LCP and participated in mobilization efforts that led to the passage of the Juana Tejada law.

That Tejada was able to shift policies and galvanize migrant domestic workers and their allies into becoming advocates for change was no small feat. Bernie Salonga, Tejada's sister, who was also a caregiver, discussed Tejada's profound impact on migrant domestic workers, stating that migrant domestic workers "were amazed how my sister, a simple caregiver, had made a significant impact on the plight of all migrant workers in Canada" (*Philippine Reporter* 2009).

The ensuing furor surrounding Tejada's case and the mass mobilizations that took place across Canada as a result exerted pressure on Immigration Minister Jason Kenney to support the Juana Tejada law and to conduct consultations with migrant care worker organizations across Canada to ascertain what improvements could be undertaken within the LCP. All of the migrant care worker organizations cited participated in these consultations, seeing in them the opportunity to decisively shape the LCP and perhaps to even instigate the same radical changes that took place in 1981, when migrant care workers were granted the right to apply for permanent residency through the FDM. These consultations magnified the fractures within the migrant care workers' movement. They had several points of disagreement, outlined below.

First, the activists from the Philippine Women's Centre network pushed for the need to scrap the LCP and drew attention to the structural problems that caused the LCP to be necessary in the first place. The increasing number of Filipina women coming to Canada as migrant care workers through the LCP motivated the PWC to seriously consider its normative position. Emanuel Sayo stated:

> This was when the debates started within PWC—whether the program itself is a good idea. The domestic workers themselves liked the program, but when you look at our analysis—the intersectionality of class, gender, and sex in the context of Canada—the conditions are exploitative. Filipino workers were really used. Part of the research we gathered during this time

showed that people come here in Canada, and Canada will tell them that they are lucky to be able to get here, so they just need to suffer for a bit. So what we ask is, Why do we need to suffer when Canada needs us? Why couldn't we just come with open visas and all that? Here, we have the exploitative nature of these programs.

The difference in the way migrant care workers were treated under the LCP and the way they were treated decades earlier, when European women dominated the migrant care work industry, served as further impetus to the PWC to oppose migrant care worker programs. From that point onward, the PWC believed that only by making "different, radical" demands that sought the elimination of migrant care worker programs could justice prevail. Cecilia Diocson in an interview conducted in 2011 argued that the research the PWC undertook on migrant care work and multiple conversations with thousands of Filipina women working as migrant care workers made her see why migrant care worker programs are exploitative and that the PWC's insistence on abolishing them was similar to American abolitionists' call to eliminate slavery in the United States. Though she understood why some migrant care workers were reluctant to call for abolition because they sought better futures, she felt that it was imperative for the PWC in its activist work to explain to these women why migrant care worker programs are present and part of Canada in the first place. Once these women saw the structural imbalances created by these programs and the individual harms that emerge from them, then they would be able to see why these programs, much like slavery in the United States, were evil.

Consequently, members of the PWC saw the consultations held by Kenney in 2009 as a flawed process that did not even begin to solve the problems of live-in domestic workers. The PWC disseminated press releases condemning the conversations and, after the changes were announced, held rallies in protest. One such rally was held in front of the KCC's offices in Toronto, where Kenney first announced the changes.

The second group consisted of the AAFQ, the WCDWA, the KCC, MWFRC, and the CAC.[17] All of these groups saw the importance of focusing solely on the plight of migrant care workers. At that time, while these organizations likely agreed with the structural analysis offered by other organizations, the most immediate advocacy concern rested on current policies that were negatively impacting migrant care workers. These organizations worked together to form the Coalition for Change, which, according to Eric, was devoted to the information and resource exchange, the widening of networks so individual migrant care workers who were members of one organization within the coalition would be "reassured that they will have support in different places," support for leadership-training events for migrant care workers, and policy coordination. Using a devolved leadership structure, the Coalition for Change therefore sought the input of each of its members in order to ascertain the best policies to put forward. Although members of this group were not averse to picketing and rallying, they were more willing to strategically liaise with policy officials than the PWC.

Third, there were the Migrante Network and Gabriela-Ontario. Both organizations believed, like the PWC, that structural issues were at the heart of the problem and ultimately saw the abolition of unequal power structures as being necessary to resolve the issues facing all migrant workers (including migrant care workers). In fact, until ideological disagreements on reform versus abolition emerged in the 1990s, organizers from the PWC, Migrante, and Gabriela were part of the same movement. Unlike PWC, Migrante-Canada and Gabriela-Ontario still ultimately felt that the LCP should be reformed and not abolished. Although they would eventually have liked to see the end of all labor export programs, they also did not want to curtail people's ability to work abroad, because they understood that labor migration was necessary for a lot of people because of a lack of economic options in their home countries. As Chris Sorio from Migrante-Ontario stated,

> Live-in domestic workers themselves say that they do not want this and tell us, "How can we enter this country if the program gets abolished?" So why will we close the door? Our job—like me, as an activist—is to protect them, to help them, to support them. They have no choices economically. If we abolish the programs, what would happen? It would be nice if everyone can enter as immigrants, but that's not happening. We need to make sure that those who eventually want to be immigrants have the opportunity to come here.

Beth Dollaga from Migrante-BC agreed with Sorio: "Workers can speak. Workers would not call for [the abolition of the LCP] because this is the only way that they could come to Canada. . . . This is the most open way for them to come. . . . This is the easiest way for them to come, with the carrot of permanent residency." Calls to reform the LCP, of course, absolutely did not mean that Migrante-Canada and Gabriela-Ontario were in favor of reform over revolution or that they sanctioned state-led changes. These organizations' stances on reform perhaps best resonates with Harsha Walia's observations that "nonreformist reforms" can create conditions for greater justice in the future (Dilts and Walia 2016). As she asks, "From an ethical orientation towards emancipation, I think a guiding question on non-reformist reforms is: Is it increasing the possibility of freedom?" For Migrante-Canada and Gabriela-Ontario, securing improvements to the LCP ensured the security of status for migrant care workers and their families, which can then create conditions for later changes.

Hence, Migrante-Canada and Gabriela-Ontario worked both against and with the state in order to get support for their policy recommendations. They regularly held protests and rallies but also kept channels of communication open with Canadian policymakers, whom they lobbied for support. Close ties, in fact, existed between some NDP members of Parliament, Migrante-Canada, and Gabriela-Ontario, with all three parties in agreement on the harms of the LCP and on ways to resolve these harms. During the 2009 consultations, representatives from Migrante-Canada and Gabriela-Ontario gave their feedback and even participated in joint discussions with the Coalition for Change to brainstorm policy recommendations.

The fourth and final group was made up of the CRC and its allies, including the organizers of the Fil-Core Support Group, which organizes the Miss Caregiver beauty pageant. Unlike the previous three groups, the CRC was decidedly politically and socially conservative, with some of its members vocal supporters of the Canadian Conservative Party. Although the CRC believed that there were policy improvements that were needed within the LCP, it did not want to push too strongly for reform because it ultimately felt that migrant care workers should be grateful for the opportunity to come to Canada through the LCP. The CRC shunned political actions that deliberately challenged its authority. It was against what it called "radical" protest activities such as marching and picketing, believing that the best way to ensure that migrant care workers' voices are heard is through "civilized discourse," as Terry Olayta, the executive director of CRC, stated. Olayta further commented, "We're not the ones who are out on the streets, who distribute pamphlets. Those are nice to read, but so what? What impacts do they actually have?" Olayta believed that it was by working with government officials that migrant care workers could ensure that their rights as migrants, as workers, and as women were protected. Olayta dismissed the activities of their counterparts, seeing these activities as being unnecessarily disruptive and unsavory, and maintained close communication with policymakers. They used their relationships with policymakers as leverage for their policy demands and as a way to find quicker resolution to the problems faced by their members.

In addition, unlike the other groups, CRC and its allies were vocal about their close ties with Christian evangelical and Catholic churches. Although individual members of other organizations may have been members of churches, CRC members did not shy away from being vocal about their religious beliefs. Christian teachings, including believing in the power of prayer as a tool for advocacy and also as a way to help distressed migrant care workers to find respite, were integral to their work.

Following the consultations, Kenney announced changes to the LCP in April 2010. The changes that were put into place included giving live-in domestic workers four years—rather than three years—to complete their requirements. Also, live-in domestic workers had the option of counting the number of hours rather than years that they worked under the LCP. The changes also made it mandatory for employers to pay for live-in domestic workers' transportation costs to Canada and to assume live-in domestic workers' health insurance costs before provincial health insurance can be claimed. Finally, the new legislation made it mandatory for employers to keep a log of the hours live-in domestic workers have worked on a weekly or monthly basis (Moyal 2010).

Activists' responses to these changes were predictable. PWC condemned these changes and interpreted them as evidence that the consultations were invalid, with the Canadian government cherry-picking the community recommendations that best suited their interests. CAC and its allies, as well as the Migrante and Gabriela networks, recognized the positive changes that were introduced but were disappointed that major policies, such as the provision of landed status on arrival, were not introduced. CRC and its allies applauded these changes, seeing them as evidence of the Conservative Party's concern for domestic workers and the validity of its cautious approach to advocacy. All organizations saw these changes as a springboard for future campaigns.

In the aftermath of these announcements, CRC initiated proceedings to form the FOACC in Toronto in 2011, which strategically maintained close linkages with the Conservative Party and sought ways to lobby for changes through creative initiatives. For example, the winner of the Miss Caregiver pageant had the opportunity to visit Ottawa and speak to Conservative members of Parliament and CIC officials about migrant care workers' concerns. In Vancouver, Marla Jose (a pseudonym) founded the Godmother Network in 2011. Disillusioned by the consultation process, which persuaded her that the government through its policy changes could not really significantly improve the lives of migrant care workers, the Godmother Network provided migrant care workers the opportunity to be part of an organization that had at the core of its mandate a political insistence on being apolitical (i.e., on refraining from participating in policy lobbying). The Godmother Network's focus on ensuring the financial stability of its members also showed that migrant care worker activists have begun looking at other ways to guarantee their security.

The increase in the number of organizations associated with FOACC and the successes of the Godmother Network in recruiting members are thus reflective of the way conservative and neoliberal values have now become a more visible part of the Canadian migrant care workers' movement. While I see their emergence as occurring in reaction to migrant care workers' frustrations with the 2011 consultations, I also see the increased entry of live-in domestic workers in the mid-2000s as creating representational gaps. The member organizations that are part of FOACC, with their emphasis on religion and assimilation, as well as the Godmother Network therefore aimed to meet the needs of live-in domestic workers seeking alternatives to existing organizations.

In addition, the growing demand for settlement services generated by new cohorts of live-in domestic workers, coupled with a government funding environment that has been unreceptive to supporting organizations that are deemed too radical (Rice and Prince 2013), affected the activities undertaken by organizations like KCC and inspired existing organizations such as MWFRC to prioritize service provision over activism. Hence, responding to live-in domestic workers' needs and to a more restrictive funding environment has also made some organizations focus less on lobbying.

Community Consultations and Policy Changes in the Caregiver Program, 2014–2021

In 2013 the economic recession brought on by plummeting oil prices led to massive employment lay-offs. In addition, Canada's temporary foreign worker programs were placed under scrutiny after news media reported that Canadian workers at the Royal Bank of Canada (RBC) were laid off and replaced by temporary foreign workers (Tungohan 2017). Subsequent public reactions against the Temporary Foreign Workers Program (TFWP) devolved into a reaction against the presence of *all* labor migrants (Tungohan 2017).

Thus alerted to the possibilities of impending changes to the LCP, migrant care worker organizations mobilized to see whether and how they could influence policy discussions. At the time, there was a sense of urgency that was pervasive among migrant care worker activists, as well as among church leaders, settlement service providers, immigration lawyers, academics, and migrant care workers. Now was not the time to heed ideological divisions. Many felt that a broad alliance was needed to preemptively combat policy changes.

Over the course of June and July 2014 in Toronto, representatives from migrant care worker groups held weekly gatherings, first to share information and then to brainstorm on possible policy proposals, which they hoped to present to then Immigration Minister Chris Alexander. The PWC, true to its abolitionist stance, was not in these meetings. These gatherings, which were eventually called the Federal Domestic Workers Program Task Force, were organized by Pastor Jon (not his real name), a Conservative Filipino community leader, director of a settlement service organization, and future Conservative member of Parliament candidate. Because Pastor Jon had obtained an invitation from Chris Alexander to attend a consultation, many of those attending the task force's meetings hoped to influence the proposals that would be presented. The meetings had a decidedly hierarchical and masculinist dynamic. Each meeting began with a prayer, with everyone attending holding hands and expressing their gratitude to God for allowing them to come to Canada. Then, Pastor Jon or one of the meeting chairs, who was always a male community activist, went through the agenda, which was predetermined prior to the meeting. Although everyone—including the migrant care workers and migrant care worker activists—who was present technically had the opportunity to give feedback, I noticed that it was the male leaders of the community, who were not migrant care workers and who in fact occupied high-status professions, who spoke the most.

These procedures were in contrast to grassroots migrant care worker organizations' procedures. In the caregiver meetings I attended, migrant care workers always assumed leadership roles in these meetings (and in fact were often the ones leading discussions), and input from everyone was proactively solicited. In some meetings, procedures were enshrined to ensure that migrant care workers' voices were centered. For example, when deciding who should get the floor, the meeting chair can decide that it will always be migrant care workers who are called first.

As a result of this feeling that they were not being heard, the numbers of migrant care workers and migrant care worker activists from all ideological sides decreased at each ensuing meeting. Because Pastor Jon's gatherings assigned two Filipino Canadian lawyers the task of drafting separate policy proposals, subsequent meetings were spent debating the merits of each of these proposals rather than seeking feedback from migrant care workers on what they would like to see. The proposals themselves provided incremental improvements to the LCP, with suggestions that sought a reduction in the amount of time domestic workers would have to live with and work for their employers before qualifying for permanent residency.

During these meetings and over email, participants—including those from progressive and conservative migrant care worker organizations—contested these proposals. Progressive groups raised the question: Rather than imposing proposals on domestic workers, why not ask migrant care workers themselves? In the end, migrant care workers from Gabriela-ON, Migrante, and Caregivers Action Centre (CAC) left the Federal Domestic Workers Program Task Force.

Gabriela-ON, Migrante, and CAC decided to mount their own advocacy campaigns, which involved attempting to shift public opinion in support of the LCP and putting public pressure on the Conservative government to improve the LCP. Rather than seeking to be included in private consultations with the immigration minister, these organizations decided to engage in other campaigns. For instance, the CAC's Pura Velasco created a short video showing an interview with an elderly woman who attested that without the LCP, her care needs would not be met. Gabriela-Ontario members created a website where people could sign their names onto a form letter asking that domestic workers be given landed status on arrival. The letter was then automatically sent to their MPs and to former immigration minister Chris Alexander.

The Conservative government's announcement of changes to the LCP on October 31, 2014, devastated migrant care workers for reasons outlined below. In its public announcements, the Conservative government heralded how the live-in requirement would now be optional under the new Caregiver Program (CP). The removal of the live-in requirement, according to Chris Alexander's public statements, was a sign that the Conservative government truly wanted to ensure domestic workers' welfare. In addition, the CP created two caregiving streams: the childcare stream and the high medical needs stream. In order for domestic workers to obtain Canadian permanent residency, they must pass English or French Language Level 5 for the childcare stream and Level 7 for the high medical needs stream. In a further attempt to professionalize the CP, attaining these language levels required "intermediate" fluency, a point that activists pointed to as showing the Canadian government's desire to create more barriers for care workers. As Adela observed, "Knowing the grammatical way to write a 'professional letter,' which these tests claim is what intermediate language speakers can do, isn't necessary in our work!"

In addition, those under the high medical needs stream might need to obtain a license to practice their profession in Canada depending on what type of medical care they were asked to provide. Personal support workers, licensed practical nurses, and other care practitioners normally require licenses to practice in Canada. This was the first-ever instance of migrant caregivers having to meet a language and licensing requirement, creating a higher barrier for immigration for migrant care workers.

A more fundamental change that differentiated between previous migrant care worker programs and the CP was that care workers who completed their requirements (including the new ones that were set) no longer had the guarantee that they would successfully become permanent residents. Rather, the Canadian government set a quota of 2,750 permanent residency entries under each stream, totaling 5,500 entries a year. If the Canadian government had filled its quota of permanent residency applicants that year, then further applicants would no longer qualify.

As a result, in 2017, the first year when applications for permanent residency under the CP were accepted, the barriers for entry under the CP were so high that care workers started applying for the permanent residency under the childcare stream, which had lower entry requirements, rather than the high medical needs stream (Keung 2017b). According to Pinay's Evelyn Calugay, these changes have effectively led to the shutdown of the Caregiver Program in Quebec. As a result, families in Quebec needing care have resorted to hiring women from other immigration streams, such as the refugee stream. This has consequently led to a shift in type of advocacy role taken up by Quebec organizations. Pinay, for example, now also advocates on behalf of refugee women working as domestic workers. The AAFQ renamed itself the Association pour la Défense des Droits du Personnel Domestique (APDD). It no longer provides specific programs for migrant domestic workers but instead allocates its resources to policy lobbying and to mounting a legal challenge that ties domestic workers with their employers, arguing that this provision contravenes the Canadian Charter of Rights and Freedoms.

Hence, by creating more strenuous requirements, the Conservative government removed a fundamental assumption of the FDM and the LCP: that domestic workers are "citizens-in-waiting" who deserve to permanently settle in Canada. Migrante-Alberta's Marco Luciano said that this was a morbid case of "trick or treat" on the part of the Canadian government: "They announced the changes on Halloween, making it seem as though their removal of the live-in requirement was a 'treat' they were providing; in reality, the other changes that came along with it showed that they were actually tricking domestic workers."

Although migrant caregiver activists privately acknowledged that their lobbying efforts likely resulted in the creation of a program that at least provided a pathway to permanent residency for domestic workers, they nevertheless were upset that the changes resulted in increased vulnerability for domestic workers.[18] Despite the ideological divisions between different migrant care worker organizations, all of the migrant care worker organizations with whom I was in contact united again because they saw these changes as impeding the shared interests of migrant care workers. All of the communications sent by First Ontario Alliance for Caregivers in Canada (FOACC), the PWC, and the Migrante and Gabriela networks stressed that the removal of the live-in requirement was a positive development that highlighted the successes of caregiver activists' long-standing efforts to draw attention to the abuses faced by domestic workers when living in their employers' households. Yet all the other policy changes, they argued, harmed domestic workers. To care for care workers meant to gather together once more in order to fight against these changes.

Once again, migrant care worker activists from different organizations gathered to protest. On November 22, 2014, a huge Justice for Domestic Workers rally was held in front of federal government offices in downtown Toronto. Longtime caregiver advocates Coco Diaz and Pura Velasco spoke, tying in the experiences of domestic workers today with the experiences of previous generations of domestic workers under the FDM and the LCP. Reminding everyone present that the right to apply for Canadian citizenship was only given after domestic workers fought tirelessly for them, Diaz and Velasco emphasized the importance of always being vigilant about holding the Canadian government accountable. "Changes are never given out of the goodness of the government's hearts," Diaz mentioned, "but because we fought for them." Pet Cleto from Gabriela-Ontario mentioned that countries such as the Philippines had labor export programs that pushed people to seek jobs as domestic workers and migrant workers abroad and reminded the audience members to also consider conditions of global economic inequality. Others from Caregivers Action Centre (CAC) and Care Workers Connections, Education and Support Organization (CCESO) spoke, including former domestic workers who shared their struggles under the LCP and current domestic workers who mentioned that their harrowing experiences under the program continued. In order to care for the migrant care worker activists who struggled before them, for present-day fellow migrant care workers and their families whose lives were upended by these changes, and for future migrant care workers and their families who will face similar struggles, it was important to keep fighting for change.

Following the rally, all of the caregiver activists gathered at a restaurant downtown to celebrate and to strategize. Seasoned leaders of the movement caught up with each other, fondly reminiscing about previous struggles while also congratulating younger caregiver activists who spoke up about their experiences for the very first time at the rally. There was a palpable sense of joy that emanated among those who gathered. Despite the reality that they were compelled to come together because of a negative event, activists expressed pride in their ability to organize a large rally and, more crucially, were inspired to think of what else they could achieve in the future. Affirming Martin Manalansan's observations that migrants, contrary to their depictions as being perpetually tragic, are "pleasure-seeking" (2008), the rally and the dinner afterward showed me the commingling of excitement, anticipation, anger, and distress that accompanies community-building within the migrant care workers' movement.

The 2014 changes became a catalyst for more vigorous movement organizing. In Toronto, Montreal, Edmonton, Calgary, and Vancouver, I witnessed organizations invigorated by the need to fight against the proposals. The ensuing election of the Liberal Party in October 2015 and the defeat of the Conservative Party after nearly a decade in power led to cautious optimism. Yet migrant care worker activists were sharply aware that they could not be complacent. Migrante-BC's Erie Maestro observed that while "the Liberals are definitely better than the Conservatives" in that they at least nominally appeared to be open to listening to migrant activists' perspectives, in the end, it was "the movement from below that is going to make the changes. It's not the folks on top. They will once they see how strong you are and how loud you can get."

Maestro's observations were prescient. In the years since the Liberal government got elected, migrant domestic workers faced the challenges of having to shift policies that had already been put into place. New generations of migrant care worker activists founded their own organizations, including Eto Tayong Domestic Workers (Domestic Workers, Here We Are) and Caring for Domestic workers (C4C) in Ontario. Using a modified version of the demand "good enough to work, good enough to stay" by asserting that it was migrant care workers' ongoing *presence* in their communities that merited residency rights, migrant care worker activists frequently came together in short-term coalitions seeking faster processing times for migrant care workers' citizenship applications.[19] They also sought the removal of the "excessive demand" provision under the Immigration and Refugee Protection Act (IRPA), which immigration officials used to justify denying Canadian citizenship to the disabled children and spouses of caregivers. Casting aside ideological differences, migrant care worker organizations' campaigns successfully led permanent residency applications to be processed more quickly.

The campaigns also led former immigration minister Ahmed Hussen to announce that the excessive demand provision would be raised so that applicants with medical costs below $19,965 would be given permanent residency

(Keung 2018). Defining "excessive demand" as involving costs above this amount allowed more migrant care workers to sponsor their disabled spouses and children to come to Canada. For instance, Mercedes Benitez, whose application for permanent residency was rejected because immigration officials saw her disabled son as requiring medical care that would be a burden on Canada's public health care system, was granted Canadian citizenship and was thus able to sponsor her family to join her in Canada. Although migrant care worker activists sought the removal of the excessive demand provision, the activists whom I spoke to recognized that Hussen's reversal was a partial policy victory.

What kept migrant care worker activists going was the hope that they could apply additional pressure points on the government in power to lead to policy changes. In 2018 migrant care worker organizations mobilized to outline the harms emerging from the new Caregiver Program, participating in consultations with the Liberal government. Once again, migrant care workers united in short-term coalitions to gain more traction. These efforts culminated in a substantive victory.

On February 23, 2019, Hussen acquiesced to migrant care workers' long-standing demands. He announced the following provisions: First, migrant care workers now have visas that are untied to their employers, allowing workers the mobility to leave abusive employers. Second, migrant care workers can now come with their families. The Canadian government will also assess domestic workers' eligibility for permanent residency prior to their arrival in Canada, preventing the situation where domestic workers only find out that they are ineligible for permanent residency after completing the CP. Although the new program still maintains existing language and licensing requirements and only accepts 5,500 applicants per year—changes that caregiver activists sharply contested when they were proposed in 2014 and continue to fight against—the fact that the new program responds directly to activist demands highlights the impact of the migrant domestic worker movement in shaping policies. The Canadian government also established the Interim Pathway, which ended in October 2019. It allowed caregivers, including those who lost status, to apply for permanent residency, thus heeding the demands of caregivers who argued that measures to regularize the status for undocumented migrant caregivers were needed.

Currently, Canada's migrant care worker programs are divided into two main streams, which are a modified version of the 2014 CP: the Home Childcare and Home Support Worker Pilot (Canada 2022). The ever-increasing licensing and educational requirements and language requirements under both streams continue to be a point of contention for migrant care worker activists. The Migrante and Gabriela networks seek the removal of these requirements while simultaneously offering free classes to help migrant care workers pass the language tests (either the Canadian English Language Proficiency Program or the International English Language Testing System). The additional requirement that care workers complete the equivalent of one year of Canadian postsecondary studies adds an additional barrier for migrant care workers, particularly since third-party credential assessment centers are inconsistent in their interpretation of workers' degrees.

Revising licensing, educational, and language requirements became especially urgent during COVID-19. In 2020 and 2021 migrant care worker activists such as Vilma Pagaduan, who founded Domestic Workers, Here We Are, critiqued these requirements as presenting an undue burden to care workers, without whom Canadian society would be unable to meet its caregiving needs. Pagaduan points out that in normal times, making mandatory the attainment of scores to show an intermediate level of English before migrant care workers could apply for permanent residency was cruel because migrant care workers were already able to perform their jobs capably without proving their competence in intermediate English. During COVID-19, during which there was an even higher demand for migrant care workers, insisting on the continuation of this policy was not only cruel but also short-sighted on the Canadian government's part. Hence, in order to recognize the essential care work undertaken by migrant care workers during COVID-19, Pagaduan holds that migrant care workers should all be given Canadian citizenship and accordingly lobbied the federal government to change policies.

Other organizations, such as Gabriela-ON, wrote policy briefs that called for the revocation of licensing, educational, and language requirements, calling these "discriminatory" because they are inaccessible (Gabriela-ON 2021). They wrote an open letter to Prime Minister Justin Trudeau and Immigration Minister Sean Fraser that argued that "systemic failures in the health system and labour and migrant policies" were ultimately the reasons why migrant care workers suffered tremendously during COVID-19 (Matatag 2021). They also raised these points in a widely circulated petition that was sent to these officials (Change.org 2021). In the same vein, the Caregivers Action Centre (CAC), the Vancouver Committee for Caregivers and Domestic Workers Rights (CCDWR), and the Care Workers Connections, Education and Support Organization (CCESO) wrote a report that explained that the "cascade of crises" facing migrant care workers during COVID-19 resulted from an immigration program that entrenched migrant care workers' vulnerability (CAC, CCDWR, and CCESO 2020, 6). The report ends with recommendations for "full and permanent immigration status for all and landed status now," along with "interim measures to ensure rights for migrant care workers" that stress "real access to permanent residency" through the abolition of the educational and language requirements, a reduction of the work experience requirement, and more robust labor and income supports (34–35). Migrante-Canada, Pinay, and the APDD endorsed these calls.

The centralization of immigration decision-making within the office of the immigration minister means that parts of the Caregiver Program—which, in its current iteration, is deemed a "pilot program"—might very well be altered, depending on the minister's agendas. While the COVID-19 crisis has led to many speeches from federal government officials recognizing care workers (including migrant care workers), whether these will be translated into the policy changes that organizations are seeking remains to be seen. Policy changes announced without much warning mean that migrant care worker activists have had to mobilize quickly. Given the intensification of care activism during the pandemic and the growth of the movement, migrant care worker activists are ready to act and make their demands heard.

Conclusion

The history of care activism in Canada shows how migrant care worker activists were at the forefront of policy improvements to Canada's migrant care worker policies. Despite—or because of—the arduous labor conditions that they faced, their ongoing realities of family fragmentation, and their vulnerability to physical harm, migrant care workers formed organizations that would help them fight for change collectively. Despite lacking Canadian citizenship, migrant care worker activists used whatever tools of movement organizing were at their disposal. They leveraged transformative historical events to their advantage. Within the Canadian migrant care workers' movement, the seven Jamaican mothers and Juana Tejada campaigns functioned as unifying events that drove increased movement activism.

Care activism in Canada, however, is far from being unified. As I showed in this chapter, there are key ideological divisions between migrant care worker activists. Every year, there are increasing numbers of migrant care worker organizations being founded, each representing different vantage points. From an advocacy perspective, the presence of more migrant care worker organizations is a positive development. With more migrant care worker organizations demanding greater attention to migrant care workers' needs (albeit with different interpretations of how these needs should be met by the Canadian government), their demands get amplified.

I do not wish to overstate differences between organizations, of course. Ultimately, what unites the migrant care workers movement is the need to care for migrant care workers and their families, including previous movement leaders whose legacy migrant care worker activists seek to uphold, as well as current and future migrant care workers who are experiencing or will be experiencing challenges. Furthermore, existing ideological divisions do not preclude the possibility of new coalitions. With new leaders emerging and with sociopolitical and economic contexts shifting, ideologies can shift. The COVID-19 pandemic highlighted the urgent need to value care work and, by extension, to care for migrant care workers and their families, which creates the possibility of overcoming long-standing divisions.

With this influential history of care activism in mind, I now turn to a more in-depth analysis of the present and future of the migrant care worker movement in Canada. Chapters 2 to 4 examine organizational tactics and strategies, beginning with key organizations in Canada and broadening to examine the transnational dimensions of this activism. Chapter 5 then shifts to consider the everyday care activism that I observed at the individual level, which I argue is often overlooked in favor of more conventional political actions such as protests.

Chapter 2

Care Activism within Migrant Advocacy Organizations

JENNY CRUZ (A PSEUDONYM; DOMESTIC WORKERS RESOURCE CENTRE): At the center of our movement is making sure that there is communication with the Lord. Prayers here and there is important. It is only when I got here that I started to see our strengths in bringing in the word of God with our activist work. Because when trouble comes, you have someone to talk to. That one also helps me out—if I can't rely on a friend or if I don't have anyone to talk to, there is a God up there who is listening. You get the feeling of your spirit getting boosted. When you speak to the Lord, you feel like there is strength, that you aren't drowning in your problems. This is an important part of our work and our organization. We make sure that the spiritual dimension is there too.

MARCO LUCIANO (MIGRANTE-ALBERTA): Our goal is to create a mass movement of people who see how the struggles of migrant workers—of migrant domestic workers—are linked to larger struggles by migrants in other countries. It's not just about changing policies here or in the Philippines. It's about defeating larger structural forces—of bureaucratic capitalism, of neoliberalism, of imperialism.

On a sunny spring day in May 2012, I was sitting at the deck of Bahay Migrante (Migrante House) in Vancouver.[1] Migrante-BC was able to make the down payment for the house after receiving a settlement from a class-action lawsuit that it helped file on behalf of abused temporary foreign workers. While sitting there with a group of people, eating Filipino street food and drinking pop, I was struck with how comfortable it felt to be there. This was an actual home. As I was thinking about how good it was to be in a space that was specifically owned by a grassroots migrants organization, one Migrante-BC member interrupted my thoughts. She pointed to the lopsided deck and joked that this sometimes caused confusion whenever she had a number of alcoholic beverages because she would not know if she was slipping because she was inebriated or because of the uneven floor. As everyone laughed in agreement, other people there discussed the work that went into maintaining the house. It was clear that all of the Migrante-BC members felt a sense of collective ownership over the house.

The importance of having a space of their own—whether it be an actual physical space like Bahay Migrante or a "community of care" (Francisco-Menchavez 2018) with whom one can share moments—was one of the crucial contributions of migrant care worker organizations in the lives of migrant care workers. The physical constraints that migrant care workers face spatially, as Dani Magsumbol (2018) notes in her research on how requirements that migrant care workers live in their employers' households lead to the invisibilization of the labor abuses occurring within the private sphere of the home, make especially urgent the ability for migrant care workers to have a space where they can "just be." Such spaces may be physical, as Bahay Migrante shows, but they can also be created through the creation of communities where migrant care workers can be with each other. In fact, while organizations' advocacy efforts yielding policy changes were important, as I addressed in chapter 1, migrant care worker organizations' importance in the lives of migrant care workers extends far beyond their ability to lobby. Migrant care worker organizations are crucial in providing migrant care workers with a space to call their own. They represent migrant care workers' needs in ways that other institutions—whether they are sending states like the Philippines, receiving states like Canada, labor unions, or other social justice organizations—cannot or will not. Care activism for migrant care worker activists entails providing care for an organization's members by assuming the role of "fictive kin" for migrant care workers who have no other sources of support in Canada.

Beyond providing each other with a supportive network, migrant care worker organizations create spaces of dissident friendships. Similar to the friendships that develop between HIV-positive queers discussed by Michael P. Brown, the spaces created by these migrant care worker organizations become sites of "radical democracy" where the very act of "being there" for each other creates a "new space for political engagement" (1997, 153). The twelve years I have spent observing and even working alongside migrant care worker activists reveal to me how care for each other and for an "imagined community" of previous, current, and future migrant care workers in Canada and in other countries is truly at the center of their advocacy. In a political environment where members of the public see the presence of "others" as a threat, the ability of oppressed communities to form communities of care in the face of such opposition becomes a powerful political act. In these spaces, migrant care workers are not beholden to anyone—their presence is not instrumentalized to serve a larger end, whether to serve their families through the sending of remittances, to serve their employers through their social reproductive labor, or to serve the sending state as "national heroes" who provide economic contributions or the receiving state as "essential care workers." Communities of care are empowering for migrant care workers because here they are valued for who they are and not for what they bring.

In this chapter, I delve into the work of five migrant care worker organizations, each of which has different ideological beliefs, but all of which create powerful communities of care for their members. In keeping with the reality that the majority of migrant care workers in Canada are Filipina, all of the organizations have substantive numbers of Filipinas as part of their membership. Because of their mandate, the Migrante-Canada and Philippine Women's Centre networks represent Filipino migrants. The migrant care worker activists in all of these organizations are more than fellow activists and more than workers in solidarity with each other. Migrant care worker activists are *kasamas*, a Tagalog term that is usually translated to mean "comrade" but that actually refers to deeper, affective ties between people who are part of each other's journey.[2] The data for this chapter are derived from my ethnographic work with each of these organizations; this ethnography involved a mix of one-on-one and focus group interviews and participant observation of meetings, rallies, and social gatherings. I chose to feature these organizations to highlight how different approaches to care activism result in the creation of different communities of care. I discuss the historical context for their organizing, their goals and "normative" vision or their dreams of what social justice looks like, and their activities.

The Godmother Network (Vancouver, BC)

Marla Jose (a pseudonym) was frustrated with the restrictions that government-funded organizations faced. As a longtime Filipino community activist and a former program director for a settlement services organization for immigrants,

migrants, and other newcomers to Canada, she saw these organizations as being limited in the work that they did. They could only assist a set number of immigrants, depending on how much funding they received from the government each funding cycle, which meant that they could only serve a fraction of the individuals who sought help. Furthermore, Jose was frustrated because such government funding was limited to helping either Canadian permanent residents or Canadian citizens, leaving behind temporary migrants and citizens-in-waiting like migrant care workers. Thus, to fund their programs for temporary migrants and live-in domestic workers, settlement service organizations had to rely on very limited funding given by corporations and individuals. For Jose, this was a major source of frustration, because "running the caregiver program was [her] favorite because it needed [her] the most." Although Jose was sympathetic to the hardships faced by immigrants, domestic workers' situations were worse and consequently merited more attention. As Jose argued:

> Immigrants don't have family issues because everybody came together. Live-in domestic workers have to face intense family reunification issues. It is really, really, really disheartening. And the immigrants can come here for greener pastures, but most of them had a [relatively] good life back home; they just come to Canada because they want a better one. For live-in domestic workers, if you look at their profiles, you will start crying. Oh my God! What is this? A lot of them are here because they have no choice, so it annoys me when people say, well, they should have just come here as immigrants. Do you think these people would come here if they had the choice?

Jose further believed that "everybody is helping the immigrants. No one is helping the domestic workers and the temporary foreign workers. Domestic workers' issues are really big, but there are so many funding problems preventing us from addressing their problems."

Jose was also critical of the model of service provision used by settlement services. These organizations only saw those who had problems. Because it was important to "reach domestic workers before they reached this point," Jose tried to proactively prevent the problems that migrant care workers faced by organizing events such as immigration and employment workshops, but funding limitations meant that these events were rare.

She was also frustrated by the absence of economic opportunities that migrant care workers faced after leaving the migrant care worker programs. That domestic workers' foreign degree credentials and work experiences abroad did not count in Canada led numerous former migrant care workers to continue being economically vulnerable. As Jose observed, this meant that many of them remained in the care work industry despite attempts to transition to other spheres of employment. The stigma that current and former migrant care workers felt as "nannies," coupled with the difficulties they faced in getting long-term, stable employment, meant that settlement service organizations were ill-equipped to address migrant care workers' economic needs. While such organizations were able to sponsor workshops on preparing for job interviews and were able to provide one-on-one career counseling, they did not have the capacity to solve domestic workers' problems of economic marginalization.

In addition, Jose felt that a lot of the challenges faced by domestic workers were seen superficially by organizations as being only "legal" in nature, consequently minimizing the actual harms felt by live-in domestic workers and, in some cases, their families. Relatedly, prioritizing legal solutions to problems that had a deeper cause discouraged migrant care workers from understanding the "real" issues at stake. To expand on this point, Jose explicated how settlement service organizations and legal organizations saw the issue of marital separation as only requiring a legal remedy. If, for example, a live-in caregiver was facing marital difficulties, organizations only talked to her about her legal options, such as filing legal separation papers if her partner was in the Philippines or filing for divorce if her husband was in Canada. For Jose, such challenges were only partially legal problems; instead, they pertained more fundamentally to issues of "morality." Because "normally, domestic workers need legal advice, though sometimes they also need moral advice," Jose believed that organizations thus had to be better equipped to handle questions of "ethics and values." For her, it was important to care for migrant care workers by giving them both a space to connect with each other to remind each other of their moral values and the opportunity to secure their economic livelihoods.

As a result, Jose decided to leave her job. She started the Godmother Network in 2011, which she explained was a way for her to "proactively" address domestic workers' economic, moral, and personal needs. The Godmother Network, unlike the other organizations featured in this chapter, is unique in that it is a for-profit organization and is officially registered in BC as a recruitment agency. It primarily earns money as a care-giving, cleaning, and housekeeping service. It is different from other companies offering such services in that it is structured like a co-operative, whereby each caregiver owns a stake in the organization after paying a nominal sum as investment. Migrant care workers were inspired by Jose's vision of forming an alternative organization such that within three months of starting, the Godmother Network already had ninety-three members. While it is similar to the economic livelihood organizations featured in chapter 4 in that its focus is on guaranteeing migrant care workers' economic security, its horizontal decision-making structure ensures that migrant care workers can set the agenda.

Accepting that "most, if not all" of the Godmother Network's members are Christian and use Christian teachings as the basis for their conduct, Jose sees adherence to Christian values as an important part of the Godmother Network's mission. As the "godmother" at the center of this organization, Jose saw her role as an amalgamation of a moral arbiter and business partner. She believed that she was a moral authority figure who was in charge of "instilling good values" in her members. For instance, she felt that it was her prerogative to continuously remind her members to exhibit "proper behavior" in public. A point of pride for Jose, in fact, was the "good behavior" constantly exhibited by the Godmother Network members; she related an anecdote of how one Filipino community member praised the way the Godmother Network members "behaved" in social events compared to "other" groups of domestic workers who "were so wild and were more interested in going to discos." Hence, one of the Godmother Network's goals is to ensure the preservation of "moral values" among live-in domestic workers.

Another one of the Godmother Network's goals is to help current and former migrant care workers in Canada become economically stable. Jose believed that rather than waiting for employment opportunities, migrant care workers needed to create their own. Caring for migrant care workers meant looking out for their financial stability. From a normative perspective, the Godmother Network, according to Jose, "seeks the full economic empowerment of former and current migrant care workers in Canada." As an organization that provides a social space for live-in domestic workers with similar moral values and that helps live-in domestic workers earn money, the Godmother Network therefore provides live-in domestic workers with a way to protect their interests without being "political." Jose saw "being political" as involving lobbying policymakers and engaging in protest actions and other actions that advocates commonly take in the public sphere. There are migrant care workers, she reasoned, who were not at all interested in doing so and consequently needed their own space to be with friends who shared similar values and to earn more money.

In pursuit of its first goal of being a moral force for domestic workers, the Godmother Network has initiatives designed to preserve "family unity." For example, Jose worked with Couples for Christ in Canada to develop programs for live-in domestic workers in Canada and their spouses and families in the Philippines. She said that there will be "workshops for the domestic workers [in

Canada], and the same workshops will be given to their families back home." In one such workshop, Jose explained that

> we teach the domestic workers not to feel guilty and not to say yes to every-thing their family asks for. Couples for Christ then teaches the family about the hardships their mothers are facing and reminding them that they have to be sympathetic to her situation; the family gets reminded that their mother doesn't pick up money off the streets; they tell the kids that the stuff they are asking for is expensive and that they shouldn't burden their mother that way. The workshops are a little different, but the goal is that when they finally see each other, they will understand.

Through these transnational workshops, Jose argued, both the caregiver and her family back in the Philippines could begin the process of understanding reunification even before the family came to Canada. By conducting simul-taneous workshops, the problems that domestic workers and their families may face upon reunification are therefore addressed, allowing the Godmother Network and Couples for Christ to be proactive in preventing problems from arising for their members.

Christian practices infuse the Godmother Network events. For example, all of its gatherings start with a prayer, and all of its sponsored social events, such as picnics and dinners, are on the "wholesome" side. For Jose, these social events are geared toward helping domestic workers establish a community in Canada so "they won't feel so alone." Jose further argued that while churches usually offer live-in domestic workers a supportive community, "the problem with the church is that it consists of different people," which means that domestic work-ers may feel alienated. The Godmother Network thus helps live-in domestic workers connect with other domestic workers sharing the same moral values.

To pursue its second goal of economically empowering domestic workers, the Godmother Network functions as a cooperative employment agency. As a cooperative, domestic workers have the incentive to advertise the Godmother Network's services widely in order to get a return on their investment, because the more money the Godmother Network earns, the more money domestic workers receive in turn. Although its members are still in the care work indus-try, Jose argued that "the impact is different because they are owners. It's not as though they were just ordered to clean someone's house; they are owners of a company, and cleaning the house is just one of the tasks that they have to do to build up their company."

Jose also underlined the Godmother Network's responsibilities toward its members' long-term financial well-being by describing how everyone is obligated to attend financial planning sessions. Jose additionally demanded that everyone who is part of the Godmother Network start their own "nonwithdrawal" savings account, which they can only access once they have reached a certain goal, such as accumulating enough savings, or once an important life event occurs, such as the arrival of their family members from the Philippines. Jose believed that having a system of "enforced savings" provides the Godmother Network members the opportunity to plan in the long term. Eventually, the goal is for the Godmother Network members to "realize their dreams" either by helping the organization grow or by "branching out" and planning a new venture. Ultimately, for Jose, being a member of the Godmother Network will facilitate migrant care workers' economic integration into Canada. It creates national and transnational "moral" and Christian communities of care that allow its members to keep each other in check.

Caregiver Action Center (Toronto, ON)

Pura Velasco was one of the Caregiver Action Center's founders. Velasco was a longtime community activist. Having come to Canada in 1990 as a domestic worker, Velasco experienced the dehumanizing and objectifying nature of care work. Rather than being treated as a human being, she observed that her employers treated her like an object without needs or labor rights (Velasco 1997). Migrant workers, according to Velasco, are treated abysmally by both sending and receiving states. Sending states like the Philippines see migrant workers as "productive milking cows" from whom they can extract remittances, whereas receiving states like Canada place "skilled and talented immigrant women" in low-wage care-giving jobs to maximize labor flexibility (Velasco 2002, 133, 134). The everyday ordeals migrant care workers experience in the face of state indifference led Velasco to organize workers. She was president of Intercede and was later part of the Community Alliance for Social Justice (CASJ) and the Coalition for the Promotion of Domestic Workers Rights.

Velasco began organizing again in the wake of Jocelyn Dulnuan's murder, setting the stage for the founding of the Caregiver Action Center (CAC). Dulnuan, a live-in caregiver employed by an affluent family in Mississauga, was murdered on October 1, 2007, days after she confided in her friends that she feared for her safety (Doolittle and Wilkes 2007). Dulnuan's case reaffirmed to Velasco the precariousness that characterized the lives of migrant care workers in Canada: "When Jocelyn Dulnuan was murdered in Mississauga, our community came together, and I became involved. I started seeing that there needed to be more activism undertaken on behalf of live-in domestic workers, that there was a need to take their concerns seriously. The murder of Dulnuan and the risk that her case was going to be dismissed because she was 'just' a live-in caregiver affected me greatly." Velasco believed that Dulnuan's case catalyzed other live-in domestic workers into being more proactive in fighting for their interests. In addition, she saw in the Dulnuan case an opportunity for the federal and provincial governments to finally pay attention to live-in domestic workers' issues: "The community of live-in domestic workers and its supporters has never wavered in its advocacy and lobbying efforts over the years. But with the federal and provincial governments that seem to be always in the hands of either the Liberals or the Conservatives, our demand for changes is ignored. Instead, these politicians continue to listen to the strong lobby of the Fraser Institute and the In-Home Coalition of Employment Agencies and Parents Coalition who are rooting for another hundred years of the backward and privatized Live-In Caregiver Program." Thus galvanized, Velasco began doing weekly "community consultations," gathering groups of live-in domestic workers together to network, to give each other information, and to exchange advice and resources. During these consultations and other CASJ events, Velasco was inspired to form a grassroots organization advocating on behalf of migrant care workers.

Having observed how organizations tended not to center migrant care workers, in 2007 Velasco started CAC (previously known as the Domestic Workers Support Services). Workers Action Centre (WAC) members who were key figures within the labor movement, such as Mary Gellatly and Deena Ladd, provided much support. That Gellatly and Ladd also emphasized centering migrant care workers' voices was important for Velasco. For Velasco, care activism necessitated ensuring that it was truly the voices of migrant care workers that were at the center of all actions. Migrant care workers—and not labor union leaders or even migrant justice organizers—had to lead the movement for change.

CAC is a progressive migrant care workers organization that consists of current and former live-in domestic workers and their allies "advocating and lobbying for fair employment, immigration status, and access to settlement services" (CAC 2012). While it has office space and received support from the WAC, as a grassroots organization, it has a full-time organizer and a group of community leaders and members who make decisions as a nonhierarchical collective. Its goals are to give domestic workers landed status on arrival; to "regularize" the status of domestic workers under the CP; to provide "decent wages, dignified working conditions, and the right to organize into unions"; to offer "protections from recruitment agencies"; and to gain the "recognition and respect for caregiving as real and important work" (CAC 2018). When it engages in policy lobbying and policy consultations with policymakers and politicians, the CAC is clear that it holds them accountable after the meeting. Given that many advocacy organizations experience consultation fatigue stemming from the multiple and repeated rounds of consultation that the federal government has organized over the years, CAC has become more adamant about engaging in "meaningful" conversations that lead to actual policy changes before choosing to partake in these consultations. Its analysis of the problems stemming from care work frequently looks at ongoing structural issues, such as the power imbalances between states that lead to the exodus of migrant workers needing to find work abroad. Along with Migrante-Canada, Gabriela-Ontario, and other progressive migrant organizations, it is part of the Migrants Rights Network, which is a national coalition in Canada of migrant organizations that demands "permanent resident status and family unit for all migrants and refugees here, and landed status on arrival for those that arrive in the future" (Migrants Rights Network 2022). Unlike Migrante-Canada and Gabriela-Ontario, however, which have a transnational reach, all of the CAC's activities are centered around policy and program improvements that are needed in Canada.

CAC members quickly mobilize in response to proposed policy changes, frequently organizing press conferences at the last minute to ensure that domestic workers' viewpoints are juxtaposed against government statements. CAC's activities include political lobbying and protests. Members are clear on their agendas and seek accountability from policymakers. They are clear that politicians cannot co-opt their presence in consultations or in public meetings to further their political careers. In addition, CAC members are adamant about centering the voices of migrant care workers in all of their actions.

I have also observed numerous instances when CAC members attended a partisan event that allowed migrant care workers' issues to be placed on the agenda. For example, in October 7, 2015, former employment minister Jason Kenney convened a gathering at an Evangelical church in Toronto that was meant to announce so-called improvements to the Caregiver Program. Because the federal elections were taking place in a few weeks, members of CAC, as well as those from other migrant organizations, were dubious about the "improvements" that were being announced. They feared that Kenney was merely using the event as an opportunity to have a photo op with the domestic workers who were gathered there to benefit his reelection campaign. Thus galvanized, CAC members planned to be at the event to make a point about the Conservative government's treatment of domestic workers. When Kenney opened the floor for questions, CAC leaders, including Pura Velasco, were the first to make pointed queries, highlighting the restrictions domestic workers faced under the new Caregiver Program, long waiting times when processing migrant care workers' permanent residency applications, and ongoing issues with recruitment. While they spoke, CAC members held up placards that included their calls for action. CAC's questions set the stage for later queries. Representatives of other caregiver organizations, some of whom represent more conservative viewpoints, inquired about ongoing problems with the Caregiver Program. Perhaps sensing that the event was not going as planned, event organizers quickly ended the proceedings soon thereafter and made no attempts to organize a photo op with Kenney.

CAC members were also actively involved in policy discussions. As mentioned in the previous chapter, because Immigration, Refugees and Citizenship Canada (IRCC) had announced on its website in 2018 that it would no longer accept permanent residency applications in November 30, 2019, from domestic workers, CAC members renewed their mobilization efforts to oppose these changes. Working in coalition with other organizations such as CCESO, Migrante-Canada, Gabriela-Ontario, and Eto Tayong Domestic workers, CAC convened a leadership workshop to discuss impending changes and activist strategies. Through their brainstorming sessions with other organizations that took place at their headquarters at the Workers Action Centre, CAC decided that now would be a good time to present a viable policy platform that would show the Canadian government the viability of the following: giving domestic workers landed status on arrival, giving them work permits that are not tied to their employers, and permitting them entry into the country with their families. Thus, during the policy consultations that were organized by the Liberal government on the Caregiver Program in the spring of 2018, CAC presented its policy proposals and sought a more accountable process. IRCC representatives also committed to an ongoing dialogue with domestic workers that summarized the results of all of IRCC's consultations with other caregiver organizations and that outlined the next steps. All of the care workers present decided the following: rather than passively telling IRCC officials what they sought, CAC strove to ensure that these consultations are substantively meaningful. CAC leaders expressed consultation fatigue and were wary that consultations were only being conducted with a predetermined outcome in mind. And while the resulting policy changes did not go as far as CAC and other activists sought, as I discussed in the preceding chapter, the CAC and its allies were successful in ensuring that a more even dialogue was engendered. CAC hoped for a more representative consultation process that would emphasize that the Canadian government's accountability to migrant care workers, who are deeply affected by the government's policies, showed a heightened awareness of what was at stake. For the CAC, consultations are meaningless unless Canadian government officials can explain how the feedback that migrant care workers shared would be integrated into new policies. During COVID-19, CAC maintained its ongoing policy advocacy work and was, in coalition with the Committee for Domestic Workers and Caregivers Rights, the Care Giver Connection Education Support Organization, and the Migrant Workers Alliance for Change, the first migrant care worker organization to release a report, "Behind Closed Doors," outlining the vulnerabilities facing migrant care workers during the global health pandemic (CAC, CCDWR, MWAC, and CCESO 2020).

CAC also has regular press conferences to highlight needed policy changes. Since 2012 until 2020, I have attended thirteen of CAC's organized press conferences. I was always impressed by its ability to bring together caregiver members who were willing to speak publicly about their experiences and an immigration "expert" such as a lawyer or a union leader who can contextualize the experiences that domestic workers were sharing.

Beyond policy lobbying, a crucial plank of CAC's work involves leadership training. CAC holds regular leadership workshops and political leadership activist training sessions for migrant care workers. One of its first workshops, called the Community Leaders' and Advocacy Training sessions, was held on January 20, 2008, in Toronto (Philippine Reporter 2008a). During this workshop, former and current migrant workers spoke, describing their experiences under the LCP and the impetus behind their decision to become activists.

After these speakers, audience members were divided into different groups, with each group role-playing scenarios involving them meeting decision-makers such as government officials, having to set up a meeting with an MP, and organizing a delegation to march in front of parliament. All throughout the sessions, participants were taught how to speak more authoritatively on policy recommendations for the LCP. Overall, participants disclosed a "sense of readiness . . . to pursue the campaign and to win" at the end of the sessions (Philippine Reporter 2008a). These sessions show how training is needed to inspire community mobilization; more pertinently, as Velasco argues, these sessions ensure that those participating in the movement become empowered. Over my years of observing CAC's work, I have witnessed the profound impacts of their approach to leadership: many of the migrant care workers who were previously fearful of being politically involved but who approached the CAC for support later became migrant care worker organizers for CAC.

In fact, the CAC's underlying philosophy is that the presence of "educated and empowered" live-in domestic workers can ensure that social transformations takes place (CAC 2012). In that spirit, migrant care workers spearhead all of their activities, from "reaching out to other domestic workers to inform them of their rights at work and to support them when their rights have been violated" to "organizing focus group discussions, roundtables, and information sessions to raise public awareness on the issues facing live-in domestic workers and the need for change" (CAC 2012). They are also the ones who enlist volunteers enabling them to hold free legal and tax clinics. Beyond its advocacy work, CAC organizes many social events for its members. It regularly organizes events such as movie nights, art workshops, and potlucks. During COVID-19, CAC had virtual meetings, offering migrant care workers a space to be together online.

Thus, the CAC is a progressive organization that is led by migrant care workers. Unlike the Godmother Network, it engages deeply in 'political' work. It sees care activism as involving advocacy work led by migrant care workers and as involving the creation of social networks that give migrant care workers a space to be together.

First Ontario Alliance of Domestic Workers Canada (Southern Ontario)

The First Ontario Alliance of Caregivers in Canada (FOACC) is comprised of the following organizations: Association of Domestic Workers Thornhill; Domestic Workers Information Technology and Web Development Group; Domestic Workers Niagara; Domestic Workers Resource Center; Domestic Workers Resource Center Rainbow; Domestic Workers Resource Centre Seniors; Caregiver Waterloo Region Resource Network; Domestic Workers Writers Guild; Fil-Core Support Group; FOACC Cultural Arts and Center; Gateway Domestic Workers Resource Center; Milton Society of Domestic Workers; Parents, Youth, Families, and Friends in Action; Samahan ng Lahing Filipino; Scarborough Domestic Workers Resource Network; Society of Domestic Workers Woodbridge; and United Filipino Mothers Association.

Terry Olayta arrived in Canada through the FDM in 1987. Because one of the requirements for migrant care workers to become permanent residents is to provide evidence that they can support themselves in Canada, Olayta decided to enroll in a health aide course, where she met other migrant care workers. Olayta explained that taking this course helped her connect with other migrant care workers and understand that the experiences she was undergoing in Canada were common. As a result, she started feeling less isolated: "In this class I saw that 1 percent were men and 99 percent were women, and only 1 percent were non-Filipinos. This was the first time when I truly realized just how much the FDM affected Filipino women—Filipino women like me. I was overwhelmed by the fact that you're by yourself in your employer's house, and then when you go to class during the weekends, wow, there are so many of us! So you can see the power—you can feel the power in numbers."

Meeting other migrant care workers helped Olayta become involved within the migrant care worker community. Olayta was involved in numerous organizations, including organizations already mentioned in this book. But she soon grew wary of what she saw as the acrimonious and "overly political" nature of these groups. Similar to the Godmother Network's Marla Jose, Olayta felt that more visible modes of care worker organizing that involved political actions such as marching in protests did not reflect what the migrant care workers in her community wanted to do. But unlike Jose, who deliberately created an "apolitical" organization, Olayta still wanted an organization that was political but did not rely on marching in the streets and protesting. She decided to start her own organization, the Caregivers Resource Centre (CRC), in 2007. Together with Merfa Yap-Bataclan, another community activist and a member of the Filipino-Canadian Community House, Olayta elicited the support of volunteers to establish the CRC as an organization that created a Christian community of care for migrant care workers and that promoted "constructive" means of promoting their needs. Central to their work is the notion of being on a "mission" to create a community of migrant care workers who can support each other and who can "save" each other from abusive workplace situations, all the while maintaining the boundaries of "acceptable" political behavior (i.e., lobbying and "constructively engaging" is okay, but protesting and being "disruptive" is not).

Jenny Cruz, CRC Niagara's chairperson and FOACC's vice chairperson, shared Olayta's vision. Cruz was a migrant care worker in Hong Kong, where she first became exposed to the issues facing Filipina migrant care workers. In Hong Kong and, later, in Canada, Cruz was determined to reach out to fellow migrant care workers and help them with their problems. She felt that the "hardships" she underwent as a migrant care worker gave her insights into migrant care workers' problems and also inspired her to prevent other migrant care workers from going through the same ordeals. As well, she stressed that her identity as a Christian motivated her to help those in need: "These Christian principles and these Christian values, I always carry in myself. So I always think of how to help people, especially live-in domestic workers."

When Olayta and Cruz met at a domestic workers' meeting, both women immediately connected. Knowing that Olayta had extensive experience organizing migrant care workers, Cruz sought Olayta's help in organizing migrant care workers in the Niagara region and in other parts of southern Ontario.

Cruz argued that because it was difficult for migrant care workers to travel to Toronto for care worker events, there was a need for migrant care workers to have their own organizations in the areas where they lived and worked. From there, Olayta and Cruz worked together to mobilize migrant care workers in different parts of southern Ontario. When discussing their outreach efforts, Cruz said, "Once we made connections with other live-in domestic workers, we never let go of these connections. We did—and still do!—networking in every city. It's almost like planting a mission . . . planting a church mission . . . you never give up. Even if you have to spend all of your money or you have to risk your life to help people, you still move forward and do it. That's just what you do." Eventually, the two activists were able to inspire different migrant care workers to create their own organizations in their regions.

The CRC's mantra, "touching one life at a time," captures Olayta's belief that any organization representing migrant care workers should prioritize care workers' interests and needs instead of larger political considerations. Olayta (2009), in fact, stressed that the CRC operates on the basis of "democratic participation," where "dialogue" rather than discord takes place. When she described her involvement with other organizations, she made repeated references to how these organizations' constant in-fighting and agitating were "bad for the heart." The CRC, in turn, held activities that Olayta depicts as being "fun and productive." Thus, in making explicit the contrast between the CRC and the acrimonious proceedings characterizing other migrant care worker organizations, she made clear that the CRC provides migrant care workers a space of "love" and "healing" where ensuring migrant care workers' welfare is the only priority. In fact, because the CRC's leadership and membership consist solely of live-in domestic workers, Olayta believed that the CRC is truly "representative" of live-in domestic workers' preferences.

When Olayta and Cruz started organizing migrant care workers, there was a dearth of migrant care worker organizations in southern Ontario. In addition, the CRC promoted itself as an organization that offered a multitude of different events (including many social gatherings). For these reasons, it was relatively easy for Olayta and Cruz to recruit care workers and other care worker organizations to be part of a coalition. All organizations that became part of their network, which they named the First Ontario Alliance of Domestic Workers Canada (FOACC), shared the CRC's mandate. Although the CRC and its member organizations were working together actively before that, it was officially launched as a network in 2011. Forming a network consolidates the agenda of like-minded migrant care worker organizations. It does so by creating a call for action that sees the migrant care workers in its network as Canadian "nation builders" who will "fully participate in all aspects of Canadian society through political engagement, economic involvement, and social action." When I asked her about this call for action, Olayta addressed the need for live-in domestic workers to see themselves as being part of Canada and to be "proud" of their contributions to Canada. Olayta pointed to Jason Kenney's (2011) letter to FOACC "thanking all domestic workers for nurturing our parents and children and caring for our vulnerable and disabled" as proof that migrant care workers, as Kenney stated, "provide a service beyond measure."

Encouraging migrant care workers to be grateful does not mean, of course, that its members do not cater to the many problems migrant care workers face under the LCP. They believe, though, that such actions have to be realistic. All of the groups that became part of Olayta and Cruz's network shared the same desire to engage in "productive" political actions that concretely helped live-in domestic workers and facilitated migrant care workers' transition to Canada. The Kitchener-Waterloo Filipino Domestic Workers Association (KWFCA), for example, seeks to ensure the empowerment of migrant care workers through their "successful assimilation into the mainstream" (KWFCA 2012). By educating, training, and convincing migrant care workers to engage in volunteer work in the larger Canadian community, the KWFCA hopes that migrant care workers can then become "well-adjusted individuals" who "contribute to the progress of the community" and who "enjoy the benefits of being a [Canadian] citizen" (KWFCA 2012).

On a similar note, the Society of Domestic Workers—Milton advocates "making adjustments to [migrant care workers'] attitudes to promote a positive approach to thinking about and enacting care work." In addition, it seeks to instill "positive behavior" in migrant care workers' "moral, social, and intellectual" lives. A poem written by Joyce Sarol (2011), secretary of Domestic Workers Niagara, encapsulates the belief that migrant care workers should always be positive and be "thankful": "Be thankful . . . for all the complaining you hear about a government because it means that there is freedom of speech . . . for the taxes you paid because it means that you are employed . . . for your limitations because there is room for improvement . . . for trials and sufferings because it makes you feel you are human and makes you depend on God." Sarol's poem, in fact, points to how FOACC encourages migrant care workers to place spirituality and religion at the center of their lives as a way to cope with life in Canada.

FOACC's primary goal is to provide migrant care workers with a safe, nonjudgmental space. Participation in overtly "political" activities, which FOACC defines as marching in protests and lobbying, is optional. With about half of the groups in FOACC's network consisting of social groups, migrant care workers are not forced to be politically active; they can engage in campaigns only if they want to, which for Olayta is yet another reason why her organization is different from other groups: "The key things to our activist work is education, friendship, fun—that should be the elements that is moving the movement. These should form the basis for the spirit of our activist work. Domestic workers shouldn't just sit there and go, 'Oh this is so boring. We don't care.'" FOACC holds events such as Christmas pageants and writing workshops. It even had, until 2018, an annual Miss Caregiver beauty pageant.

The Miss Caregiver beauty pageant was started in 2006 by the Fil-Core Support Group (Tiosen 2011), an organization that became part of FOACC and that was soon adapted as one of FOACC's marquee events. The winner of Miss Caregiver represents migrant care worker organizations in lobbying meetings with policymakers. When the federal Conservative government was in power, one of Miss Caregiver's prizes was going to Ottawa to meet Conservative members of Parliament and to lobby them for policy improvements on behalf of care workers. For example, Alma Tacuboy, Miss Caregiver 2010, headed FOACC's delegation to meet members of Parliament and former immigration minister Jason Kenney. During this meeting, Tacuboy discussed FOACC's recommendations on the LCP. Such lobbying effort is an excellent example of how the migrant care worker organizations that form part of Olayta and Cruz's network interpret "constructive" political advocacy.

Because the migrant care workers in its network prioritize escaping from the drudgery of live-in care work over participating in political campaigns, FOACC ensures that it is responsive to these demands. Unlike other organizations, which tend to see social events as a secondary part of their work, FOACC makes them a central component of its work. That its social events explicitly do not have a political agenda distinguishes FOACC events from those of other groups. For example, although the winner of the Miss Caregiver pageant lobbies policymakers in Ottawa, beyond this encounter, it does not have a larger political goal. This is unlike the Migrante Network's Mother-of-the-Year contest, which is a "political" beauty pageant aiming to expose the hardships faced by migrant mothers. Such an emphasis on "fun," as Olayta described it, induces migrant care workers to be part of their network. For FOACC, showing care for migrant care workers thus entails creating a community of care free from the stresses of work, work that can include the types of advocacy and protest actions undertaken by migrant care worker activists in the CAC and the Migrante Canada network.

As Olayta stated, these tactics give migrant care workers "relief from emotional pain" and help them "build friendships and build hope." While one could argue that doing so makes migrant care workers complacent and denies them the opportunity to fight for their interests, Olayta believed that adopting this attitude is ultimately more productive. Rather than constantly seeking redress for the abuses they suffer under the LCP, migrant care workers are able to be more realistic about their situations. As Olayta emphasized, "You can fight, but you have to fight strategically." Each member organization within the FOACC network thus emphasizes the need for migrant care workers to assimilate into Canada by becoming more "positive" about their experience, echoing Olayta's belief that migrant care workers need not be too "militant" in their approach to activism. Rather than being frustrated by agitating for migrant care workers' rights—oftentimes to no avail—FOACC believes that encouraging migrant care workers to have a "positive" attitude toward their situation will be more productive in the long run. Olayta argued that "if we break this 'cancer' of the mind—if we see things too negatively—then we can start seeing our circumstances differently. Our mindset is not just confined to this and that and petty things." Seeing their assimilation into Canada as a necessary prerequisite to their well-being, Olayta and Cruz thus encourage migrant care workers' ongoing involvement in community events, which they argue not only will help migrant care workers adjust to Canada but also will help Canadian society at large accept them and recognize them as valid citizens of Canada.

In contrast to the other organizations discussed here, FOACC is distinct in its insistence that migrant care workers should be grateful to the Canadian nation-state for giving them the opportunity to live and work in the country; hence, gratitude and "strategic fighting" rather than taking part in what they characterize as acrimonious politics should define their work. Care activism for FOACC thus involves instilling among migrant care workers a more "positive" and more "realistic" mindset. It is less important for us to imagine what the world could be; instead, we should constructively seek changes within the world as it is. In sum, as a conservative organization, FOACC sees value in lobbying for policy improvements in a "constructive" (i.e., nondisruptive) manner. FOACC fosters the creation of Christian communities of care for migrant care workers, centering gratitude, joy, and hope in its activities.

The Migrante Canada Network
(Vancouver and Victoria, BC; Calgary, Edmonton, and Fort McMurray, AB; Winnipeg, MB; Toronto and Ottawa, ON; and Montreal, Sherbrooke, and Quebec City, QC)

The furor surrounding Filipina domestic worker Flor Contemplacion's hanging in Singapore in 1992 was decisive in mobilizing migrant workers in the Philippines. Contemplacion was found guilty of murdering Delia Maga, a fellow

Filipina domestic worker, and the child under Maga's care. Because of the Philippine government's reluctance to intervene on Contemplacion's behalf, she soon became a symbol of the failures of the Philippine government's labor export programs (Rodriguez 2002, 341–42). Migrant workers in particular were appalled by the disjuncture between the Philippine government's portrayal of migrant workers as modern-day "heroes" making vital contributions to the Philippine economy and its indifference to the plight of migrant workers. Contemplacion's struggles served as the catalyst for migrant workers' political awakening. The "collective rage" they felt toward the Philippine government stemmed from the realization that "those on top were not doing what they should do: showing compassion and looking after the welfare of its citizens abroad" (Rafael 1997, 278).

Galvanized groups of migrant workers subsequently started to initiate discussions on the issues facing them, ultimately leading to the formation of Migrante in 1996 (Migrante 2012). Since then, Migrante's reach has extended beyond the Philippines, where its headquarters is still located, and it has become active in other countries. The successes of Migrante–Hong Kong, which became the first Migrante chapter overseas, led migrant workers to organize chapters in other countries. To oversee the operations of its chapters abroad and to coordinate its activities, Migrante-International was soon created. With over ninety organizations in twenty-two countries, Migrante's influence is widely dispersed. The vast scope of its network gives migrant workers access to the various events sponsored by Migrante chapters abroad and, more crucially, provides them with assistance when facing labor abuse.

Although there were organizations in Canada that were affiliated with Migrante-International, it was not until 2008 when Migrante-Canada was established. The activists who played a major role in establishing Migrante-Canada had different reasons for doing so. There were leaders who came to Canada as exiles from the Philippines due to their suppression under the Ferdinand Marcos regime. There were others who were broadly interested in migration issues because of their or their families' personal, harrowing immigration histories. Yet a substantial number of Migrante's members consisted of migrant workers themselves, including those who were currently involved in struggles to regularize their status and to overcome abusive employment conditions. Over the years, I have also witnessed a new generation of Migrante's leaders whose parents were migrant workers. In particular, leaders whose parents were migrant care workers were galvanized because of their experiences of years living apart from their parents and the difficulties they faced when adjusting to life in Canada.

Even prior to Migrante-Canada's official founding in 2008, there were discussions under way on the need to create a larger, unified migrants' coalition among activists. For instance, the Jocelyn Dulnuan murder in 2007, discussed in the previous chapter, compelled migrant workers to form an organization. Former NDP MP Peggy Nash approached Christopher Sorio, a longtime community activist whose experiences as a student activist during the Ferdinand Marcos regime catalyzed his advocacy on behalf of migrants' issues in Canada. Nash told Sorio that she wanted to initiate legislation on behalf of migrant workers. Nash's request, along with others from the community who sought legislative changes, incentivized migrant activists to work together to understand the situations of live-in domestic workers and to devise policy recommendations. This coalition eventually became known as the Coalition for the Protection of Caregivers' Rights (CPCR), and put different migrant activists in contact with each other. At the same time as CPCR finalized its list of recommendations, Migrante-Canada was launched on the same day as what would have been Dulnuan's fortieth birthday.

While migrant activists were working together in Ontario to devise a list of recommendations for the LCP, there was discord among the members of SIKLAB-BC, an organization that was part of the Philippine Women's Centre network. Even before Migrante-Canada was established, SIKLAB-BC was a member of Migrante-International. A desire to be more "strategic," however, convinced some of the members of SIKLAB-BC to leave Migrante-International (Lindio-McGovern 2013, 97). Because the dissenting members within SIKLAB-BC wanted to remain part of Migrante-International and agreed with its mandate, these members founded Migrante-BC in 2009. According to Ordinario, the process of organizing the "Solons tour," which involved making arrangements for three Philippine opposition party members to speak about human rights abuses in the Philippines (*Philippine Reporter* 2008b), widened Migrante's reach, leading to more members.

Eventually, as the advocacy work of Migrante-Canada became known in other parts of Canada, migrant activists became inspired to establish their own organizations. The first Migrante chapter was founded in Toronto, but soon after, other chapters were established in different parts of Canada. Given that migrant workers and, in particular, migrant care workers are not a monolithic group, migrant activists sought ways to represent these specific needs.

For example, Binnadang-Migrante was launched in 2011 as an organization "by, of and for, the Philippine Cordillera indigenous peoples" (Cleto 2011). Its goals were to simultaneously support "migrant workers' rights," the call for Philippine national liberation, and, most importantly, the struggle for the self-determination of Philippine indigenous groups. During its launch, guest speakers such as Vernie Yocogan-Diano, who is part of Gabriela-Philippines and the chairperson of Innabuyog, an alliance of indigenous women in the Cordillera region, reminded the audience of how Canadian mining companies have been actively plundering indigenous land in the Philippines. Yocogan-Diano reiterated the importance of being aware of these transnational connections and asked the Binnadang-Migrante members, most of whom were migrant care workers from indigenous Filipino groups, whether this was "the home [they] would like to return to?"

Another example was the formation of Migrante-Youth, which directly addressed the issues facing the children of migrant workers, especially the children of migrant care workers, who had to adjust not only to life in a new country but also to a life with formerly absent parents. By organizing social events for youth members such as sports events—for example, Migrante-Youth in BC has a youth basketball league—migrant youth's feelings of isolation are decreased. It also has art workshops that give migrant youth the opportunity to express their feelings through art. For instance, Bert Monterona, an internationally acclaimed muralist, held classes teaching Migrante-Youth members how to paint. Monterona was able to get funding from the city of Vancouver to support this endeavor. Beth Dollaga, a Migrante-BC member, spoke highly of this event: "Sometimes, it is very difficult for our youth—especially those who have just come and have been reunited with their families—to express themselves. With visual arts, there is no limit to their expression. It's just like music. Art is something that has no limits. Migrant youth were able to express their political and socioeconomic ideas through visual art." In addition, Migrante-Youth holds workshops that help migrant youth contextualize their experiences of family separation and family reunification amid the structural realities of economic inequalities between countries, which acted as "push" factors compelling their parents to seek jobs abroad. These workshops not only help alleviate migrant youth's feelings of abandonment but also inspire them to be engaged politically.

Hence, the various organizations that form part of Migrante-Canada respond to its members' particular needs and their specific political beliefs. According to its leaders, the vast scope of Migrante-Canada and the ability of organizations to respond to the specific needs of its members are sources of strength. It is worth noting, of course, that its campaigns on the LCP specifically and on behalf of migrant workers generally are inextricably linked to its larger advocacy for democratic reform in the Philippines and its belief in ameliorating global structural inequities. Its membership in the International League of Peoples' Struggles (ILPS), a transnational grassroots network that "promotes, supports and develops the anti-imperialist and democratic struggles of the peoples of the world against imperialism" (ILPS 2022)—of which the International

Migrants Alliance (IMA), discussed in the next chapter, is a part—creates linkages between Migrante-Canada and other grassroots organizations with a similar vision.

Migrante-Canada's activism is multiscalar, engaging a variety of actors in Canada, in the Philippines, and in transnational grassroots and mainstream forums. While it is active in ensuring that migrants' needs are met by organizing events, programs, and workshops for domestic workers and by actively campaigning for policy reforms in conjunction with various allies, its goals to find alternatives to labor migration and to end global structural inequities ensure that its activism is also equally focused on larger, structural campaigns. To be clear, Migrante-Canada does not draw a line demarcating labor migration and global structural inequities. For Migrante-Canada, the very existence of structural inequities makes developing countries vulnerable to economic exploitation by developed countries, leading to the rise of labor export programs, of which migrant care work is an extremely lucrative part. Hence, its campaigns always strive to make clear the linkages between structural inequities, Philippine politics, and the community-level and individual harms created by migrant care work. Normatively, Migrante-Canada seeks to end labor export programs, create true democracy in the Philippines with an equitable distribution of wealth and a national industrialization program, and eradicate power discrepancies between developed and developing countries. Migrante-Canada's ties with the national democratic movement in the Philippines, including with mass organizations such as the Bagong Alyansang Makabayan (Bayan) and its affiliate chapters abroad, including Bayan Canada, show that its work is tied to the larger project of ending poverty through ending power structures such as feudalism, capitalism, and imperialism.[3]

Migrante-Alberta's Marco Luciano describes activism as necessarily taking place on "united fronts," which necessitates using all possible means at one's disposal to engender social justice for migrants. Taking a united front approach to activism consequently entails forming broad alliances, lobbying policymakers, protesting, participating in legal actions, taking part in media campaigns, holding art shows, and so on. These activities are designed to reach multiple stakeholders and elicit change.

On the policy advocacy front, Migrante-Canada actively lobbies the Canadian government and the Philippine government for improvements in policies. Its members meet regularly with government officials on behalf of its members facing distress. It submits policy briefs on various issues, such as extending provincial employment standards regulations to domestic workers and giving domestic workers landed status on arrival.

When advocating directly for its members, Migrante-Canada also supports migrant workers who file legal cases against abusive employers and recruiters. The down payment for the house for Bahay Migrante, which I discuss in the beginning of this chapter, was paid for using part of the settlement from a lawsuit that migrant workers filed against the restaurant chain Denny's. Migrante-BC members, 98 percent of whom were migrant domestic workers, contributed the rest. According to Migrante-BC's Erie Maestro, one migrant caregiver who was at that point currently under the LCP gave $1,000 because she felt a "sacred trust and love" for Migrante-BC.

Having an actual space that is owned by Migrante members is crucial in helping distressed migrant workers. Maestro explains that since taking ownership of the house, they have had the opportunity to provide shelter for migrant workers who have been trafficked, migrant domestic workers who were fleeing situations of abuse, and other members who simply needed a place to live. She stated, "We wouldn't have been able to give this support without the house."

Migrante-Canada's extensive network benefits its members tremendously, allowing the organization to widen its communities of care. Maestro discussed, for instance, the case of Letitia Sarmiento, a migrant caregiver who filed human trafficking charges against her employer. A Migrante-BC member met Sarmiento in a shelter where she was volunteering and told Sarmiento about Migrante-BC. Migrante-BC then found her a lawyer, put her in touch with sympathetic politicians, and supported her throughout her case, which ended with the court finding her employers guilty of human trafficking.

Migrante-Canada's network is also national. Migrant workers, for example, have access to a toll-free 1-800 hotline, which different Migrante-Canada leaders take turns handling. Migrante-Canada, like a lot of other migrant worker organizations, also conducts rescue missions, during which they fetch migrant care workers fleeing abusive employers and take them to a safe place. The organization's connections then allow it to help these workers find other jobs. Migrante-Canada also sponsors seminars and workshops contributing to its members' professional development and transition to Canada.

Aside from direct public advocacy, Migrante-Canada sees that one of the difficulties facing migrant workers generally—and migrant care workers specifically—was the question of educational and professional accreditation. To meet these goals, Migrante-Canada has several partnerships with labor unions. For example, Peter Leibovitch from the United Steelworkers (USW) helped classify Migrante members as an "affiliated community of workers," thereby allowing migrant care workers to take courses that were given for union members

(IWworkers 2011). The Education Without Borders campaign, which Migrante-Canada cosponsored with the Workers Action Centre and the United Food and Commercial Workers (UFCW), is another example of how Migrante-Canada has benefited from close ties with a labor union. The Education Without Borders campaign gives all Migrante-Canada members free access to the online college courses offered by UFCW; in addition, Migrante-Canada members are eligible to apply for migrant workers' scholarships.

Migrante-Canada also helps facilitate educational courses that would help migrant care workers pass the language requirements imposed following the 2014 changes to the caregiver program. Migrante-Alberta, for example, has a regularly scheduled course that helps caregivers pass International English Language Testing System (IELTS) level 5, which they require for their citizenship application. Given that most IELTS training programs are expensive, Migrante-Alberta's ability to offer this course for free ensures wider accessibility for migrant care workers. At the end of the course, Migrante-Alberta has a graduation ceremony for its students, celebrating that this was a course that migrant care workers were able to finish despite the onerous demands on their time. Through rituals like graduation ceremonies and regular celebrations (e.g., Mother's Day), Migrante-Canada consciously creates a space of care for migrant care workers that honors their accomplishments.

Like other organizations, Migrante-Canada sponsors events that contribute to its members' political socialization. Similar to CAC and to the PWC, critical political education is a crucial part of Migrante-Canada's work. To care for migrant workers is to show them that others share their experiences and, more importantly, that these experiences emerge out of a long history of colonial exploitation. Global South countries like the Philippines are economically dependent on Global North countries, supplying Global North countries with goods (including human capital) in order to meet their economic needs. Understanding these structural inequities can thus help migrant workers to see that there are larger issues at hand, that their individual experiences are connected to long-standing inequities. Such topics become part of the curriculum for the regular Migrante schools. Interestingly, some of its current members have also participated in Migrante schools outside Canada, either in the Philippines before they migrated abroad or in other countries where they worked prior to coming to Canada. A few even sent their children to Migrante schools in the Philippines before their children joined them in Canada to ensure that their children were aware of the realities of migration and settlement before moving. These educational classes are crucial so that migrant workers and their families can contextualize their circumstances.

Continuous linkages with Migrante chapters in the Philippines and in other countries through Migrante schools and other campaigns remain a vital component of Migrante-Canada's work. Migrante-Canada regularly organizes relief efforts giving aid to Filipinos in need, which it sends to its partner organizations in the Philippines. In November 2013, for example, much of its work was dedicated to amassing contributions for people who were victims of Typhoon Haiyan.

Migrante-Canada has links with Migrante Partylist, a political party in the Philippines seeking to elect candidates into the Senate and into Congress, and has hosted events in Canada such as helping Filipinos residing abroad register as absentee voters to compel Filipinos in Canada to continue being politically active in the Philippines. It also regularly has events discussing and campaigning against incidences of political corruption and political oppression in the Philippines. In October 2013, for instance, it held a "pork barrel" forum contesting pervasive corruption in the Philippine Senate. Migrante-Canada members regularly hold vigils and protests in front of the Philippine embassy in support of their political stances.

In recent years, Migrante-Canada, similar to other Migrante chapters worldwide, has been actively organizing against former Philippine president Rodrigo Duterte's regime. Because many of its members were anti-Marcos activists who were politically tortured under the Marcos regime, they draw many parallels between the human rights abuses under Marcos and under Duterte. In September 2018 Migrante-Ontario, for example, held an event commemorating martial law. In her prepared remarks, Migrante-Ontario's Maria Sol Pajadura discussed how the Philippines' labor export program, first established by Marcos and continued by ensuing presidential regimes, continues to be a lynchpin of the Philippine government's economic development program under Duterte. Hence, Migrante-Canada, arguably more so than any of the organizations featured in this chapter, remains extremely engaged with Philippine politics. It is a fundamental part of its mandate. Chapter 5 discusses how Migrante's activism in the Philippines reinforces the advocacy work other Migrante chapters undertake worldwide, including with Migrante-Canada.

In addition, Migrante-Canada consciously creates spaces for its members to use art and pageantry as ways to make their individual experiences visible. For example, it holds an annual story-writing competition. All of the entries in the 2011 competition showcased tales written by migrant care workers, whose experiences of labor abuse under the LCP and family separation and reunification resonated with the other Migrante-Canada members who read them.

In this vein, Migrante-Canada has occasionally organized the Mother-of-the-Year competition. Structured as a "political" beauty pageant, this competition includes representatives from each of the Migrante-Canada organizations, all of whom have to compete in several categories, including "talent" and "question-and-answer." During the talent portion, all contestants showcased one-woman acts featuring aspects of their migration experience. One contestant, for example, acted out a skit that showed the different stages of her relationship with her children, highlighting how she was once close to her children when she still lived with them but then gradually became estranged from them upon moving abroad to work as a migrant care worker. Another contestant sang a song that expressed the harrowing plight of migrant workers. During the "question-and-answer" portion, all contestants made references to their personal experiences as migrant care workers and discussed what they ultimately hoped to achieve in Canada, with most mentioning that they want to find stable jobs and be reunited with their families. For the contestants, participating in the Mother-of-the-Year competition bolstered their confidence and gave them an outlet to express their frustrations. For the audience, most of whom were also migrant care workers, seeing their friends affirm the hardships they were also going through under the LCP was a cathartic experience. These artistic initiatives highlight how care activism involves the creation of spaces for affirmation. In these spaces, migrant workers can express themselves artistically. The migrant workers looking at the artwork, reading their stories, and watching Mother-of-the-Year can also then see their own experiences represented in these mediums, thus enabling mutual feelings of catharsis.

Moreover, while Migrante-Canada is a secular organization, unlike FOACC and the Godmother Network, religious rituals are embedded in some of its work. Migrante-BC organizes a regular "migrants' station of the cross" during Lent, where each "station" draws parallels between Jesus's experiences and those of migrant workers. It has signed a statement of unity with other churches and labor unions in support of migrant workers. Migrante-Ontario sometimes co-organizes migrants' masses with churches that have a high number of parishioners who are migrant workers. In doing so, it recognizes that religious and spiritual life is an important source of strength for migrant workers.

With more Migrante chapters being established annually, the increase in Migrante-Canada's membership base means that as an organization, it is gradually growing stronger. The autonomy accorded to each of its member organizations allows Migrante-Canada to be responsive to the diverse needs of its individual members. When asked why people are interested in being part of Migrante-Canada, Migrante-BC's Erie Maestro referred to the multifaceted nature of its organizing efforts. Creating a community of care is key: "People want to join. Even those who weren't active. There was someone who wants to join. I asked why. She said because we were the only ones who don't fight. We're not just an organization that organizes rallies, that goes to the Consulate, that marches, that protests, that lobbies. All of that is important, but we also provide people with a space. We also have a basketball team, we have a Mother's Day event, we have volleyball, we have art. We even have events with the church."

Migrante-Canada's politics are aligned with CAC, often working with CAC on numerous campaigns through its ongoing work within the Migrants Rights Network. Unlike the Godmother Network and FOACC, Migrante-Canada sees the importance of using a variety of political tactics—from direct lobbying to protest actions—to push for change. As a progressive network with national, cross-national, and transnational networks, Migrante-Canada lobbies for policy change, seeks structural transformation, and creates generative communities of care for its members.

The Magkaisa Centre

The Magkaisa Centre is comprised of the following groups: the Philippine Women Centre of BC (PWC-BC), the Philippine Women Centre of Ontario (PWC-ON), and the Filipino Canadian Youth Alliance (Magkaisa Centre 2021).[4] For the purposes of this chapter, I will be primarily focusing on the work of the Philippine Women's Centre (PWC).

Prominent community and migrant activists Cecilia Diocson's and Emmanuel Sayo's exposure to migrant care work began in the 1980s, when they started meeting women who were part of the FDM. During that time, most of the migrant care workers they met were not just from the Philippines but also from southern European countries such as Italy, Portugal, and Spain. Based on these women's experiences of abuse and exploitation under the FDM, Diocson and Sayo began organizing them into a movement by informing them of their labor rights and by providing support for them by being there when they were needed. While they also gave the same support to Filipina migrant care workers, the work they undertook with these Filipina women was also invariably linked to the anti-Marcos, prodemocracy struggles that were taking place at that time.

The presence of Filipina migrant care workers in Canada, Diocson and Sayo believed, was one of the many harmful consequences of Marcos's regime. As Sayo explained, "From the very beginning, organizing domestic workers—you have to understand—involved providing our support and solidarity for the Filipino struggle going on at that time. There was a struggle for the restoration of civil liberties, for democracy in the Philippines. So part of that work is to look at these Filipinos as people who were displaced because of the martial law regime in the Philippines. So that was part of our organizing." It soon became obvious to both women that the situation of Filipina migrant care workers was so dire that they gradually began to focus more thoroughly on the issues facing migrant care workers. As Sayo described it, "We started formally organizing domestic workers along progressive lines."

In 1987 conversations between Diocson and other migrant care workers planted the seeds for the foundation of what became the Philippine Women Centre in Vancouver, founded officially in 1989. The urgent needs of migrant caregivers inspired its founding.

The PWC's normative vision seeks the end of class struggles and neoliberal exploitation, leading to the full equality of all women. From the very beginning, one of the PWC's main agendas was to "reclaim the history of the working-class woman" and to "look at the struggles of the working class, which has been and continues to be a gender issue."[5] The FDM and, later, the LCP were to Diocson and Sayo a blatant example of class exploitation, where affluent, white families in Canada benefited from the labor power of poor, working-class women from developing countries. Creating an organization where working-class women like migrant care workers were at the helm and were not relegated to menial tasks became a priority.

The PWC's analysis, however, remained rooted in structural critiques. Contrary to the perception offered by sending and receiving states that migration presents a "golden economic opportunity" for migrants, the PWC condemns the "severe crisis in the global economy" that individualizes one's understanding of the problems facing migrants and that distracts from the larger problem at hand, namely, the perpetuation of capitalist exploitation (Sayo 2011). For the PWC, it is therefore important to see the duality of the struggles against capitalism. Using the analytical framework of a "counterspin," which it holds as a corrective to the tendency of "the dominant discourse to spin to the right," the PWC prioritizes looking always at the structural forces underpinning labor migration while focusing its advocacy endeavors on organizing in Canada. As Sayo argues, "We are here to stay in Canada and our struggle for societal change and transformation is here. This struggle takes on different forms and expressions and, in the end, it is part of the whole process of the struggle for socialism in Canada." Part of the work of helping create a socially just Canada involves working alongside Black, indigenous, and queer communities, leading the PWC to co-organize with these groups. The PWC, for example, had a campaign on Cancel Canada Day in 2021 in solidarity with indigenous communities (Magkaisa Centre 2021).

The eradication of exploitative programs such as the LCP consequently plays an important part of the PWC's vision. Throughout the years, the PWC has not abated its stance against the LCP, becoming one of the most forceful voices seeking its abolition.

Diocson described the PWC's early days as being difficult but inspirational. With only six members to start, five of whom were migrant care workers and one of whom was a professional, the group did not have a formal space at that point and so borrowed space from supportive religious organizations such as the United Church of Canada. According to Diocson, the PWC's primary goal during this time was to "help domestic workers respond to their situations. For most of them, we start with their stories, asking what is happening in their employers' homes, and just telling stories." Once they had amassed enough members, they were then able to hold workshops discussing Filipina migrant care workers' roles as "women, as women workers, and as women immigrants." By discussing how gender, class, and race oppression operate on individual and structural levels, the Filipina migrant care workers present during their meetings were thus better able to contextualize their situations in Canada.

The PWC's use of intersectional analysis occurred before it became popular among academic and activist circles, and it continues to form the basis for the group's understanding of migration. Diocson described the analytical framework they developed back then: "Aside from workshops and giving them the perspective that they are women workers who are members of an ethnic minority and are thus triply discriminated against, we also said that racism was part of the program. We said that we should really look at the policy as part of a racist policy targeting women. Way back, we were already talking about these issues." Because of its networking successes, the PWC was soon well-known not just within the Filipino community but also within Vancouver and across the country. It dispensed advice to migrant care workers facing abusive living and working conditions. In some cases, the PWC also provided its members with contacts who could refer migrant care workers fleeing their employers to places with shelter; later, when the PWC acquired office space, it provided these women with temporary housing.

Aside from providing services, an integral part of the PWC's activities is research. By understanding more thoroughly the experiences of marginalized communities, including live-in domestic workers, the PWC hopes to create programs that more effectively meet these communities' needs and, more crucially, to understand the sources of oppression that can thus form part of their activist pursuits. The acquisition of research funding allowed the PWC and its allies to pursue its action-oriented research agenda more substantially. While the PWC has regularly undertaken research endeavors since its inception, getting support helped make the PWC more prolific. Through these funded research endeavors, the PWC was able to use the research it gathered in its lobbying and protest efforts as a mode of community mobilization and also as a way to spread awareness.

The use of participatory action research (PAR), which the PWC argued is "based on the principle of starting and learning from the experiences of the community and its members, collectively analyzing and synthesizing these experiences and planning action for social change and participation," enabled the "empowerment of disempowered groups" (NAPWC-ON 2008, 18). It received funding from Status of Women-Canada (a government agency) in 1999, after which it received more funding in 2000 to organize a conference in Winnipeg looking at Filipino migrants and immigrants. The 2000 conference addressed experiences of "economic marginalization, immigration problems, recognition and accreditation of skills and foreign education, and youth issues." In 2001 the PWC organized a conference in Vancouver. Centering the concerns of the Filipino Nurses Support Group (FNSG), it "critiqued the LCP as stalling the full development of women who come under the program" and sought "the recognition and accreditation of Filipino nurses doing domestic work" (NAPWC-ON 2008, 14).

The strengths of the PWC's work in these areas enabled it to obtain funding from Canadian Heritage and Multiculturalism (a government agency) from 2006 to 2009 for "Filipino Community and Beyond: Towards Full Participation in Multicultural Canada." This was a program that assessed Filipinos' "settlement and integration" in Canada, further expanding the scope of the PWC's research and advocacy work to look more fully at the key barriers that its leaders and members found negatively affected the Filipino community's integration into Canada. Because of this funding, the National Alliance of Philippine Women in Canada (NAPWC), consisting of different Philippine Women Centres across Canada, was formed. NAPWC obtained an office and staff (NAPWC-ON 2008, 22), making it a more established organization that was widely recognized by the Filipino community and by members of Canadian society. This also led to the establishment of three centers: the Kalayaan Centre in Vancouver, the Kapit Bisig Centre in Montreal, and the Magkaisa Centre in Montreal. Having access to a physical space within these three cities enabled the PWC and its allies to be more present within each of these communities, consequently allowing them to reach out to more Filipino community members.

More significantly, this project consolidated the PWC's previous work on marginalized communities and more clearly set out the PWC's research and advocacy priorities, which involve examining the following issues:

1. The causes and factors leading to the economic marginalization of the community, which includes assessing the non-recognition of skills and foreign education; the non-accreditation of professional training; de-skilling; streaming into low-paying occupations; the lack or slow enforcement of equity policies and programs such as affirmative action in public employment;

2. Racism, discrimination, and social exclusion, which include looking at the Filipino community's tendency to ghettoization and their low participation in civil, social, and political affairs;

3. Women and gender issues, which encompass understanding why the majority of Filipinos in Canada are women and scrutinizing the stalled development of women, especially those under the LCP;

4. Youth issues, which addresses why Filipino youth have one of the highest drop-out rates in high school, Filipino youth's sense of social and civic alienation, and their rights and responsibilities. (NAPWC-ON 2008, 14–15)

The PWC believes that these four areas "are key variables that must be addressed in order to achieve full participation and contribute to the strengthening of social cohesion in a multicultural society like Canada" (NAPWC-ON 2008, 16).

On the basis of these priorities, the PWC and its allies organized multiple conferences across Canada that served as platforms for data gathering, community mobilization, and awareness-raising. I attended the November 2006 launch of the project in Toronto through its conference, "Making the Filipino Community Count." Its November 2008 conference, "Filipino Community and Beyond: Towards Full Participation in a Multicultural and Multi-ethnic Canada," provided an update on the results of the project and initiated collaborative data analysis with conference attendees.

A significant cross section of Filipino and non-Filipino community members attended the initial conference in 2006, with over one hundred students, professors, migrant care workers, factory workers, activists, and professionals represented. The activities organized were comprised of academic and activist panels explaining the situation of the Filipino community in Canada and delineating research from academics and activists documenting Filipinos' economic, political, and social marginalization in Canada, and "break out" brainstorming sessions where attendees were given the opportunity to address the challenges they were facing and the advocacy efforts they could pursue to mitigate these challenges. The energy and the enthusiasm that emerged from this initial conference were palpable for everyone I spoke to, with all indicating a willingness to be part of a community organization that formed part of a "movement" that created concrete changes for Filipino community members and, by extension, other communities of color. In particular, the sessions on Filipino youth, which showcased research illustrating how Filipino youth (including the children of migrant care workers) were underachieving in schools compared to their Canadian and immigrant counterparts galvanized everyone in attendance, many of whom were under the impression that Filipino youth, like their immigrant parents, had high rates of academic success.

The 2008 follow-up conference resulted in the same expressions of solidarity. With even more people attending, the 2008 conference disclosed the results of its research and community-building activities through activist and academic panels on the issue areas identified earlier. Between panels there were artistic performances that made political points. For example, during a fashion show called "Scrap: A political fashion show to stop violence against Filipino women," various models posed in scenarios that highlighted Filipina women's abject position in Canada, including scenarios specific to the LCP.

In addition, like the 2006 conference, there were break-out workshop sessions, this time on systemic racism, discrimination, and social exclusion, which tackled Filipinos' continuing experiences of deprofessionalization and deskilling. Sessions on family reunification and migration were inspired by narratives of pain and loneliness expressed by live-in domestic workers and their children, and sessions on youth dropouts, education, and employment disclosed Filipino youth's issues in integrating into Canada. In keeping with its mandate to create a mass movement consisting of Filipino migrant care workers, laborers, youth, activists and Filipino community members, the PWC has what it calls a "comprehensive model of organizing," which analyzes the types of oppression facing different sectors of the Filipino community and, in particular, Filipina women based on a feminist intersectionality approach. The sustainability of the movement the PWC helped create is for Diocson and Sayo a source of pride, for they believe that their refusal to compromise and their adherence to progressive politics enabled the PWC and its allies to "make their own history." Care activism for them involves being uncompromising and being staunch in their refusal to shy away from ongoing structural critiques.

Nevertheless, Diocson and Sayo also recognize that for the movement to grow, the causes they look at have to also shift. Focusing on the issues facing Filipino youth was a particular concern. As Diocson argued:

We also say that we really need to look at the other issues in our community because our community is not just live-in domestic workers. If we do not look at the issues of the younger generations and just focus on the LCP, it's not enough. That's why we need to move on and get the young people on board. They'll be able to articulate the issues of our domestic workers, our mothers, because we know—and we have the capacity—deep inside, there are so many issues and traumas that they experience that they can't cope by themselves. But the children—and you can now see the children of the domestic workers out there defending their moms—they are articulating their needs.

Including issues of family separation and reunification in its work thus allows the PWC to be more responsive to the needs of its members, providing them with the opportunity to understand and get support for their situations.

For example, as part of its project to understand family separation and reunification issues, the PWC participated in several research projects with Geraldine Pratt (2012), which later formed the basis for the play *Nanay*. Members of PWC were part of this theatrical production, which offered them the opportunity to express their feelings about how the LCP fragmented their families in a manner that is more impactful and more visceral than rallying or writing op-eds. The catharsis experienced by Canadian participants and audience members (including migrant care workers and their children) during the play enables greater understanding of these family issues, which then encourages more people to be sympathetic to migrant care workers' needs. Live-in domestic workers watching the play also experienced affirmation that their experiences were the norm, thereby decreasing feelings of isolation.

The creation of a space of their own was an important component of the PWC's activism. Through regular gatherings such as Sinigang Sundays (sinigang is a sour Filipino soup), which included a study series that helped community members discuss issues such as culture and identity, the history of the Live-in Caregiver Program, and contradictions under capitalism (NAPWC-BC 2016), the PWC and its organizations created a space where people could gather, eat, and hang out.

In sum, the ability of the PWC to see care activism as involving not only migrant care workers but also their children, other immigrants, and youth members highlights its strengths as a collective. Its analysis of the structural causes of labor migration aligns closely with Migrante-Canada and with CAC. A key difference, however, revolves around the question of whether to end migrant care worker programs. The PWC's uncompromising stance has meant that it continuously pushes public conversations to consider the often fraught question of Canadian complicity in the continuation of labor migration programs. The PWC's successes in forming its own organizations that center its members' needs shows that its abolitionist vision resonates with many.

Similarities and Differences between Organizations

Care activism involves placing at the very center migrant care workers' needs and widening one's understanding of advocacy to include the creation of communities of care for migrant care workers and their families. All of the organizations in this chapter do so, showing care for migrant care workers by giving them a space of their own. Having their own space means that migrant care workers can put themselves first: they can be part of a community of fellow migrant care workers who deeply understand their circumstances and can all collectively bear witness to each other's travails. They can create networks that can allow them to support each other when they are in distress (e.g., when they have to flee an abusive employer or when they have to find a new job). These networks also celebrate successes and important milestones (e.g., finally receiving Canadian citizenship). Migrant care workers who are part of advocacy organizations can do advocacy work in a way that makes the most sense to them. With the possible exception of the PWC, all organizations also provide a space for migrant care workers to attend to their spiritual and religious needs. Attending to migrant care workers' spiritual and religious needs does not necessarily involve liaising with specific religious dominations. Rather, these organizations recognize that many migrant care workers find strength in being part of a collective faith community and in the belief that there is a "higher power" looking out for their well-being (see Fresnoza-Flot [2010] on how religiosity can be a source of empowerment and also of social control for Filipina migrant workers).

Despite these similarities, there are differences in how migrant care worker organizations conceptualize care activism. Understanding these differences is important because this shows that there is no singular definition of care activism. As a movement, it is wide enough to encompass different organizations, all with distinct histories, goals, normative visions, and activities.

In many ways, the Godmother Network is an outlier compared to all of the organizations I examined because it deliberately paints itself as being apolitical. Jose believes that it is important to carve a space for domestic workers that does not involve activist politics. Indeed, finding ways to improve domestic workers' economic situations is what is most needed. By organizing domestic workers into an employment collective that also organizes social events and "keeps domestic workers and their families away from trouble" (to use Jose's words), the Godmother Network meets domestic workers' economic, social, and moral needs. I suggest that its explicitly apolitical stance is in itself political, because refraining from participating in policy debates and political discussions concerning care work and migration has political repercussions, as seen in elections where minimal voting turn-outs enable the election of governments that do not truly have a popular mandate. In addition, I wonder about the ability of the Godmother Network to achieve its goals of economic empowerment, because prior research shows the limitations of entrepreneurial programs in ensuring migrant care workers' long-term economic success (Weekley 2004), which is affected in part by the existence of a "stratified labour market" (Parrenas 2021) that places care and domestic work at the bottom of the labor hierarchy. Yet I recognize that the Godmother Network meets the needs of the many domestic workers who are not politically organized and who dislike advocacy work. The economic benefits that they derive may not give them much more than their salaries as migrant care workers, but knowing that they are owners of a business may be what matters more.

FOACC represents a conservative approach to migrant activism, where the focus is placed not on marching or rallying or protesting but on strategic and less confrontational forms of lobbying. While FOACC organizations endorse reforms to migrant care work policies, its leaders adhere to a form of "model minority" politics whereby its members always have to demonstrate their gratitude to Canada for accepting them into the country. Criticizing sending states like Canada for its complicity in the global brain drain and for its temporary labor migration policies that lead to forms of "global apartheid" (Sharma 2006) whereby some migrants are acceptable and others are not is contrary to FOACC's mandate. In fact, FOACC emphasizes the importance of Christian teaching in its work. It uses discourses of sacrifice, humility, and prayer to overcome adversity in prominent ways.

CAC, Migrante-Canada, and the PWC all represent more progressive approaches to caregiver activism. Unlike the Godmother Network and FOACC, they take part in political lobbying and in protest activities. Yet CAC differs from Migrante-Canada and from the PWC in that its members and leaders are exclusively domestic workers. And while CAC, like Migrante-Canada and PWC, sees the problems facing migrant care workers as being tied to structural issues, its foremost goals are about improving the situations of domestic workers in Canada through policy change, through educational and information awareness campaigns, and through the creation of social networks. Its lobbying activities take place primarily in Toronto and pertain mostly to combating Canadian policies.

In contrast, Migrante-Canada and PWC, as Filipino organizations consisting of leaders either who come from an anti-Marcos activist background in the Philippines and thus have a heightened awareness of the injustices facing Filipinos abroad or who worked or currently work as migrant domestic workers, have a broader scope. Migrante-Canada and the PWC share a similar structural analysis of the underlying problems with migrant care work. While migrant care worker policies themselves cause problems for migrant domestic workers, the roots of the problem—namely, neoliberal capitalism, colonialism, and feudalism—go much deeper. Differences between the two, however, emerge on the question of normative visions. Migrante-Canada takes a more critical reformist stance to the issue, acknowledging that Canada's caregiver program is deeply flawed yet remains a crucial pathway for migrant workers into Canada. As a nonreformist reformer (Dilts and Walia 2016), Migrante-Canada sees reforms as being necessary to securing greater emancipation for migrant care workers in the future. PWC, in contrast, assumes an abolitionist approach that calls for the "scrapping of the LCP." Enabling a program that remains, at its heart, a racist, antimigrant program is to sanction injustice.

The collective acts of resistance exhibited by the migrant care worker organizations listed in this chapter—acts that at times complement and at other times conflict with each other—show that care activism has different manifestations. Far from being compliant victims, migrant care workers show that they form organizations that can effectively meet migrant care workers' needs because they are aware of the limitations of sending and receiving states' abilities to do so. The increased demands presented by COVID-19 on migrant care workers, who faced a higher workload, greater risks of exposure to COVID-19, increased anxiety and stress created by financial precarity, and higher rates of labor abuse (Gabriela-ON 2021; CAC, CDWCR, MWAC, and CCESO 2020), galvanized migrant care worker organizations. During the pandemic, migrant care worker organizations became active in checking in with migrant care workers, providing support to them and their families by organizing food drives, sending personal protective equipment (PPE) and raising funds, and creating virtual spaces of support. While in-person meetings were difficult, these organizations found ways to form community. By being there for each other in ways that states and other civil society organizations cannot and will not, migrant care workers create communities of care that instill among migrant care workers the security of knowing that they are not alone in their struggles.

Chapter 3

Scaling Up Care Activism in Transnational Spaces

BETH DOLLAGA (MIGRANTE-BC) DISCUSSING THE PASSAGE OF CON-
VENTION 189: I believe that it is always the people who will make the
convention worthwhile. It is always the people—particularly domestic
workers—who should empower themselves amongst themselves and
make use of this as an instrument to ensure empowerment.

GABRIELA PARTY REPRESENTATIVE LUZ ILAGAN SPEAKING DURING
THE INTERNATIONAL MIGRANTS ALLIANCE MEETINGS ON JULY
3, 2011: Neoliberalism must be crushed. IMA must fight against the
continuing attacks on the rights of migrants.

In the midafternoon of June 16, 2011, during the annual International Labour
Conference (ILC), I was in a cavernous room at the United Nations headquarters in Geneva, Switzerland, waiting to hear whether ILO Convention 189
(C189), Decent Work for Domestic Workers, would pass.[1] C189 offers specific
protections for domestic workers and requires states to implement measures
for ensuring decent working conditions for this group. I was at the back of the
room, where members of the public, civil society representatives, and domestic
worker activists were seated. It was exhausting to listen to country representatives and members of the employers' groups and workers' group dissect each
clause and subclause. It was also frustrating to watch attempts by country representatives or employers' group representatives to weaken the text by proposing
that nation-states be given the right to opt out of key provisions.

Yet the stakes for me as an observer of the proceedings were lower compared to those for the domestic workers and migrant care workers present. As Jennifer Fish (2017), Eileen Boris (2019), and Adelle Blackett (2019) underscore, the creation of C189 was a culmination of years of concerted advocacy by domestic workers and migrant care workers to ensure that domestic work is recognized. Domestic work is frequently seen as work that does not deserve to be regulated or even compensated, so having a convention that recognizes the importance of domestic work is a watershed moment.

The domestic and migrant care workers whom I got to know at this time all shared with me that they traveled long distances and even took unpaid time off in order to be there. The moment was significant not only because of the passage of an international legal document conferring protections to care and domestic workers, a document that many activists were aware would be subjected to a longer process of ratification. What mattered most was the symbolic recognition made that domestic work and care work were valid forms of work and mattered. Despite the potential backlash they faced in being vocal about the deficiencies of national and international law with respect to domestic work, the activists were compelled to care for the larger care worker community by advocating on behalf of the larger imagined community of previous, present-day, and future domestic and care workers.

The painstaking work that they had put into ensuring that C189 got on the ILO's agenda all culminated in this moment. For them, C189 was about more than just a convention. If it passed, not only would C189 allow them greater leverage in their advocacy efforts in national spaces, but it would also mean that they could help ensure the fair treatment of present and future care and domestic workers. Essentially, C189 would help them care for an imagined community of fellow care workers by giving them legal protections. Because the ILO's tripartite structure meant that only country delegates and employers' and workers' groups representatives could vote on whether the convention would pass, the domestic workers and migrant care workers present were all too aware that their fates were in the hands of others.

After a nerve-racking process of hearing from all of the countries being represented, followed by representatives of employers' and workers' groups, it was clear that C189 had passed. When the last vote was counted, all of the observers and members of advocacy groups seated at the back of the room, all of the workers' group representatives in front, and about half of the country delegates spontaneously stood up and cheered. All around me, domestic workers and migrant care workers, activists and worker group representatives were hugging. Many were crying. In complete contravention of norms of decorum that dictated that people had to behave formally when attending UN meetings, others started spontaneously undulating, dancing, and singing.

A group of care workers from Trinidad and Tobago sang the following catchy song:

My mother was a kitchen girl!
My father was a house boy!
That's why I'm a unionist, I'm a unionist, I'm a unionist.[2]

I hugged Pinay's Evelyn Calugay, Migrante-BC's Beth Dollaga, and Migrante-HK's Eman Villanueva, who were sponsored by labor organizations to attend the meetings as workers' group representatives. All three of us soon joined in the singing. Domestic workers and migrant care worker activists gathered around Halimah Yacob, the workers' group representative, and hugged her. It was clear to all of us present that C189 was not only a legal victory for domestic workers and migrant care workers but also a way for them to pay tribute to previous generations of domestic and migrant care workers, some of whom were members of their own families.

The song excerpt included above highlights how transnational care activism is grounded in a desire to care for care workers in the past, in the present, and in the future. The legacy of previous generations of care workers influence activists today, who are driven by the desire to improve conditions for an imagined community of care workers. It was a victorious moment, one that Fish (2017) notes was a long time coming. Coordinating between different domestic worker and migrant caregiver organizations across different continents, all with various agendas, was challenging. The near impossibility of the task, however, did not deter migrant care worker activists. They all saw the importance of establishing international standards regulating domestic work. Moreover, all of them were aware that transnational forms of activism could yield decisive improvements in domestic workers' and migrant domestic workers' lives.

Transnational forms of activism, of course, go beyond mainstream organizations such as the UN and the ILO. Grassroots transnational assemblies such as the International League for Peoples' Struggles—of which the International Migrants Alliance (IMA) is a part—provide equally fertile grounds for resistance. Representatives of Migrante-Canada and Gabriela-Ontario participate in both transnational mainstream and grassroots gatherings. For them, both are vital parts of care activism.

In this chapter, I examine how Migrante-Canada and Gabriela-Ontario engaged in care activism in transnational spaces. Given that part of Migrante-Canada's and Gabriela-Ontario's advocacy work involves transnational advocacy, I investigated how such transnational care activism takes shape across two distinct cases: when undertaken within a mainstream international organization such as the ILO versus a grassroots organization such as the International Migrants Alliance. The "transnational" in both cases are distinct from each other. Thus, activists navigating both spaces have to be strategic and use different activist tactics. I call such forms of activism "multilayered care activism" because it entails the use of diverse, at times contradictory, tactics.

These transnational engagements are crucial to understanding how care activism as a framework for migrant organizing goes beyond the national. This is especially the case when considering how migrant care workers have transnational lives in that they live in Canada but are supporting families in other parts of the world. Through their participation in these forums, migrant care worker activists embody what Robyn Rodriguez (2013) calls "migrant labour transnationalism," in which they seize "counter-hegemonic" forms of nationalism that contest "homeland-oriented, citizenship-based" forms of membership. By being part of these transnational spaces, migrant care worker activists contest the neoliberal economic project that sending and receiving states are complicit in, pointing to how it is these economic structures that facilitate their labor migration and their separation from their families. Rather than accepting, as given, the affective forms of belonging that sending states attempt to engender among their nationals—as seen in discourses of migrant "heroism" that are designed to compel migrant workers to keep sending remittances—transnational fora provide migrant care workers the opportunity to find community with other groups of migrants. The creation of transnational communities of care is consequently a crucial dimension of care activism.

To examine the transnational scope of care activism as practiced by Migrante-Canada and Gabriela-Ontario, I draw from ethnographic research that I conducted at the 2010 and 2011 ILO C189 meetings in Geneva and the 2011 IMA meetings in Manila, Philippines, interviewing participants and observing proceedings. I also conducted follow-up interviews in 2012 with migrant care worker activists from other countries who attended the meetings to get their thoughts on transnational care activism. My observations and interviews highlight vast differences in migrant care worker activists' tactics in both spaces. Because the ILO was a mainstream international organization, activism involved lobbying delegates who were voting on C189 to ratify stronger policies that applied to all workers. Such activism also involved holding parallel events that took place between sessions and sometimes even outside the United Nations. In contrast, as a grassroots space for migrant workers, IMA's delegates consisted of representatives of migrant organizations from around the world. Here, migrant care activism involved consideration of advocacy strategies, including how best to support and amplify each other's campaigns. More crucially, these spaces created generative conversations surrounding alternatives to migration and toward radical futurities. Ultimately, I argue that Migrante-Canada and Gabriela-Ontario's involvement in both spaces shows how transnational advocacy is a crucial component of care activism.

International Labour Conference Meetings on the ILO Convention on Domestic Work in Geneva, Switzerland, June 2010 and June 2011

Getting a mainstream international organization to recognize domestic work was not an easy task. Historically, domestic work was not seen as "real" work and thus was considered not deserving of protections. ILO secretary-general Juan Somavia's decision in 1999 to concentrate on "decent work and fair globalization" with an explicit focus on women's labor during his mandate created the institutional conditions needed for ILO bureaucrats and civil society activists to place domestic work on the agenda (Boris and Fish 2014, 427). The director of ILO's Conditions of Work and Employment program, Manuela Tomei, furthered Somavia's agenda by creating the report "Decent Work for Domestic Workers," framing her argument for treating domestic workers "like any other workers in terms of Somavia's decent work agenda" (427). In addition, in the late twentieth century, the emergence of grassroots organizations representing domestic workers—including migrant care workers—in different countries created a political consciousness among domestic workers that their interests needed recognition (429). Interestingly, in Canada, the rise of Intercede, Pinay, and other organizations in the late twentieth century, as I outlined in chapter 1, follows the same global pattern. Collectively, the rise of these national organizations scaled up and were precursors to the "global mobilization of domestic workers" (429). The International Domestic Workers Network, which was officially founded in 2009, served as an umbrella organization that united different national domestic workers' organizations in a campaign calling for the creation of a convention on domestic work (WIEGO 2018). Hence, to explain the emergence of C189, one has to consider the "interplay between local struggles, transnational networks, and institutional action" (Boris and Fish 2014, 413).

The inclusion of migrant care workers' concerns in C189 was an important win for migrant organizations. Alexis Bautista with Migrant Forum Asia (MFA), a regional grassroots migrants network consisting of migrants' organizations and unions that has its national office in Quezon City, Philippines, contextualized C189 when we met in 2017. He explained that prior to the 2010 and 2011 ILC meetings on domestic work, migrants' organizations in different global regions were putting in the legwork to ensure the inclusion of migrant domestic workers. They held regular conference calls with other migrants' organizations to keep each other updated on developments around the proposed convention. Bautista observed that they "really had to make sure that [they] were visible in all spaces relevant to the discussion around the convention" so that migrant care workers' concerns were not omitted from the agenda.

ILC delegates' constant and ongoing references to migrant care workers during the official sessions of the 2010 and 2011 deliberations highlighted the successes of migrant organizations' efforts. Rather than only seeing domestic and care work as a labor issue taking place within states, migrant care worker organizations made it a point to keep reminding delegates about the larger context of global wealth disparities and the resultant need for Global South nationals to seek employment opportunities abroad. In doing so, they discussed how migrant care worker activists were vulnerable not only because they worked in a poorly paid and poorly regulated sector but also because they are temporary migrants who faced the constant threat of deportation if their employers chose to end their contracts. During the sessions, migrant care worker organizations had the opportunity to share their concerns during workers' group meetings that were convened before each official session. The Canadian Labour Congress (CLC) supported Migrante-Canada's Evelyn Calugay's and Beth Dollaga's attendance at these meetings as representatives of the CLC. This meant that they were able to sit in the proceedings as workers' group delegates.

In fact, the interventions that they made, along with other migrant care workers and their allies, ensured that the interests of migrant care workers were discussed. Their feedback was also decisive in making clear the importance of protecting all domestic workers. The major debate during the 2010 and 2011 proceedings centered on whether to give domestic workers and migrant care workers labor protections through "universal standards." Much of the tenor of the discussions between country delegates, employers' group representatives, and workers' group representatives—all of whom discussed and later voted on the convention as per the ILO's tripartite structure—centered on whether labor standards should factor in "national circumstances." These debates, in fact, illustrated how discussions on global labor standards are highly contentious, especially when these discussions pertain to women's work (Boris 2019).

There was tension among ILO delegates when discussing the creation of universal standards for domestic work. For workers' group representatives and migrant advocates—including the migrant care workers from Migrante-Canada and Gabriela-Ontario—ensuring that universal standards were created was crucial so they could hold employers and policymakers to account. Having standards that give employers and policymakers an excuse not to enforce strong labor standards would work against their interests. For employers' group representatives, the opposite was true: generally, they did not want to be bound by universal labor standards that they felt would compromise their flexibility.

This split was also reflected between countries, depending on whether they were migrant-sending or migrant-receiving states. There was a split between labor brokerage states (Rodriguez 2010) that encouraged their nationals to work abroad to bolster their national revenues and richer countries that relied on migrant labor. Some countries, such as Canada and some "Fortress Europe" states such as Great Britain, as migrant-receiving states initially sought the establishment of a set of nonbinding recommendations on domestic work rather than a convention. For these countries, at issue was the need to protect their national interests as migrant-receiving states; they feared that a legally binding convention would not be attentive to domestic circumstances. Although these countries were outvoted—with two-thirds of the committee agreeing on the need to create a convention—the same debate on creating universal standards versus recognizing national and cultural context (and thereby weakening the existing text) persisted throughout the 2010 and 2011 discussions.

During both sessions, the question of state sovereignty was a decisive issue for sending and receiving states. In particular, member states of the European Union were vocal about maintaining the integrity of "Fortress Europe," as activists called it, which they felt was being threatened by the influx of non-European migrants. The fact that prominent members of the EU such as Great Britain eventually voted against the convention shows their continuing fear about the loss of their national autonomy.

The EU, as well as the employers' group, repeatedly sought to dilute proposed clauses by asking that articles be followed "according to national laws and regulations," thereby significantly weakening the impacts of the proposed texts by giving member states the option to not fully implement the recommendations at hand. These tensions were evident during discussions of certain articles of the convention, some of which I discuss here.

Article 8, which addressed the concerns of migrant domestic workers, led to a particularly thorny discussion about the scope of the convention. The transnational dimension complicated the question of labor protections, particularly when legal standards differed between migrant-sending and migrant-receiving states. Yet migrant care worker activists were adamant that migrant domestic workers be included in the final convention. During workers' group meetings and during individual lobbying meetings with different country delegates, Migrante-Canada's Evelyn Calugay and Beth Dollaga debunked the widely held perception among delegates that Canada's Live-In Caregiver Program (LCP) was a "model" that other countries should follow because the LCP provided domestic workers with access to citizenship. Calugay and Dollaga argued that the potential to acquire Canadian citizenship at the end of their two-year contracts actually magnified employers' power over domestic workers, making domestic workers reluctant to voice their opposition to abusive treatment lest their citizenship applications get jeopardized. Ensuring that Canada did not get a free pass in its treatment of domestic workers was an important intervention because it drew international attention to the significant limitations of Canadian policies. Activists' interventions also amplified the calls made by other migrant care worker organizations that an article addressing the issues facing migrant domestic workers be included. The result of these deliberations, Article 8, reads as follows:

ARTICLE 8

1. National laws and regulations shall require that migrant domestic workers who are recruited in one country for domestic work in another receive a written job offer, or contract of employment that is enforceable in the country in which the work is to be performed, addressing the terms and conditions of employment referred to in Article 7, prior to crossing national borders for the purpose of taking up the domestic work to which the offer or contract applies.
2. The preceding paragraph shall not apply to workers who enjoy freedom of movement for the purpose of employment under bilateral, regional or multilateral agreements, or within the framework of regional economic integration areas.
3. Members shall take measures to cooperate with each other to ensure the effective application of the provisions of this Convention to migrant domestic workers.
4. Each Member shall specify, by means of laws, regulations or other measures, the conditions under which migrant domestic workers are entitled to repatriation on the expiry or termination of the employment contract for which they were recruited. (ILO 2011)

The question of whether domestic workers should be allowed to negotiate their living arrangements (Article 9) was contentious because of the tension between enforcing universal standards and complying with national legislation. Some states believed that allowing domestic workers the freedom to negotiate the terms of the contract violated national norms. Canada and Japan, for example, were reluctant to endorse this proposition because both countries felt that doing so would compromise their respective migrant domestic worker programs. As previously discussed in chapter 1, Canada's LCP, which has since been replaced by an in-home child care and in-home personal support worker stream that does not have a live-in requirement, mandated that all migrant domestic workers have to live with their employers, because the Canadian government's first priority is to meet the caregiving needs of its citizens, regardless of whether doing so heightens the risk that migrant workers become vulnerable to abuse. For Migrante-Canada delegates, it was crucial that employers' power over migrant care workers was minimized. One way that employers' power was magnified was through the mandatory live-in requirement. Migrante-Canada was also concerned with how employers exercised power over workers by keeping hold of their passports and copies of their contracts.

The final wording of Article 9 reflected these concerns, showing the impacts of migrant care worker organizations' input:

ARTICLE 9

Each Member shall take measures to ensure that domestic workers:

(a) are free to reach agreement with their employer or potential employer on whether to reside in the household;

(b) who reside in the household are not obliged to remain in the household or with household members during periods of daily and weekly rest or annual leave; and

(c) are entitled to keep in their possession their travel and identity documents. (ILO 2011)

The debates surrounding the remuneration and recognition of migrant domestic workers (Articles 10 and 11) further highlighted tensions between employers and migrant-receiving states and workers and migrant-sending states. Exactly what counted as "domestic work" and whether these should be recognized was at the crux of these debates. The employers' group and some states argued that establishing universal guidelines on recognizing domestic work was unreasonable. For them, domestic work existed in a unique category that usually required irregular hours of work. For these delegates, assuming that households functioned like firms would make universal standards regarding compensation and rest periods unrealistic. In addition, some migrant-receiving states observed that there were cultural norms regarding the scope of domestic work. For example, giving domestic workers time off was, according to some delegates, unrealistic, given different cultural contexts. Thus, for them, standards should reflect cultural and national norms. Emphasizing difference, then, was a tactic to prevent the imposition of universal standards.

Tactics used by employers and some states were stymied by the workers' group and other states that asserted that cultural difference was often used as a red herring, masking abusive practices. In addition, the issue of appropriate remuneration needed to be addressed directly, given that some of the biggest forms of labor abuse that care and domestic workers experienced pertained to the nonpayment of wages. They criticized the pervasive belief that some forms of domestic and care work should not be remunerated, and how this led to some delegates' resistance to establishing set standards for remuneration. When reflecting on these discussions with Migrante-Canada delegates later, we were struck by how the reluctance to appropriately compensate care workers appeared to have been born out of two existing stereotypes: that women and people from certain cultural backgrounds were innately more caring and thus voluntarily undertook tasks that were not considered part of "work."

In the end, Articles 10 and 11 were the result of delegates' attempts at compromise:

ARTICLE 10

1. Each Member shall take measures towards ensuring equal treatment between domestic workers and workers generally in relation to normal hours of work, overtime compensation, periods of daily and weekly rest and paid annual leave in accordance with national laws, regulations or collective agreements, taking into account the special characteristics of domestic work.
2. Weekly rest shall be at least 24 consecutive hours.
3. Periods during which domestic workers are not free to dispose of their time as they please and remain at the disposal of the household in order to respond to possible calls shall be regarded as hours of work to the extent determined by national laws, regulations or collective agreements, or any other means consistent with national practice.

ARTICLE 11

Each Member shall take measures to ensure that domestic workers enjoy minimum wage coverage, where such coverage exists, and that remuneration is established without discrimination based on sex. (ILO 2011)

Delegates addressed the feasibility of enforcing standards during discussions on the issue of illegal recruitment and whether the convention could create standards to cover these illicit activities. The situations of migrant domestic workers were especially complex. If, in fact, recruitment agencies operated in one country yet sent workers to another country, who would be accountable for monitoring their activities? During the workers' group meetings, Migrante-Canada was especially active in ensuring that recruitment be placed on the agenda, even if questions of feasibility emerged. Pinay's Evelyn Calugay (who was also part of Migrante-Canada and was there as a CLC delegate) disclosed the difficulties of going after recruiters and employment agencies that abuse migrant domestic workers. She cited the example of the employment agency Super Nanny in Montreal, which recruited Filipina women from the Philippines and from other countries in Asia where they worked as migrant domestic workers to work in Canada. Super Nanny representatives promised them a caregiving job in Canada provided the women paid the company $4,000 in recruitment fees, which are illegal in Canada. When the women arrived in Canada, though, they found that there were no jobs waiting for them. Pinay's attempts to file a court case against Super Nanny, however, was thwarted because the owner of the agency died. His daughter took over operations but denied being involved in trafficking. Calugay's observations, along with other delegates, encouraged the workers' group to examine the question of what can legally be done for the trafficked migrant domestic workers in these cases.

Article 15 outlines what member states can do to protect domestic workers—including migrant domestic workers—who were victimized by abusive recruitment practices, thereby showing the collective impact of the points made by Calugay and other workers' group representatives:

ARTICLE 15

1. To effectively protect domestic workers, including migrant domestic workers, recruited or placed by private employment agencies, against abusive practices, each Member shall:
   (a) determine the conditions governing the operation of private employment agencies recruiting or placing domestic workers, in accordance with national laws, regulations and practice;
   (b) ensure that adequate machinery and procedures exist for the investigation of complaints, alleged abuses and fraudulent practices concerning the activities of private employment agencies in relation to domestic workers;
   (c) adopt all necessary and appropriate measures, within its jurisdiction and, where appropriate, in collaboration with other Members, to provide adequate protection for and prevent abuses of domestic

workers recruited or placed in its territory by private employment agencies. These shall include laws or regulations that specify the respective obligations of the private employment agency and the household towards the domestic worker and provide for penalties, including prohibition of those private employment agencies that engage in fraudulent practices and abuses;

(d) consider, where domestic workers are recruited in one country for work in another, concluding bilateral, regional or multilateral agreements to prevent abuses and fraudulent practices in recruitment, placement and employment; and

(e) take measures to ensure that fees charged by private employment agencies are not deducted from the remuneration of domestic workers. (ILO 2011)

To be clear, delegates had heated debates on the content of other articles. Yet what was interesting to witness when comparing the deliberations in 2010 versus 2011 was that who was sitting as representatives mattered when it came to negotiations. While discussions were more heated in 2010, with representatives of employers' groups appearing to be reluctant to compromise, the discussions in 2011 were more constructive. One migrant activist from Asia told me that the change in leadership of the employers' group was not a coincidence, with other members of the employers' group seeking someone who took a more conciliatory stance.

Such a desire for compromise and for negotiations was also reflected in workers' group deliberations. It was inspiring to witness how much careful strategizing took place during these sessions. Different workers' group representatives—many domestic workers themselves—took pains to explain different contexts, providing a sense of how universal standards can be created while also taking into account diverse circumstances. During these discussions, domestic workers at times referred to each other as "sister," showing the affective ties that they have built toward fellow domestic workers. By explaining context, migrant care worker activists were able to highlight why it was crucial for convention deliberations to cover different areas of care and domestic work.

Analyzing the Journey to Ratification: Establishing Transnational Care Activism and Communities of Care

Ultimately, the 2010 and 2011 meetings showcased the ILO's strengths in fostering multisectoral dialogue and in creating a convention that recognized the validity of domestic work. Nevertheless, while the resulting convention was a crucial victory, in many ways, it was the journey of getting C189 ratified that was more impactful for migrant care worker and domestic worker activists. C189 gave them an opportunity to gather and create transnational communities of care.

Migrant care workers who were not part of the workers' group were also active. They attended workers' group and official convention meetings and used the breaks to lobby delegates. When watching their lobbying efforts, I took note of the various tools that they used to gain support for their stances. For instance, I noted how both NGOs and grassroots migrants' organizations kept referring to domestic workers' "difference." Because ILC delegates were most familiar with labor organizing, which tended to involve predominantly male workers in formal labor sectors, those lobbying for the passage of C189 emphasized domestic workers' difference to gain traction. At times, emphasizing difference promoted stereotypes of the "oppressed" Third World woman (Boris and Fish 2014, 439). The ironic juxtaposition of strong and savvy domestic worker activists handing out brochures and brandishing placards that showed pictures of "oppressed" Third World women was in fact not lost on me. Yet these activists knew that "constructions of difference make effective lobbying tools to challenge the wider global system that reproduces severe power differentials between women positioned as workers and employers" (440). Simultaneously, however, migrant care worker activists also emphasized migrant care workers' similarity to other workers: even though domestic work is often not read as "real" work, some of their working conditions (e.g., the power employers exert over their well-being, the risk of not getting fairly compensated for their work) are similar. Watching migrant domestic worker activists deploy the frames of "difference" and "similarity" showed a sharp awareness of knowing how to adapt your message to ensure support.

Activists' actions during the 2010 and 2011 deliberations demonstrated what multilayered care activism should look like. Rather than sticking to one tactic, migrant care activism consciously used a variety of seemingly contradictory tactics. Migrant care worker activists and domestic worker activists did not limit their advocacy work within the confines of the ILC. They used the forums inside and outside the ILC and gatherings to bring attention to their concerns. When observing representatives from Migrante-Canada, for example, I took note of how they gave voice to the way temporary labor migration generally and migrant care work specifically had become a "permanent" policy solution for countries facing economic problems. Alongside other activists, they showed how larger macrostructures needed to be altered in order to instigate change.

One such event that showed the need for larger structural changes occurred during an organized protest in 2011. This protest brought together different migrant advocacy organizations. In the middle of the 2011 convention, representatives of migrants and domestic worker organizations, including Migrante-Canada, went outside the United Nations building to protest ongoing cases of human rights abuses, including abuses to migrants' rights. These protests and gatherings were notable because of activists' attempts to broadcast their message using engaging tactics that were in sharp contrast to the somewhat sterile environment that characterized the ILC debates. These tactics involved more traditional forms of protest, with activists displaying signs and distributing pamphlets, and more unconventional forms, such as musical and artistic performances. That the activists participated in the ILC while also protesting the very existence of these deliberations shows their awareness of their flexibility in using different forums to transmit their message.

These spaces opened the conversational space to consider alternatives to the status quo. While most of the NGOs, unions, and grassroots migrants' groups that were present at the protest could not identify the exact policy prescriptions to create these alternatives, the point of these conversations was more emotive. The fact that everyone present sought alternative arrangements showed that the desire for large-scale structural changes was present. Though C189 was too limited in scope to encompass these concerns, the act of articulating these concerns in a public forum and establishing networks with other organizations that felt the same way was empowering. This, in fact, may very well have led some of the actors to envisage ways to transcend structural inequities. Seen in this light, the conversations being held at the ILC hinted at the conversations that would subsequently take place at the International Migrants Alliance (IMA) meetings, which deliberately created a space to envisage these alternatives. I discuss this further in the next section.

Aside from taking part in ILC deliberations and in protests, migrant care worker and domestic worker activists also formed communities of care with each other. Over the two weeks that the ILC discussions took place in 2010 and in 2011 (four weeks in total), many of the women there seemed to form dissident friendships (Chowdhury and Philipose 2016). Although NGO-sponsored side events scheduled between official convention meetings, as held by Amnesty International and Anti-Slavery International, additionally created a space outside ILC meetings to bond, many of these friendships were outside official meetings.[3] Over the four weeks, I observed and at times participated in lunches, dinners, and sightseeing excursions that strengthened friendships. The high costs of eating in restaurants in Geneva made cooking meals more cost-efficient, so some migrant care worker activists shared their food with each other.

In these gatherings, I witnessed many domestic workers extending care to each other by affirming the validity of their experiences. The ability to compare experiences was decisive in strengthening political consciousness and the sense that they were in this together. Understanding their vulnerabilities as women undertaking precarious work in countries where they were ethnically and culturally different became a prominent discussion point for some women. By breaking bread with each other and sharing stories, migrant care worker and domestic worker activists affirmed that they mattered. More than the discussions on specific articles of C189 or the women's participation in protests, the establishment of these communities of care was vital in strengthening their bonds of solidarity with each other.

In the end, the final terms of the convention reflected a balance between protecting domestic workers and ensuring that member states' concerns regarding adherence to national norms were kept in some parts of the document. With 396 votes in favor of the convention, 16 votes against it, and 63 abstentions, the international community decisively showed its support for domestic work. For the migrant care worker activists who were present during the sessions, the ratification of the convention affirmed to them that their experiences were valid and that international legislation has been created to protect them. The outpouring of emotion that migrant care worker activists expressed once the final vote was announced—manifested in dozens of activists chanting, crying, singing, and dancing within the UN chambers—showed the symbolic significance of the ILO Convention.

For the domestic workers and migrant domestic workers present, C189 was a historic moment. It denoted international recognition that domestic work was "real" work and that the work the women did was valuable. For Calugay and Dollaga, the ability to use C189 in their activist work in Canada was crucial. They were aware, however, of the many advocacy hurdles that they faced. As Dollaga stated in an interview we held in 2012, a year after the Geneva meetings, "Usually, the government will always have ways to deny our requests: 'It's already a convention, so why ratify it?' We have lots of conventions, but has it been ratified? Even when it has been ratified, is it being enforced? It is, again, the community and the people themselves who will make it happen. Thus, the convention is only useful to a certain point, but it is up to us as grassroots actors to make use of it."

International Migrants Alliance Meetings, Quezon City, Philippines, July 2011

The International Migrants Alliance (IMA) is drastically different from the ILO. The IMA was founded by migrant activists in 2008 during the International League of Peoples' Struggles (ILPS) meetings in Hong Kong, and its founders were motivated by the need to draw global attention to the situation of migrants through the establishment of a transnational, grassroots coalition. IMA consists of migrant activists from different organizations whose members include migrants, refugees, and displaced persons from different countries. Although the IMA is a relatively young coalition, its membership base increased between 2008 and 2011: in 2008 IMA had 55 member organizations, while in 2011 it had 83 members. At the time of writing in 2021, there are 120 member organizations in IMA. The ability of existing IMA organizations to reach out to other organizations, coupled with changing economic circumstances that led to the rise of more militant migrants' organizations, explains this increase in membership. As Eni Lestari, the newly elected chairperson of IMA in 2011, told me, "IMA provides the opportunity for different groups to look for new alternatives, new realities. The global economic crisis and the continuing increases in temporary labor migrants, refugees, and displaced persons make IMA even more necessary. We can't get representation within other international forums, so we need to create our own organization." The critical stance IMA takes against existing economic and political arrangements and state policies is for all of its members a source of its legitimacy. Unlike the ILO, whose initiatives in promoting migrants rights are based primarily on the demands of states, IMA does not directly engage with state representatives, although its allies include sympathetic politicians and policymakers. In fact, it distinguishes itself from other similar coalitions by taking a "progressive, anti-imperialist" approach.

According to its Basis of Unity, which was adopted during the First General Assembly in Hong Kong in June 2008, "The deepening crisis of world capitalism leads to a more vicious exploitation and oppression of millions of people in the world. . . . [T]hese internal conditions leave the people of oppressed and underdeveloped countries, poverty-stricken and persecuted, without any option: migrate or leave their country and family in order to be safe and survive" (IMA 2008). Keynote speeches during the Second General Assembly in Manila in July 2011 similarly indicted the existence of global inequities. Chairperson Gerry Martinez argued, "The phenomenon of labor migration is the result of the increasing under-development of nations who have long ago opened their doors to neo-liberal policies under the banner of globalization. . . . It has intensified the commodification of the labor force and service sectors of underdeveloped nations at the expense of genuine national development."

It is the desire to seek alternatives through "genuine national development" that makes IMA a grassroots coalition. The necessity of substantially changing the political and economic status quo motivates IMA member organizations whose members insist that the realities of migration merit serious attention.

Because international and domestic initiatives have thus far failed to take into account that migration is unsustainable and reinforces conditions of dependency between rich and poor countries, it is incumbent upon IMA to hold mainstream international organizations such as the ILO and the UN and states accountable to their policies and also to think of new arrangements. While there is no consensus on what these alternative arrangements would look like, IMA member organizations are clear on the need to put a stop to cyclical migration by perhaps supporting national development projects, rejecting free trade arrangements, and including migrant workers in existing decision-making structures. A key tension among IMA members, of course, pertains to strategizing. As the discussions during the 2011 IMA meeting show, it was a challenge to understand how IMA could both criticize the system that creates labor migration and represent labor migrants who are dependent on this very system. The question then becomes one of practicality: How can IMA wage campaigns seeking alternatives to migration and to existing power structures when its members rely on migration for their livelihood?

To be clear, different organizations are aware of how these structural inequities perpetuate the oppressive conditions found in migrant domestic work. As part of my ethnographic research, I attended the 2011 IMA meetings and, during the conference, had one-on-one interviews with ten activists and informal conversations with about a dozen more. All of the activists whom I interviewed, including representatives from Migrante-Canada and Gabriela-Ontario, recognize that migrant care worker programs only arise because of peripheral, developing countries' reliance on developed states in the center for their economic needs. The lived experiences of the activists I spoke to who are or were migrant care workers are microcosms of these structural relationships of dependency. Petronila Cleto from Gabriela-Ontario insightfully saw the parallels between the situation of migrant domestic workers and that of developing countries like the Philippines by observing, "I'm dependent on richer countries like Canada to give me work much like the Philippines relies on other countries to help solve its economic problems."

Nonetheless, the need both to find alternatives to labor migration and to protect the rights of migrants is perhaps a potential source of discord for IMA. On the one hand, IMA delegates during the 2011 sessions spoke of the need to solve the microlevel problems faced by specific groups of migrants. The plight of migrant care workers, immigrants experiencing racial profiling following the passage of stricter immigration laws in Europe and North America, refugees dislocated by political uprisings, and migrant farm workers—to name but a few—was extensively discussed during the sessions. Understanding the similarities in the experiences of various migrants was crucial in helping IMA see how joint campaigns can be waged. On the other hand, the current realities of economic and political turmoil cannot be denied, thereby making migration a necessity. While IMA criticizes the very system that makes migration inevitable, it is also aware that for all of its members, migration serves as an opportunity for economic betterment and/or political stability. This tension, while not fully resolved among IMA members, points to the debate in many IMA discussions.

One such debate during the IMA meetings that captured these dynamics involved the question of whether IMA should include support for the United Nations and the ILO within its program of action. Some representatives suggested that doing so ensures that member organizations are compelled to promote UN and ILO treaties. Others suggested, in contrast, that supporting the UN and ILO dilutes IMA's grassroots initiatives and may compel IMA to be beholden to these organizations.

Ultimately, while IMA members voted in support of the ILO C189 and reiterated their support for the UN Convention on the Rights of Migrant Workers and Their Families, IMA chose not to formalize its support for these bodies. Delegates eventually agreed that IMA should both work with and work against mainstream international organizations, depending on the types of campaigns being waged. This strategic approach, in fact, reflects the actions taken by migrant care worker organizations that both seek changes to Canada's migrant care worker programs and criticize systemic inequality, as I addressed in chapters 1 and 2. Debates on whether to work with or against mainstream organizations at this transnational scale, in fact, replicate ongoing debates within Canada's migrant domestic workers' movement. While IMA's 2011 statement of action included support for the UN International Convention on the Rights of Migrant Workers and Their Families and the ILO C189, there was no mention of the creation of formal ties with both the UN and the ILO. Instead, IMA delegates agreed that the work of both bodies through their conventions would be a useful framework of action for their activities.

When I discussed this issue with migrant activists, it was clear that migrant activists saw their involvement in different forums strategically. Eman Villanueva, representing Migrante–Hong Kong at both the 2011 ILC meetings in Geneva and the 2011 IMA meetings in Quezon City, told me that participation in these disparate venues was crucial for his organization's advocacy work. Each venue allowed for networking opportunities and addressed different concerns. Having an internationally recognized convention such as C189 helped with their political lobbying and might even help spur changes in national laws, whereas participating in grassroots networks like IMA helped with on-the-ground changes and also opened the doors for alternative arrangements. Migrante-BC's Jane Ordinario agreed with Villanueva's assessment, adding further that participating in both transnational mainstream and grassroots forums enable a fuller realization of Migrante-BC's overall goals: "Having the Convention helps us keep track of how Canada's policies towards domestic workers need to be kept in line with international standards, so it becomes a good tool to pressure governments, but being here at IMA helps us meet other migrants' groups and dream about the future."

IMA's focus on migrants' lived experiences and on the possibilities of systemic change set it apart from the ILO meetings. In fact, I was struck with how discussions during the cultural events, political rallies, and art shows that took place during IMA pointed repeatedly to the harmful effects of labor migration on individuals, families, and communities and on sending states. While delegates understood the human costs of domestic work and care migration during the ILC meetings, the discussions centered on factual information. (In fact, as Jennifer Fish [2017] observed, domestic worker activists who became too emotional during ILC sessions were told to "behave themselves" by the ILC organizers.) In contrast, the IMA meetings foregrounded the emotive. During the art and poster exhibit held at the end of the IMA sessions, a huge papier-mâché airplane with the words "No to labour export policy" emblazoned across the body of the airplane hung above the room. Below the airplane were placards that further emphasized the artists' opposition to labor migration policies, with signs stating, "Stop forced migration." Above these placards were more pictures of migrants protesting and photographs of Filipino workers queuing at the airport in Manila, departing to work abroad.

Performances bolstered the messages being imparted in the art exhibit. A political fashion show that featured different models striding down the runway and carrying suitcases that showed that they were heading abroad made the poignant point that the Philippine government was manufacturing workers who were sent abroad to support the country. Artists sung songs that referenced migrants' lives abroad. The audience members' visceral reactions to these artistic performances highlighted how seeing an artistic rendering of their experiences as migrants or as the sons or daughters of migrants was cathartic.

Taking the discussions during the IMA sessions together with the art exhibit and cultural performances illustrates how the lived realities of labor migration are felt every day by migrant workers, their families, and their communities. The hardships of labor migration cannot simply be understood by reading dry reports and statistics. Instead, it was crucial to recognize and to affirm the complex emotions that migrant workers and their families experienced as a consequence. The importance, then, of IMA was that it provided migrant workers and their allies a "safe space" that was similar to the one provided by the migrant caregiver organizations that I discussed in chapter 2, a place to affirm the validity of their experiences and to understand that migrant workers from different countries around the world shared similar struggles.

At the backdrop of these discussions, art exhibits, and performances was the recognition that the status quo was unsustainable. Ordinario's earlier statements about how IMA provides a space for delegates to "dream" about the future is relevant because they reflect the desire within IMA to envisage new equitable structural arrangements. Conversations during IMA gatherings touched on the following: rather than a world that prioritizes unequal economic growth between states and between people, can there ever be a world where the vicious and unending cycles of capitalist accumulation are abandoned? What would a society that does not take for granted the need for families to be separated because of labor migration look like? Can the Philippines as a sending state harness national development policies that can be used to generate growth instead of a reliance on labor migration? How can receiving states like Canada recognize their complicity in perpetuating imperial arrangements that place the needs of poor, developing, sending states like the Philippines below theirs? During these conversations, I realized that I now truly understood intersectionality scholars' argument that structures and experiences of oppression are "mutually constitutive" (Cho, Crenshaw, and McCall 2013, 786) and thus required transformation. As the Combahee River Collective states, "The liberation of all oppressed peoples necessitates the destruction of the political-economic systems of capitalism and imperialism as well as patriarchy" (1983, 267–68).

Conclusion

The ILC meetings on the creation of C189 and the IMA meetings were two diametrically opposed sites of migrant caregiver activism. Migrante-Canada and Gabriela-Ontario representatives participated in both meetings for vastly different reasons.

The ILC meetings provided these representatives with an opportunity to influence the creation of an international legal instrument that they could use to support their advocacy work. Similar to other domestic worker and migrant caregiver organizations that lobbied for the establishment of C189, Migrante-Canada and Gabriela-Ontario knew that C189 had the potential to shift the discourse on domestic work, provide long-awaited legal and political recognition of the rights of domestic workers and migrant domestic workers, and, more importantly, signal to domestic workers and migrant domestic workers that their work mattered. Migrante-Canada delegates were active in lobbying delegates, participating in protests, and sharing the experiences of migrant care workers in Canada. Having a mainstream international organization like the ILO recognize domestic work therefore legitimizes domestic work. Similar to the way the language of international human rights is used to legitimate the struggles of historically oppressed groups, the creation of C189 provided domestic workers and migrant domestic workers access to universally accepted standards. From an advocacy standpoint, being able to refer to the standards set by C189 was useful for organizations in Canada. Lobbying the Canadian government for C189's ratification thus becomes a part of advocacy organizations' playbook, giving them a useful tool to "shame" the Canadian government into amending its policies.

Yet the 2010 and 2011 meetings were significant not only because they led to the creation of C189 but also because they strengthened bonds of solidarity between migrant care worker and domestic worker activists. By sharing stories and advocacy strategies, the women who gathered understood that they were not alone. These spaces strengthened their connections to each other and to an "imagined community" of previous, present, and future migrant care and domestic workers. Consequently, when C189 passed, the migrant care workers and domestic worker activists who were present saw this moment as signifying that their collective struggles as a larger community of care workers were finally recognized. I argue that such spaces constituted transnational spaces of care activism and communities of care.

As a transnational grassroots assembly that consists solely of migrants' organizations, the IMA could not have been more different from the ILC. In creating a basis of unity, a constitution, and by-laws that dictate how IMA member organizations can support and bolster each other, IMA strengthened Migrante-Canada's and Gabriela-Ontario's advocacy goals. More importantly, however, IMA's provision of a discursive space where migrant workers and their allies could consider structural alternatives to the status quo bolsters the point that present-day inequities need not take place in the future, a point I further explore in the conclusion of this book. By encouraging migrant workers and their allies to dream of future realities, IMA allowed for subversive imaginings of more just realities. Rather than accepting the inevitability of labor migration, events during IMA—which included artistic performances and exhibits—encouraged participants to dream bigger.

Understanding the two contrasting spaces of the ILC and IMA thus elucidates how transnational spaces of care activism are crucial to Migrante-Canada's work. While the ILC allows the organization to play a role in creating an international convention that can be useful for lobbying the Canadian government, IMA helps facilitate transnational connections with other grassroots migrants organizations that can inform their advocacy work in Canada. In some ways, the community of care that was created within the ILC was more covert: these communities were formed outside and in parallel to formal deliberations, whereas the communities created at the IMA were front and center to IMA's agenda. The anti-imperialist solidarity engendered through IMA facilitated a more radical ethic of care, one that sees the creation of new worlds and the abolition of old ones as being central to the survival of one's community of migrants. Nevertheless, despite these differences, both spaces were noteworthy because they provided a space for the creation of transnational communities of care. Migrante-Canada's engagement in the ILC and IMA showed that care activism was about more than just seeking policy changes: it was about finding ways to cathartically affirm the validity of each other's experiences and seek structural transformations in order to honor the legacy of previous migrants and to ensure that present-day and future migrants face better conditions.

Migrante and Gabriela chapters and migrant care worker organizations that are based in other countries participated in these transnational efforts. Opportunities to draw linkages between the struggles facing migrant workers in different countries abounded at the ILC and IMA both during the meetings and afterward through various virtual forums. Migrant activists worked collectively to come to a more nuanced understanding of the multilayered forms of oppression emerging from labor migration and to strategize on ways to overcome structural injustice. These transnational networks facilitated a practice of "multidirectional care" (Francisco-Menchavez 2018) where members of different organizations bolstered each other's campaigns and found ways to support specific members moving from one country to another. It was not uncommon, for instance, for members of Migrante who are about to move to Canada to touch base with leaders of Migrante-Canada chapters for support.

The transnational communities of care formed in these sites engendered the possibility of thinking beyond labor migration, enlarging the possibilities for structural changes. Even migrant care worker activists based in restrictive national contexts were engaged in these conversations. The next chapter looks more deeply at migrant care activists' advocacy efforts in three different locations: Hong Kong, Singapore, and the Philippines. It shows that, notwithstanding differences in national contexts, migrant care activists are motivated by a desire to provide support for migrant care workers through the creation of communities of care.

Chapter 4

Care Activism in the Philippines, Hong Kong, and Singapore

LAORENCE CASTILLO (MIGRANTE-PHILIPPINES): Migrant domestic workers are the ones who experience the full effects of the Philippine government's labor export policies. The value of having organizations that are led by migrant domestic workers and that are for migrant domestic workers lies in their capacity for self-empowerment. For Migrante, it isn't only a matter of helping migrant domestic workers cope with their situations. It is about showing them that the cycle of exploitation needs to stop. It is about politicizing them and having them see that they cannot merely rely on the Philippine government to advance their interests. They have to see that they are part of the movement for transformation.

SHIELA TIEBA (GABRIELA–HONG KONG): Migrant domestic workers in Hong Kong are overworked and are exhausted. Yet many who we talk to don't understand why they are in the situations that they are in; what gets lost is the political context. Why are they here? So we hold educational workshops that talk about why there is forced migration. We also talk about gender. The majority of migrant workers here in Hong Kong are women. This is because of the way women occupy an inferior position in Philippine society. Women are valued primarily because they can be exported for labor. It is easier for the Philippine government to "sell" their femininity, constructing them as ideal domestic workers.

JOHN GEE (TRANSIENT WORKERS COUNT TOO, SINGAPORE): When we first started, one of the immediate concerns was that we shouldn't just focus on extreme cases of domestic worker abuse. What was of greater concern to us was this sort of . . . this daily background of a lack of consideration for domestic workers. These were things that don't make headlines but were still important.

The International Labour Organization (ILO) estimates that of the 67.1 million domestic workers globally, 11.5 million are migrants, of which 8.5 million are women (ILO 2016, 11). The vast numbers of migrant domestic workers worldwide have led to a concurrent rise in the numbers of organizations representing them. For example, the International Domestic Workers Federation (IDWF), which has its headquarters in Geneva, has regional coordinators who bring together domestic worker organizations in Africa, Asia, the Caribbean, Latin America, North America, and Europe. To use another example, Migrante-International and Gabriela-International have member organizations worldwide, with most of these organizations representing Filipino migrant domestic workers. All of these organizations vary in terms of their size, their histories, their normative goals, and their activities. They operate in different national contexts, each with distinct policies toward migrant care and domestic workers. Each activist quoted above is based in a different location and has a different migration and advocacy history. Yet the same care activist ethos persists. All three expressed a desire to advocate on behalf of migrant care workers and to create communities of care to help insulate migrant care workers from the arduous conditions of care work.

My goal in this chapter is to critically assess care activism in countries outside Canada. I explore the extent to which different national contexts affect the types of care activism that different organizations pursue. How does national context, as seen in terms of policies surrounding migrant workers' engagement in activism, shape care activism? In addition, I asked, if the ability to apply for permanent residency is taken off the table, what does care activism look like?

To answer these questions, I delve into ethnographic fieldwork I undertook in the Philippines, Hong Kong, and Singapore in 2011 and 2017. As part of this work, I conducted one-on-one interviews with migrant care worker activists, hung out at different migrant advocacy organizations' offices in each of these countries when invited, and had meals with migrant care workers in parks, malls, and plazas. I show how care activism in each of these sites is affected by national context.

The chapter is structured as follows: I first assess how migrant organizations in the Philippines, as a sending state, have attempted to carve out transnational spaces of care for migrant workers. I also detail their efforts to influence and shift policies and, in some cases, even to conceive of alternatives to labor migration. Given that labor migration has long been a reality in the Philippines, having been adopted as a "temporary" policy under former president Ferdinand Marcos in 1974 and having continued since (Rodriguez 2010), migrant organizations in the Philippines have long played an active part in contesting these policies.

After contextualizing care activism taking place from within the sending state of the Philippines, I then pivot to look at migrant care worker organizations in the receiving countries of Hong Kong and Singapore. Both Hong Kong and Singapore developed foreign domestic worker programs in the 1970s because high numbers of women entering the workforce led to a concurrent rise in demand for paid domestic workers (Hong Kong Government 2022; Anjara et al., 2017). Migrant care workers from the Philippines, in fact, most commonly head to Asian countries. Figures from the Philippine Statistics Authority in 2018 show that 86 percent of all labor migrants were bound for Asia (PSA 2018). Compared to North and South America, where only 5 percent of all Filipino labor migrants went in 2018, there are considerably larger labor migration flows from the Philippines to Asian countries.

However, migrant activism looks different in Hong Kong and Singapore. In fact, when seen in terms of the sheer diversity of migrant organizations present, the Philippines and Hong Kong are actually quite similar. In both countries, there are explicit divisions between groups on account of divergences in normative goals, ideology, and activities. A rich history of civil society protests in both countries and the presence of a democratic government encourage varied forms of political expression, somewhat mirroring the divisions existing in Canada between progressive organizations and "mainstream" or, as described in Hong Kong, "traditional" organizations that advocate reforms. Hong Kong's geopolitical location in relation to the Philippines matters here as well. Given that Hong Kong is closer to the Philippines than it is to Singapore, maintaining transnational activist ties between Hong Kong and the Philippines is easier (Wui and Delia 2015, 194). Activists in the Philippines and Hong Kong, especially those who are part of progressive movements, can more easily coordinate campaigns (194).

In contrast, Singapore's geopolitical location, which places it farther from the Philippines compared to Hong Kong, coupled with the restrictions faced by civil society organizations in Singapore because of authoritarian restrictions to organizing, constrains the types of migrant domestic worker activism present in Singapore. As such, the organizations that are active in Singapore focus primarily on migrant welfare, policy advocacy, cultural promotion, and economic livelihood. Restrictions prohibiting migrant workers from organizing mean that allies do all of the overtly political organizing work, leading one of the migrant care workers whom I interviewed to describe themselves as "silent partners."

Of course, despite variations in care activism across these three countries, I found that the multiple sites of care activism in the Philippines, Hong Kong, and Singapore show how migrant care workers prioritize the creation of communities of care. Much of the impetus behind their activism is their belief in the need to care for previous, present-day, and future communities of migrant care workers and their families. Caring for migrant care workers and their families is at the heart of their advocacy work.

This care activist orientation even extended during the pandemic, when the Philippines, Hong Kong, and Singapore—like nearly all countries globally—went through upheavals. These assorted crises did not decrease care activism. In fact, these crises intensified care activism. The heightened pressures placed on migrant care workers during the pandemic led to longer working hours, higher risks of exposure to COVID-19, restrictions on workers' mobility and thus restrictions to their activities during their days off, and higher rates of termination (Alcaraz et al., 2021; Vilog and Piocos 2021). As Joy Sales (2021) notes, activism during this period became an extension of the "essential work" that migrant workers were already performing. If anything, the pandemic intensified the activities of migrant organizations. The pandemic, more so than "normal" times, illustrated the urgency of forming communities of care.

The Philippines: Care Activism in a Democracy

The Philippines, as a migrant-sending state, has a labor export program that has been in place since 1973. It has an established government infrastructure that facilitates labor migration, with entire bureaucracies dedicated to the marketing of Filipino workers to potential employers in receiving states, accrediting potential migrants' educational credentials, managing their welfare abroad, and ensuring their reintegration into Philippine society upon their return. Dubbed by Robyn Rodriguez (2010) as a "labor brokerage" state, the Philippines has systematized labor export so effectively that other sending states hold it up as a model to follow (see also Guevarra's [2010] trenchant work on the Philippines as a labor exporting state). While the Philippine government has passed legislation to protect the welfare of migrant workers, as seen through the Migrant Workers and Overseas Filipinos Act of 1995, known as the "Magna Carta" for migrant workers, civil society organizations representing migrant workers have charged that the government is not doing enough. They have therefore emerged to ensure that migrant workers' needs are represented and to push for a vision of Philippine society that is not reliant on labor migration.[1]

Sitting in the corner of Migrante House in 2017 while waiting to speak with Laorence Castillo, a longtime Migrante-International activist, I was content to blend into the bustling environment. At the entrance of the house, new arrivals approached Migrante members who were seated behind a long desk. They were subsequently directed to different parts of the house, where they presumably met with different Migrante members who listened to their concerns. I also noticed a group of men entering the house carrying suitcases, who Castillo later explained to me were recent arrivals from the Middle East. They stopped by Migrante House because they were being forcibly sent back home. Without the funds to make the long trip back to their hometowns in provinces far away from Manila, they were hoping that Migrante could help.

Castillo asked me about my plans for later that week, because there was going to be a victory party to celebrate the success of Migrante's campaign for Jennifer Dalquez. Dalquez, a migrant domestic worker who was put on death row in the United Arab Emirates after killing her employer, was later found to have been acting in self-defense and was released from prison. Migrante's campaign put pressure on the Philippine government to actively seek her release. The campaign also led to the formation of national coalitions with other migrant advocacy organizations in the Philippines, as well as allied churches with programs that support migrant workers. For Castillo, Dalquez's acquittal "wasn't just good because she was saved from death row. It was also good because her case can be used to learn how to handle other similar cases. At the same time, it was used to expose the limitations and the problems with the Philippines' labor export programs."

I immediately asked about the case of Mary Jane Veloso, a Filipina migrant domestic worker who was charged with drug trafficking and sentenced to death. Veloso was granted a reprieve after a last-minute intervention by Indonesian president Joko Widodo. I told Castillo that I was living in Edmonton when news circulated about Veloso's pending execution. In Edmonton, members of the Filipino diaspora were furious by what they saw as a grave miscarriage of justice. Details of her case spread in person and on social media spaces such as Facebook and Twitter, with many discussing how she came from a poor family and was duped by a labor recruiter into accepting a job as a migrant domestic worker abroad but ended up having heroin planted in her suitcase. Veloso's case seemed to be especially triggering for Filipino migrant workers who left their families to work abroad because they saw themselves in Veloso. I then asked Castillo about Migrante's role in advocating for Veloso. After watching press conferences held by Veloso's parents during which they were accompanied by Migrante members, I was impressed to see them link Veloso's case to larger structural inequalities that made migrant workers susceptible to labor trafficking. That her parents later became Migrante organizers and initiated a support group for the parents of migrant workers who are on death row was a testament to their commitment to migrant advocacy.

Debunking popular sentiments that Veloso's reprieve was granted primarily because of former Philippine president Benigno Aquino Jr.'s appeal to Widodo, Castillo explained that there was a variety of factors that were in effect. He mentioned, in fact, that Philippine government officials were pessimistic about the possibility of a reprieve and counseled Veloso and her family to "just pray" three days prior to her scheduled execution. Yet Migrante and other migrant advocacy organizations persisted in their campaigning, placing Veloso and her family members front and center in their media interviews to provide a human face to Veloso's case. For Castillo, the pressure that Migrante and other advocacy groups were able to exert led the international community, most notably the United Nations, to intervene.

The national and transnational space encompassing Migrante's work became clear to me during my conversation with Castillo and other migrant advocates in the Philippines. Such multilevel forms of organizing highlight Migrante's multiscalar reach, allowing the organization to show care for migrants and even their families during all aspects of migrants' journeys. Such advocacy can be witnessed through programming. Prior to migration, migrant workers and their families can go to Paaralang Migrante (Migrante Schools), which informs them of the root causes of labor migration and their labor rights when they go abroad. When abroad, they have the support of Migrante organizations in migrant-sending states. After returning to the Philippines, they have access to programs geared toward advocating for returned migrant workers.

The multiscalar nature of Migrante's work was not unique to Migrante. Gabriela, a grassroots Filipina feminist organization, also deploys similar organizing tactics. As a progressive organization that has as its core agenda building mass movements for national democratization in Canada, advocating for migrant workers falls under this broader mandate. Care activism for Gabriela, which has a national base in the Philippines (including a political party related to Gabriela's work) and organizations abroad, necessitates providing a progressive voice for Filipina women in different countries. By recognizing the interconnections between gender oppression and structural inequalities, including militarism and neoliberalism, Gabriela fosters a progressive mindset that can be at odds with socially conservative values that are more commonly associated with Filipino ethnic organizations. Understanding that care activism takes place across multiple sites and spaces, each involving different tactics forged within varying domestic contexts, highlights the affective dimension of advocacy work, which is often neglected by social movement theorizing, which tends to focus on structural openings enabling the emergence of such activism. Contrary to the perception that migrant organizing takes place in a singular site, Migrante and Gabriela show that they have extensive reach. The form of care activism they embody is all-encompassing and thorough, perhaps showing the difference made when organizations are led and run by women and by migrant workers who understand all too well the various facets of gendered injustice, including within structures and processes of labor migration.

While Migrante and Gabriela are perhaps distinct from the other organizations featured here in that they have an arguably larger reach due to their presence in migrant-receiving countries, they share with other Philippine-based migrant advocacy organizations a conviction that care activism should involve having a base within the sending state. The migrant advocates in the organizations I discuss below sought policies that met migrants' needs and that gave alternatives to labor migration. Yet the transnational nature of their work was also clear. All of these organizations had linkages with organizations that represented migrant workers in receiving states, oftentimes maintaining transnational programs that allowed migrant workers and their families to get assistance. Most of them also participated in transnational and regional forums that enshrined migrants' rights in transnational and regional agreements.

While many of these organizations worked collaboratively, their understanding of care activism differed. Similar to how migrant care worker organizations discussed in chapters 1 and 2 had differences in normative vision and goals, migrant organizations in the Philippines also had distinct ideals. On the one hand, Migrante, Gabriela, and other "progressive" organizations saw migrant workers' problems as stemming from structural inequalities that eventually necessitated taking a more militant stance against government institutions and even transnational and regional bodies.[2] For these organizations, analyzing labor migration from an anticapitalist, anti-imperial lens enabled them to get to the root of the issues. Building a social movement led by migrant workers was one way to dismantle unequal power structures. The Tagalog term *makamasa*, which roughly translates to "being of the people," describes their orientation toward their work, which means that movement-building is as crucial as—and, in some instances, can even supersede—policy change. Part of their vision of care activism involved caring for "the people," including and especially migrant workers and migrant care workers. As organizations that were for the people, progressive organizations felt that it was important to maintain their autonomy. This means that they prefer being grassroots movements that get funding from their members rather than from external organizations that might impose requirements that run counter to their mandates.

On the other hand, there were "mainstream" organizations that saw the importance of advocating rights-based approaches to migrants' issues, which meant participating in transnational and regional fora and maintaining constructive dialogues with state officials. Some of these organizations also emphasized the importance of encouraging migrant families to participate in economic livelihood programs. For them, then, care activism involves ensuring that migrant care workers and their families had viable economic options that allowed them to be together. Unlike progressive organizations, they saw the importance of working with and not against government bodies and even mainstream international organizations that gave funding in support of their work.

Forms of Migrant Organizing

The organizations I discuss here are by no means the only examples of migrant organizing in the Philippines. Civil society organizing is a deeply embedded part of Philippine democracy. There are migrant organizations at different scales within the country, including those that are concentrated within a specific town or city and have links with hometown associations abroad and those that are religious. There are also organizations that have a national scope and those that have national, regional, and transnational scopes. Many of these organizations differ in size, activities, and membership. What unites these organizations is an ethic of care toward migrant care workers (including those who are abroad and those who are repatriated) and their families and a belief in ensuring that migrants' interests are well-represented within the sending state. What I focus on here are migrant organizations that have ideological differences.

Migrante and Gabriela, as progressive organizations, believe strongly in empowering migrant workers and their families to build sustainable movements that help rectify social injustice. Hence, their programs for "distressed" migrant workers and their families not only provide them with relief assistance but also empower them to eventually become movement leaders. Castillo described Migrante's rights and welfare program:

> Migrante endeavors to empower them on their rights and have them appreciate the value of fighting for their rights and being part of an organization consisting of OFWs [overseas foreign workers] who will fight for their rights.

We want to teach them not to be self-centered and think, Well, because I'm the victim, I need assistance. It is important for us to have them situate themselves in the larger context—that their experiences of vulnerability and exploitation are the same as others'. And this is all because of an exploitative system. They can be part of a movement while pursuing their own individual struggles. They can be part of a movement to change the whole system.

Castillo noted, in fact, that changing the whole system involved looking beyond migration issues toward advocating for larger democratic forms. Responding to my question on whether it is ever viable to find alternatives to labor migration—one of the goals that is often stated by progressive organizations—Castillo discussed how seeking such alternatives is part of progressive organizations' normative project to facilitate wide-scale democratization. Migrante and its various chapters are allied with Bagong Alyansang Makabayan, or Bayan, an umbrella of left-wing organizations in the Philippines and in other countries. Bayan was formed in 1985 in opposition to the Marcos dictatorship and thus had the larger goal of fostering the "national democratic movement in the Philippines to attain and achieve policy reforms, such as agrarian reform and national industrialization." Once these reforms are enacted, Castillo reasoned that economic conditions for all Filipino citizens would improve, thereby eliminating the "push" factors that compel people to migrate in the first place. Castillo's invocation of reforms, in fact, resonates with Migrante-Canada's approach, as outlined in chapter 2 and as discussed by Harsha Walia: reforms that push us closer to more freedom are necessary at every juncture (Dilts and Walia 2016).

Joms Salvador, Gabriela's representative whom I spoke with after meeting Castillo, agreed with Castillo:

You cannot just look at labor migration. You can't just stop it. There are all of these deeper policy issues at play. So, for example, you have to look at the question of agrarian reform. Why is it that landlords and multinational corporations control agricultural land? Why do they impose prohibitive costs on the farmers who are using the land—costs that are so high that some are forced to simply leave their communities and go abroad so they can pay off their debt? What will happen if there is agrarian reform where land is distributed for free to farmers? Also, why is it that the vast majority of our rice and other agricultural products is bound for export? Basically, once you've solved agricultural problems and also problems like industrialization and mining, you get to the roots of the issue, you stop our reliance on labor migration, and you begin the process of national democratization.

Antonio Tijuan Jr., the former executive director of Ibon Foundation, which is a progressive think tank that works closely with Migrante and Gabriela, shared an analysis of ongoing colonialism and migration that accorded with Salvador's and Castillo's analysis. We met at Ibon's offices and discussed why there never appeared to be an end point to labor export policies. As he pointed out, the fact that poor countries like the Philippines provide labor to more affluent locations like Canada, Hong Kong, and Singapore highlights the Philippines' ongoing dependency on these states. Although Tijuan stressed that not all migration is forced, it was difficult to decouple people's purportedly autonomous rationales for migrating from their stark economic conditions: "They are forced to migrate because of their circumstances, which are then the result of the contractualization and flexibilization of labor that different Philippine governments pursued to enrich their individual coffers."

Hence, for progressive organizations, migrant organizations that represent migrant workers should not only provide services for migrant workers but also criticize and eventually eradicate unequal power structures. Attempts to provide migrants' welfare through the creation of, for example, "migrant reintegration programs" that seek to give returning migrants economic opportunities, they argue, are insufficient. As Castillo explained, "The problem with these reintegration programs is that migrants still won't earn money under these programs. What we want in terms of reintegration is ending the vicious cycle of migration. To end this, we need a strong economy in the Philippines, and that will not happen through their concept of reintegration."

While progressive organizations lobbied the Philippine government, maintaining constant and ongoing dialogues with government representatives when advocating on behalf of distressed migrant workers or when seeking policy and program changes, they were not afraid to criticize government initiatives. Indeed, as Castillo noted, government representatives would prefer that migrant organizations "work peacefully with them," but sometimes "being loud and disruptive" is the only way to usher in change. Compelling the government to directly confront the ramifications of their continued policies of labor export and seeking accountability prompt consideration of the ongoing harms of labor migration to migrant workers and their families.

The approaches used by these organizations were markedly different from those of the mainstream organizations that I spoke to. Mainstream organizations were unlike progressive organizations in that they were less wedded to the idea of creating a mass movement of migrant workers. Migrant workers' immediate needs necessitated taking an arguably more conciliatory approach to migrant justice, one in which accepting funding from government and larger nongovernment organizations need not be antithetical to these organizations' goals. To care for migrant workers meant trying to work within existing structures and using the tools given within these institutions to fight for change.

To be clear, individual advocates may very well share progressive organizations' analysis of the roots of migration. When conversing with Ellene Sana, the executive director of the Center for Migrant Advocacy (CMA), I noticed that her analysis of the underlying causes of migration was similar to analyses shared by progressive organizations. Nevertheless, mainstream organizations' work was focused on advocating for policies and programs that directly assist migrant workers and their families. Given the inevitability of labor migration, it is incumbent on migrant advocates to try to carve out spaces for migrant welfare within existing structures.

Although mainstream organizations were more inclined to take a less adversarial approach to lobbying, this did not mean that they uncritically accepted government policies. Sana recognized deficiencies in government policies toward migrant workers, lamenting the way they had ignored the "forced" nature of labor migration, the effects of deskilling on female migrants who found that they could only find employment as domestic workers abroad despite their high levels of education, and the insidious nature of labor trafficking. Overall, Sana saw the role of CMA specifically—and mainstream organizations generally—as advocating for the needs of migrants to the Philippine government, which, unlike CMA, may not have on-the-ground knowledge of migrants' lived realities.

Sana also saw the importance of policy changes, because these had actual, tangible effects on the lives of migrants. Hence, working with the state was vital to CMA's work. She described CMA as the Philippine government's "critical partners on the ground" when addressing migrants' issues. She stated that because the involvement of civil society organizations such as CMA was entrenched in the Philippine Constitution—with other government documents on migration management even pointing to the "government's partnership with civil society in protecting the rights of OFWs"—the Philippine government was compelled to work with them. CMA, in fact, was distinct from other migrant advocacy organizations in the Philippines because it is officially recognized as the Philippine government's partner.

In contrast to progressive organizations' occasionally adversarial approach, which at times entailed shaming the government into action, Sana believed that a productive way forward was to do the following: "We should give the government the benefit of the doubt and negotiate in good faith. We always tell them that it isn't in our agenda to put you on the spot, to embarrass you in front of the international community. No! That's not our objective. Our objective is for you to do your job! Our goal is for you to do your job without the presence of NGOs. Usually, what happens is that the government acts on something because it is compelled by NGOs. For us, we don't actually want that." This meant that rather than going to the media with cases of migrant distress, CMA preferred keeping channels of communication open with government officials to ensure "prompt advocacy." For Sana, building a relationship of trust with the government made it easier for CMA to meet its goals.

The Philippine government regularly invited CMA to be part of its consultations when developing migration policies. CMA was part of various national coalitions, including the Philippine Migrants Network and the Philippine Alliance of Women's Rights Advocates, as well as transnational groups such as Migrant Forum Asia and the United Nations' High-Level Dialogue for International Migration, that placed pressure on the Philippine government to improve its policies and, for the latter, that attempted to establish international standards for the fair treatment of migrant workers.

CMA was also invested in establishing bilateral agreements between the Philippines and other receiving countries. As Sana rightly stated: "What is concerning is that when migrants are outside our borders, our laws don't apply to them anymore. This is when we aggressively push for bilaterals. So not only for the purposes of labor but also social security, because our migrants are getting older. . . . This is why we lobby for mandatory social insurance that is a shared contribution between sending and receiving states." CMA thus collaborated with states to produce policies and programs that it thought best advanced the interests of migrant workers.

Other mainstream organizations are more closely aligned to progressive organizations like Gabriela and Migrante. The organization Kapisanan ng mga Kamag-Anak at Migranteng Mangagagawang Pilipino (KAKAMMPI, Association of Overseas Filipino Workers and Their Families) shares other progressive organizations' critical take on government programs and occasionally protested government actions. KAKAMMPI has also supported some of Migrante's campaigns. Fe Nicodemus, KAKAMMPI's executive director, observed that the Philippine government's attempts to protect Filipinos abroad were at times insufficient. Citing as an example the mandatory Pre-departure Orientation Seminars (PDOS) that Filipinos with labor contracts abroad had to attend, Nicodemus questioned why some of the seminars were being organized by recruitment agencies, which had an ulterior motive in ensuring that migrant workers stayed put in abusive employment situations. In addition, because migrant workers who attended PDOS had to pay a fee, which, theoretically, should have been paid by their recruitment agencies but were in reality down-loaded to migrant workers, PDOS become a crucial source of income for recruiters. "I do not know why the Philippine government now wants agen-cies to run PDOS. Agencies, even the really good ones, will squeeze as much money as they can out of migrant workers," Nicodemus observed. "So from the very beginning, before they even leave the country, migrant workers are already exploited."

Nicodemus added that pilot projects such as an online PDOS that required prospective migrants to pass an online test after sitting through an online semi-nar showed that it is in the interests of the Philippine government to expedite the departure of migrant workers abroad rather than enacting programs that truly protect them. "In these cases, what do you think will happen? The agen-cies running these online programs will only give migrant workers the answers to the questions."

As an organization that advocates specifically for migrant workers and their families, KAKAMMPI was established in the mid-1980s, during which time the numbers of overseas migrants skyrocketed. Back then, it focused specifically on advocating for the rights of female migrant workers and has since wid-ened its mandate to look at all migrant workers and their families. Nicodemus explained that the organization was particularly attentive to the effects of over-seas migration on family members: "OFW families deserve recognition. Prior to KAKAMMPI, when family members of OFWs complain, they get asked, 'Well, why are you complaining? You're not the one abroad!'" KAKAMMPI created a discursive space that legitimated the difficulties faced by migrant families. By organizing leadership workshops for the children of migrant workers, holding counseling services for migrant workers and their families, and hosting a radio show entitled *Babaeng Migrante, may kakampi ka* (Female migrants, you have someone at your side), KAKAMMPI legitimized and made public migrant families' travails. After all, as Nicodemus noted, "Migration is experienced not just by the migrant but by their family members too."

Recognizing that returned migrants may not have the requisite skills to get jobs in the Philippines, KAKAMMPI started an educational training program for migrant workers. For Nicodemus, it was important to recognize the real-ity of repatriation. Migrant workers who returned to the Philippines tended to become deskilled. Thus, learning new skills enabled them to reintegrate into the workforce. KAKAMMPI's programs, which were geared in support of female migrants, recognized the importance of reskilling. To enable more female migrants to attend, KAKAMMPI also provided free childcare during its sessions.

Other mainstream organizations allocated substantial resources toward their economic livelihood projects. When I visited the offices of Philippine Migrants Rights Watch (PMRW), where I met President Carmelita Nuqui, I noticed that PMRW shared its offices with the Development Action for Women Network (DAWN). I later discovered that the two shared office space because Nuqui was also the executive director of DAWN. Although Nuqui and I spoke a little bit about the work of PMRW and its efforts to support the individual advocacy work of its partner organizations, our conversation ended up focusing primarily on DAWN.

Initially founded in 1996 to assist female migrants who worked as hostesses and as escorts in Japan, DAWN expanded its mandate in 2011 to represent the interests of migrant workers—including migrant domestic workers—and their families. While DAWN engaged in direct policy lobbying, research, and advocacy for migrant women and their families, a substantive component of its efforts lay in the development of its "alternative livelihood" projects, which provided female migrants training in sewing, weaving, and making peanut butter. While the two of us observed women weaving various items such as blankets and table runners in a room at the back of the office, Nuqui described the vulnerabilities facing migrant women abroad and the difficulties they experienced reintegrating into the Philippine job market after their return. Weaving and sewing were not only ways for returned migrant women to learn new and potentially lucrative skills, they were also therapeutic for migrant women in distress: "We provide programs for distressed female migrants, many of whom were trafficked or were forced into abusive labor situations; hand-looming allows them to feel a greater sense of belongingness and to reintegrate into their communities."

In sum, there is a diverse range of mainstream migrant organizations in the Philippines. While all of them provide programs for migrant workers, the types of programs they offer vary. Some, such as CMA, have developed close ties with the Philippine government and participate actively in national, bilateral, and transnational discussions. Others, such as KAKAMMPI, take a more critical stance on government policies and focus most of their activities on programs for migrant workers and their families. Yet others, such as DAWN, engage in lobbying but devote a lot of time and resources toward economic livelihood programs. By engaging in a variety of activities, these organizations represent migrant workers' and their families' various needs.

Migrant organizations in the Philippines differ not only in forms of care activism (see chapter 2) but also in normative ideals, strategies, and agendas. Understanding the scope of migrant advocacy in the Philippines highlights how advocates' vision of how to best care for migrant care workers also differs.

Whereas there were some organizations that believed that guaranteeing migrant workers' economic futures was the best way to show care, there were others that believed that finding alternatives to labor migration and providing training for migrants at all stages of their migration journey were crucial.

These differences notwithstanding, migrant organizations in the Philippines understood that the current system of labor migration was unsustainable and untenable. Too many migrant workers and their families have suffered and will continue to suffer. Labor export was meant to be a temporary policy but has since morphed into a permanent fixture of Philippine economic development policy. All the activists I spoke to who are members of organizations with a base in the Philippines felt all too well how migration has become an inescapable part of migrant workers' realities; in many ways, it was hard to envisage a way out. Regardless of differences, both progressive and migrant organizations understood the challenges of labor migration. As such, their care activism is grounded in a shared ethos of care for previous, current, and future migrant workers and their families.

Activists felt this shared ethos more strongly during times of intense political turbulence under former president Rodrigo Duterte's leadership. Duterte oversaw the forced arrests and political killings of progressive activists, using legislation to bring charges of terrorism and sedition against them. He seized the opportunity offered by COVID-19 to declare emergency powers (which he claimed were needed in order to curtail the spread of the pandemic) and to further restrict the actions of progressive organizations in the name of security. The Anti-terrorism Act, which took effect in June 2020 in the midst of a national lockdown, magnified his powers (Agojo 2021; Auethavornpipat and Tanyag 2021, 8). Duterte even targeted migrant workers who were critical of his regime. For example, he tried to extradite and censure a Filipina domestic worker in Taiwan who voiced her opposition to his administration's mishandling of COVID-19 in Facebook posts (Sales 2021, 603).

The backdrop of political authoritarianism, along with the Philippine government's botched response to the COVID-19 pandemic (Hapal 2021) and the challenges that Filipino migrant workers faced as a result of COVID-19 (including millions of cases of migrant death and forced repatriation [Asis 2020]), led to a counterresponse from civil society actors, including migrant organizations. While lockdown legislation made it hard for them to organize in-person protests, virtual rallies and information sessions for migrant workers affected by COVID-19 proliferated, as did transnational and national mutual aid networks (Auethavornpipat and Tanyag 2021). International networks such as the MALAYA (which means "free" in Tagalog) movement, founded in 2018 to contest extrajudicial killings and to call for human rights in the Philippines, became quite politically organized during COVID-19, drawing attention to the many human rights abuses committed by the Duterte regime, including against migrant workers (Sales 2021).

Hong Kong: Care Activism in a "One Country, Two Systems" Context

Hong Kong has a robust culture of migrant activism, with grassroots transnational migrants' assemblies such as IMA first being established there. While Hong Kong does not offer migrant domestic workers pathways to permanent residency, its robust protections for migrant domestic workers and its relatively higher wages make it an attractive destination. It offers domestic workers ample labor protections, such as the provision of weekly days off, the requirement that migrant domestic workers be given their own sleeping spaces, and the right to freedom of association. Nicole Constable (2009, 2014), whose rich scholarship has documented the lives of migrant domestic workers in Hong Kong for many years, observes that the Hong Kong government's desire to portray itself as a "world city" invested in "peaceful and subtle forms of modern governmentality" (2009, 156) means that social movement organizing, including public rallies, are accepted.[3]

On a sweltering weekday afternoon in July 2018, I met Edwina Antonio Santayo in front of a shop inside Worldwide House in Hong Kong. Santayo, who is part of Hong Kong's Mission for Migrant Workers (MFMW), was bringing me to visit Bethune House, a shelter for distressed migrant domestic workers. On our way there, Santayo spoke to me about Bethune House's history—how it was founded in 1986 and relied on donations from churches, community organizations, and supportive individuals; how migrant domestic workers who needed emergency shelter found their way to Bethune House through referrals and word of mouth; and how those who lived there all contributed to the upkeep of the house and were each in charge of buying groceries, cooking, and doing other household chores.

When I arrived at Bethune House, I took note of how the apartment was similar to other apartments in Hong Kong in that it was tiny by North American standards. The space was used efficiently: there were beds in the main area, a kitchen, and enough space for desks and a computer terminal. The women living in the shelter were all migrant domestic workers from the Philippines and Indonesia. Over tea and biscuits we looked at the crafts that they were creating and at pictures of their families and children back home, and we talked a little bit about what had brought them to the shelter. One woman shared how her employer had forced her to take care of two aggressive dogs, which attacked her, placing her in the hospital. When she returned to her employer's household, she was out of a job. Many talked about wage theft. One spoke about sexual assault. They spoke, too, about their hopes for the future. While their court cases in Hong Kong were pending, they made plans for the future. Perhaps they could get another employment contract in Hong Kong or in another country. Perhaps they could head home for a little while and get reacquainted with their children. Bethune House gave them the opportunity to escape from their abusive employers and to contemplate future possibilities. "Here, I can breathe," one woman said.

Bethune House provided a safe space for migrant domestic workers in which to shelter, one that the leaders of MFMW saw as being necessary in Hong Kong. Established in 1981, the MFMW was the first organization that provided services for migrant workers in Hong Kong. When I interviewed Cynthia Abdon-Tellez, the director of MFMW, about why MFMW got started, she noted that the high numbers of Filipino migrant domestic workers in Hong Kong led to the concurrent realization that there was a need for an organization that looked after the social welfare of migrant workers. MFMW undertook educational awareness campaigns that informed migrant workers of their rights and documented migrant workers' living and working conditions.

Abdon-Tellez was deeply connected to many of the other migrant domestic worker organizations in Hong Kong. In subsequent interviews with other migrant organizers, I noticed that they made constant comparisons between their organizations' work with Bethune House and with Abdon-Tellez's leadership. For instance, Eman Villanueva, the chairperson of Bayan Hong Kong and Macao and the secretary-general of United Filipinos of Hong Kong (UNIFIL), and I discussed Bethune House's crucial work at the start of our conversation.[4] Bethune House's leadership was also how Gabriela–Hong Kong's Shiela Tieba and I started our conversation when we met. Both Villanueva and Tieba saw the history of migrant activism in Hong Kong as beginning with Abdon-Tellez and Bethune House.

Beyond Bethune House, Villanueva and Tieba described migrant organizing in Hong Kong as diverse. "There are organizations everywhere, for everything," Villanueva stated. Both Villanueva and Tieba used the following typology for migrant organizations in Hong Kong. According to them, there were three types of migrant organizations: "critical" advocacy organizations, organizations that provided services for migrant workers, and "mainstream" organizations.

Juxtaposing Villanueva's and Tieba's typology with my participant observation of various spaces of migrant organizing in Hong Kong shows just how vibrant migrant organizing is in the city. Interestingly, there are different physical spaces in Hong Kong that migrant workers associate as being sites where certain organizations are based. Essentially, different migrant organizations take over different parts of the city on Sundays, during migrant workers' days off.[5] Their ability to take over these spaces makes migrant organizing more visible compared to, say, Canada. Because of Hong Kong's high population density, migrant workers tend to be concentrated in public spaces on Sundays, which is also when most organizing work takes place.

At first glance, it is easy to make the assumption that the groups of migrant domestic workers gathered in random spaces depending on which spaces were available. Yet conversations with Tieba, Villanueva, and others and my own explorations in different parts of the city led me to see that migrant domestic workers went to specific locations in the city depending on their countries of origin and their organizational ties. Indonesian migrant domestic workers, for example, gathered at Victoria Park. Walking around Victoria Park on a sweltering Sunday in June 2017, I noticed that Indonesian women gathered in spaces around the park, with many sitting in circles on picnic blankets and even under tents; in many cases, a banner displaying the name of their hometown association or their cultural group or their activist organization was prominently displayed so others could find the group. Throughout the afternoon, two different groups of women in traditional costumes practiced dances.

On the same day, I ventured to Central in Hong Kong and noticed similar groupings of Filipino migrant domestic workers gathered in the downtown core. Tieba told me that activist organizations gathered at designated spots in Central on Sunday, ensuring that they could be easily located by fellow migrant domestic workers who needed help. One of the chapters of Gabriela–Hong Kong, in fact, called itself "Gabriela–Hong Kong Bank" not because its members worked at Hong Kong Bank but because the group hung out on Sundays at the foot of the Hong Kong Bank building. Tieba noted that Gabriela–Hong Kong members regularly went on recruitment drives in their location by "going all around Hong Kong Bank, bringing a megaphone, disseminating flyers, and waging a public discussion."

When walking around Central, I observed that various organizations did use space in the way that Tieba described. Some activists were engaging in public discussions. Women clad in party dresses and wearing sashes saying "Miss Prospera 2017" approached various groups and asked for donations for the charitable causes that they championed as beauty pageant contestants, which I discuss later in this chapter. There were no fewer than eight groups practicing what looked to be flash dances. And there were members of UNIFIL affiliate organizations who were practicing a political flag dance, complete with banners and music. I discovered that they were going to perform as part of the annual prodemocracy event that civil society organizations in Hong Kong hold every July to criticize Hong Kong's handover to China and to publicly organize in support of human rights. As my conversations with Villanueva and Tieba showed, the bulk of migrant organizing took place in Central on Sundays. Villanueva noted, though, that migrant care worker organizations also organize in far-flung areas of Hong Kong, including the New Territories, Yuen Long, and Tsuen Wan.

Constable (2009) notes that Hong Kong stands in contrast to other Asian countries where there are sizeable numbers of Filipino labor migrants: Singapore, Malaysia, and Gulf State countries such as Saudi Arabia and the United Arab Emirates. Hong Kong's "image of peaceful and subtle forms of modern governmentality" and its desire to promote "the social stability needed for economic prosperity" have led the Hong Kong government (namely, its police forces) to tolerate migrant organizing (156). In fact, the very visibility of migrant organizing in Hong Kong, as seen through migrant organizations' use of public spaces, is noteworthy because of the way space is used for political agendas. While there are similar spaces where migrant domestic workers gather in Singapore, such as the shopping center Lucky Plaza, Singapore's prohibitions against civil society organizing mean that these spaces are not used for overt political ends.

Forms of Migrant Organizing

The space, both physical and discursive, that is provided for migrant organizing in Hong Kong has enabled the flourishing of different types of migrant organizations. The migrant activists whom I interviewed saw migrant organizations in Hong Kong as broadly being divided between three different types of organizations: progressive organizations, or "cause-oriented" groups that have an overt political agenda; "traditional" organizations, whose purpose is to provide migrants with a social network via hometown and cultural ties or a shared interest in certain activities (e.g., hometown associations, sports leagues, singing); and organizations that provide services through economic livelihood programs and counseling services.[6] I describe each of these below.

Progressive organizations have a long history in Hong Kong. The presence of Filipino migrant workers in Hong Kong has led to a concurrent rise in political organizing among Filipino migrants. Similar to Filipino migrant organizations in Canada, organizations initially formed in Hong Kong to protest the Marcos dictatorship, which was in power from 1972 to 1986. Unlike Canada, however, the relatively higher numbers of Filipino migrant workers in Hong Kong and the geographic closeness of Hong Kong to the Philippines gave added urgency to advocacy campaigns. Migrant organizations in Hong Kong, in fact, experienced the brunt of the Marcos dictatorship's policies on migrant work.

According to Villanueva, Filipino migrant workers first formed the Association of Concerned Filipinos not only to protest the Marcos dictatorship but also to campaign against its antimigrant policies. The association, along with other migrant organizations, then formed United Filipinos against Forced Remittances in opposition to Marcos's forced remittances policy, which mandated that between 50 and 70 percent of migrants' remittances be sent through institutions recognized by the government. Villanueva described the situation as follows:

> It took so long to get money, and it was hard for people to get to the places that sent the funds. What the bank would do is they would hold the remittance for a while before releasing it to the family. The worst part is that if you weren't able to show proof that in that year you remitted 50 to 70 percent of your income, there were punitive acts. For example, your passport wouldn't be renewed or your contract, if it's for renewal, won't be renewed. This is why loan sharks became so prominent. Migrant workers felt compelled to rely on them because they needed to show the government that they remitted 50 to 70 percent of their annual income.

As a result of mass actions in Hong Kong, the Philippines, and other countries where there were migrant workers, the Marcos government scaled back the provision and eliminated the punitive actions associated with the policy. The success of their protest persuaded migrant workers of the need for a permanent migrant workers' organization, subsequently resulting in UNIFIL, which united different migrant advocacy organizations in Hong Kong under one coalition. Eventually, migrant advocates began seeing commonalities in the experiences of migrants from other countries in Asia and strengthened their analysis of the effects of labor export programs on migrants and migrant families. Filipina migrant domestic worker Flor Contemplacion's sentencing to death by hanging in Singapore further strengthened migrant advocates' convictions that they needed to politically represent themselves rather than relying on other organizations and their home governments to do so. Such analysis led to the formation of Migrante-Asia and Migrante–Middle East in 1994, followed by the formation of Migrante-International in 1996. UNIFIL subsequently became the "Migrante of Hong Kong," as Villanueva described it, with the organization using both terms.

Gabriela–Hong Kong had similar transnational roots. Gabriela-Philippines was established in 1984 in opposition to Ferdinand Marcos's dictatorship and later formed partner organizations in different countries. In Hong Kong, Tieba noted that the formation of Gabriela Party-List in the Philippines, during which its members sought the election of political representatives in the Philippine Congress, led its allies to get support from Filipino nationals abroad, including in Hong Kong. The process of meeting and talking to Filipina migrant domestic workers about Gabriela's work led to the formation of Gabriela chapters in Hong Kong.

As progressive groups, organizations affiliated with UNIFIL such as the Gabriela chapters take a more militant stance against the Philippine and Hong Kong governments and do not shy away from public protests. Similar to their counterparts in Canada and in other countries, progressive organizations' ultimate goal is the abolition of labor export programs. They take an anti-imperialist stance that sees such programs as the manifestation of persisting global inequalities between states. Rather than only providing migrant domestic workers with a social network and support services, activists affiliated with UNIFIL provide migrant domestic workers with a political education that allows them to understand their situation in relation to larger structural problems. As Tieba noted at the beginning of this chapter, "What gets lost is the political context." By this, I interpreted Tieba as saying that UNIFIL distinguished itself from other organizations by instilling in its members an awareness of the larger structures of power and policies that made labor migration necessary. By providing its members with this context, UNIFIL hopes to empower its members and plant seeds of change. This form of political education may even be interpreted as a form of care activism: when UNIFIL's members become aware of the larger structures of power that compel their migration from the Philippines and that separate their families, they finally stop individualizing their situations and can see that their challenges are a result not of individual failures but of systemic factors.

Progressive organizations make continuous contact with the Philippine government and the Hong Kong government, protesting against policies one day and then holding meetings with government officials the next. Like progressive organizations' "united front" approach to activism in Canada, progressive organizations see these actions not as contradictory but as equally necessary components of activist politics. Similarities in how both progressive forms of activism emerged are unsurprising, given UNIFIL and Migrante's common ties to Migrante-International. In fact, echoing Migrante-Canada representatives' observations of their strategic approach to advocacy, Villanueva was quick to note that the rallying and protesting that UNIFIL does are strategic: "Empowerment is best expressed and achieved through mass mobilization. The sheer numbers, the level of organization, the determination to gather together as a community—these are the highest expression of our political determination to advance these causes."

Contrary, perhaps, to the perception among conservative members of the Filipino community that rallying serves no purpose except to express grievances, Villanueva was clear that rallying in Hong Kong brought results: "In our experience, our ability to get the Philippine and the Hong Kong government to respond depends on the size of the protests that we are able to organize." Philippine president Gloria Macapagal-Arroyo's decision in 2006 to require all migrant domestic workers to undergo mandatory skills training elicited massive opposition, leading UNIFIL to organize three rallies in Hong Kong in the span of one month, with each ensuing rally attracting an increasing number of people. According to Villanueva, "The first one had four thousand people, the second one was like seven or eight thousand. And then the third one had more than ten thousand. We filled up the park in front of the consulate. And people were truly angry." The rally itself led the Philippine government to make some concessions by limiting who was required to take the training session, a concession that appeased mainstream organizations but that progressive groups saw as being insufficient.

Villanueva asserted that other rallies that UNIFIL organized leading to decisive changes included its regular protests against the Hong Kong government's proposal to cut migrant workers' minimum wage, which migrant activists were successful in preventing three times between 1998 and 2003. Following their successful attempts at preventing wage cuts, UNIFIL members recalibrated and decided that it would be better not to operate from a defensive position but to reframe their campaign to actively seek for wage increases instead. Reframeing their campaign in this light succeeded in raising migrants' wages in 2007. Similar tactics led to a wage hike in 2018.

UNIFIL's ability to forge coalitions with different groups was a major part of its success. Villanueva noted that members of mainstream organizations and migrant domestic workers who remained unaffiliated with any organization still attended rallies depending on the issues at hand. Likewise, Tieba observed that "even if there are other traditional groups with different positions, even they recognize the value of our groups because of the respect that our organizations command."

In addition, UNIFIL had ties with migrant domestic worker organizations that had other racial groups as part of their membership base. UNIFIL was part of the progressive Asian Migrants Coordinating Body (AMCB), which had member organizations representing five different nationalities. Villanueva described AMCB as follows: "It is the biggest, the largest grassroots organization for domestic workers of organizations and unions. We have twelve affiliates. Five of these affiliates are umbrella organizations themselves. All in all, there are one hundred or so organizations under AMCB. There are Filipinos, Indonesians, Sri Lankans, Nepalese, and Thai." As seasoned advocates, progressive Filipino migrant activists proactively sought ways to help build migrant movements from other nationalities. Cynthia Abdon-Tellez of the Mission for Migrant Workers described how Indonesian migrant domestic workers formed their own organizations with the support of Filipino migrant worker activists. In fact, during the first protest organized by Indonesian migrant domestic workers, Filipino migrant domestic workers marched in solidarity. In doing so, Filipino migrant activists not only bolstered support for Indonesian activists' campaign but also ensured that Indonesian migrant organizers—some of whom could pass as Filipino—were difficult for Indonesian government officials observing the rally to identify because they blended in with the crowd.

Eni Lestari, chairperson of the International Migrants Alliance (IMA) and a longtime migrant organizer, noted that fellow Indonesian migrant care workers like herself were first emboldened by Filipino migrant care workers' activism. She founded the Association of Indonesian Migrant Workers in 2000, which quickly became active with the AMCB. For Lestari, their advocacy work, which spanned campaigns against the nonpayment or the underpayment of wages, protests against employment agencies overcharging migrant care workers, and public education work, made a difference for Indonesian migrant care workers: "We also began establishing networks with different institutions, like churches and mosques, so we could make sure to provide resources and shelter for Indonesian migrants who ran away from employers. After long years of education and awareness raising, I can at least say that, after 2007, the issues of underpayment and denial of rest days are improving. Fewer workers are being underpaid now, most Indonesians enjoy Sundays off, and most workers do not have their passports taken away" (Lestari and Li 2019). Lestari is also similarly adamant about how care activism should also assess the root causes of migration. Awareness campaigns that inform migrant care workers about the structural imbalances created by globalization are important in order for migrant care workers to become politicized.

Hence, for UNIPHIL, AIMW, and other progressive organizations that are part of AMCB, care activism entailed empowering migrant care workers to understand why labor migration persists and their rights and entitlements, thus planting the realization that a better world is possible. Care activism entailed moving toward a radical future where labor migration was no longer a reality.

Interestingly, UNIPHIL, AIMW, and AMCB also developed ties with groups of progressive migrant employers. In Hong Kong, there existed organizations representing migrants' employers, each with its own specific stances on issues such as migrant wages and the live-in requirement. Similar to the migrant organizations that were active, employers' organizations were divided along ideological lines. Some supported greater restrictions on migrant workers, calling for reduced wages and the revocation of migrant entitlements such as days off. Others were more moderate in that they sought the continuation of the status quo, such as the maintenance of the existing minimum wage. Progressive employers' organizations, however, took promigrant stances that supported UNIPHIL's calls for action. It was the desire to counter antimigrant sentiments that were being broadcast by employers' organizations that motivated the formation of progressive employers' groups such as Open Door.

Doris Lee, who founded Open Door in 2009, explained that when campaigning against raising the minimum wage for migrant workers, employers' groups asserted that migrant workers' wages were fine:

> There was the representative of an employer of domestic worker confederation association, and he went on interviews here and there saying, "No, no, [migrant domestic workers] are fine. Look, they have mobile phones, and they build houses in home countries, and yeah, there is some bad things happening time to time, but mostly there is a very stable and a very good system, and we should not mess things up, and they would become unaffordable." So I was already familiar with some migrant groups, and they were familiar with me, and so they would call me from time to time asking me if I could speak because I was an employer, I had a domestic worker. I would go and say some things, and then once, someone told me, "Oh, it would be good if there were an employer group that were different." I knew that in New York there were groups helping domestic workers and that some NGOs organized employers to support certain legislation. In other words, it made a difference to organize employers, so that was also motivating and inspiring for me.

Lee noted that many of Open Door's activities involved presenting alternative narratives regarding the situations of migrant domestic workers, disputing the harmful assertions made by employers' groups. Open Door advocates testified in the Hong Kong legislature in support of progressive migrant organizations' calls for a higher minimum wage and better treatment and gave media interviews. In addition, many employers' groups monopolized discussions of migrant domestic work in Chinese-language newspapers, presenting negative accounts. Open Door's statements disputed these accounts, enabling a more nuanced perspective on migrant domestic work. Lee discussed her discomfort with how some employers felt that they were "good" employers simply because they did not have hidden cameras spying on domestic workers. In an effort to encourage employers to see the indispensability of the work of migrant domestic workers, Open Door partnered with international artists to mount an exhibit that, in part, featured thank-you letters to migrant domestic workers from migrant domestic workers' employers. In doing so, Lee noted that Open Door highlighted that the problem was not employing migrant domestic workers per se but rather refusing to treat migrant domestic workers with dignity. Hence, shifting the popular discourse on what "good" employers are like and on migrant domestic work is therefore one of Open Door's mandates.

By taking an unapologetically militant stance in support of migrant domestic workers, progressive organizations in Hong Kong shifted the discourse on migrant work, achieved important policy changes in both the Philippines and Hong Kong, educated migrant domestic workers on the structural roots of labor migration, and pursued alliances that allowed them to support their short-term and long-term goals. For these organizations, lasting and sustainable change entailed building a mass movement consisting of both migrant domestic workers and their allies.

On a Sunday morning in July 2017, I was in a dim room in a karaoke bar surrounded by a group of migrant domestic workers who led "traditional" organizations, a category that the women used to describe their work. Noemi Cordero, a longtime Filipina migrant advocate, invited me to their gathering. It was somewhat awkward for me at first when Cordero introduced me as a "Filipina professor from Canada" who was their "guest of honor" and presented me with a corsage of flowers. Rather than fading into the background, I was unwittingly put in the spotlight. The late arrival of a migrant domestic worker who was featured in the documentary *Sunday Beauty Queen*, a much-celebrated documentary on migrant domestic workers competing in beauty pageants (Villarama 2016), generated much excitement among the women.[7] This took attention away from me and made me less conspicuous. Soon, over food, we chatted about how long the women had lived in Hong Kong, what their employers were like, and their families.

During our conversation, it was sobering for me to note that all of the women involved were ambivalent about their experiences in Hong Kong. One woman, who had been in Hong Kong as a migrant domestic worker since the 1980s, lamented having to give up her "love life." She was considering heading back to the Philippines but was sad about the possibility of not having a family to return to, although she noted that she would be with her siblings and the nieces and nephews she helped support. Others discussed family fragmentation. Like nearly all migrant domestic workers whom I have spoken to in different countries, the migrant women in Hong Kong were living the oftentimes lonely realities of family separation. Marital strife was commonplace, as were feelings of disconnection from one's children. Yet others talked about the abysmal economic situation in the Philippines. "If you have a job in the Philippines, don't even bother going abroad," one woman counseled. Another woman, who was there with her daughter, who came to Hong Kong as a migrant domestic worker, stated that going abroad did not help her children escape from economic strife. "We've become a family of OFWs [overseas foreign workers]," she said matter-of-factly, "and when my daughter said that she wanted to come abroad so she can support her siblings, I was against it but then thought that I couldn't stop her doing what I did. And so I arranged for her to find employment with a good family here in Hong Kong. At least when she's here, I can look out for her."

Yet the gathering was also joyful and forward-looking. As was the norm for the migrant domestic worker gatherings that I attended, there was a lot of gossiping, teasing, and strategizing. The women who were there led traditional migrants' organizations that prioritized providing their members with a community of fellow domestic workers who came together to pursue various activities such as cultural pursuits and sports. There were professional accreditation organizations, as in the case of the Integrated Midwives Association of the Philippines, which organized refresher courses for domestic workers who were midwives in the Philippines so they would not lose their accreditation. Like members of other migrant organizations, the women formed these groups because they wanted to make sure that they had a space for themselves. As one woman noted, "Sometimes, talking to our families on Skype and hearing about their problems just add to our stress. When we're together, we don't stress out too much. We can have fun."

Interestingly, all of the women at the gathering emphasized that their organizations were engaged in advocacy work. Benita, who led the Kapehan sa Paoay (Coffee with Paoay), explained why they decided to become a formal association with an explicit mandate to raise funds for distressed fellow domestic workers: "Initially, we wanted to just be a 'bonding' group, but then we realized that our gatherings on Sundays could be used for something important. We fundraise during events such as our regular 'sports-fest' and Halloween party. We use our funds to give [HK]$200 to any of our members who got terminated. We also have a 'feeding' program where we send funds to organizations in our hometowns to provide food for hungry children. At the end of the year, we split up the rest of the leftover funds between all of us." Carmela, who headed the South Cotabato Overseas Workers Association (SCOWA), discussed how members saw each other as their "home away from home" and provided emotional and financial support. All members paid monthly dues of ten dollars (in Hong Kong dollars) and raised funds through their annual Miss SCOWA beauty pageant. These funds were used toward helping support livelihood projects for members' families. For instance, the women purchased a goat for a member's family, which was then used to generate income for the family through the selling of goat milk. They also bought school supplies for children in South Cotabato, provided relief funds to the region during natural calamities, and gave funds to the families of migrant domestic workers who passed away. Carmela was clear that she saw a higher purpose in her stay in Hong Kong: "We don't just take care of our families. We also take care of our communities, of our hometown. I am lucky to be here, so I have to give back."

When asked whether the organizations participated in overtly political actions such as those sponsored by UNIFIL, the women mentioned that they were supportive of UNIFIL's campaigns and appreciated that these groups existed to advocate for the women's concerns. Benita emphasized that she was supportive of UNIFIL's work and attended rallies that it organized when needed. "There is space for both of our groups," she explained. Carmela agreed with Benita. However, she added that she sought to ensure that SCOWA remained an "independent" organization that remained unaffiliated with other groups because she did not want to lose sight of SCOWA's purpose of providing a social space for migrant domestic workers from their region in the Philippines and undertaking advocacy work.

Unlike progressive organizations, traditional organizations do not necessarily make explicit the linkages between the structural roots of labor migration and migrant care workers' experiences of labor migration. While conversations that we had during our gathering showed that migrant care workers were aware of these "push" factors that made labor migration one of the only options the women had to support their families, political education was not a formal part of their work. The scope of their organization is best characterized as being more focused and smaller in scale: their ambit of care extends toward specific care workers in their networks, in their organizations, and in their specific regions in their home countries. There are close parallels, in fact, between their practices of care activism and some of the organizations featured in chapter 2, such as the First Ontario Alliance of Caregivers in Canada. The focus for both was on meeting migrant care workers' immediate needs and establishing a community of care for migrant care workers.

In contrast to "cause-oriented" progressive organizations and "traditional" organizations, economic livelihood organizations saw their mandate as providing migrant domestic workers with tangible skills and programs that would achieve economic security and help them make money. Similar to the Godmother Network, a migrant care worker organization featured in chapter 2, economic livelihood organizations saw that the best way to care for migrant care workers is to increase their economic empowerment. Yet unlike the Godmother Network, these organizations tended to be run by allies. Though migrant domestic workers themselves assumed leadership positions, allies determined organizational agendas and priorities. While these organizations do not necessarily shun the causes that UNIPHIL supported or the cultural-social and philanthropic endeavors that traditional organizations pursued, the leaders of these groups believed that it was in migrant domestic workers' best interests to learn financial management, to upgrade their skills, and to conceive of other business ventures that would bring them more funds and perhaps eventually allow them to exit migrant domestic work itself.

Jun Concepcion, who is the director of the Alliance of Overseas Filipinos for Change, described his motivation for establishing his organization:

> I've been working for the Filipino community for more than two decades now. It makes me sad to see that there are so many recurrent problems and so many new problems that are coming up. You can't be an employee all the time. You've got to start preparing for the future. You can't be reintegrated into Philippine society unless you're ready, unless you have money and knowledge. [In starting this organization] I wanted our kababayans [compatriots] to become more selective, more mature, more intelligent, so what they do during their spare time will help with their jobs, their future, help them build savings and investment.

To ensure that workers make the best use of their spare time, Concepcion organizes workshops and conferences in Hong Kong and the Philippines that provide support for migrant domestic workers' economic livelihood projects. The alliance is a transnational network that connects migrant domestic workers abroad with either state, nonprofit, or business partners in the Philippines that allow workers abroad to invest in projects at home, perhaps even with the assistance of their family members there. For example, in August 2017 the alliance organized a conference in the Philippines. It was attended by Philippine government officials who discussed the programs that they have for migrant workers (including financial investment programs and programs for migrant workers in distress) and corporate and nonprofit representatives who talked about livelihood and investment opportunities. Conference proceedings were livestreamed in Hong Kong, enabling migrant workers in Hong Kong to participate virtually. Other workshops that the alliance has sponsored discussed potential investment opportunities in industries as varied as the mushroom farming industry and real estate.

Lenlen Mesina, the former executive director of Enrich HK, explained that Enrich HK was founded because there were no financial literacy and financial planning programs that were geared specifically for migrant domestic workers. The organization subsequently received a grant from Oxfam Hong Kong that allowed it to develop a pilot program on financial literacy for migrant domestic workers and hold workshops in assorted places around Hong Kong where migrant domestic workers gathered, such as churches. Following the success of this pilot program, the organization grew. There was an increasing number of migrant domestic workers participating in various projects such as its "money-smart migrants" program, which taught financial management. Migrant domestic workers also participated in one-on-one mentorship programs where they were paired with corporate mentors who provided advice on workers' business and investment plans.

Economic livelihood organizations' unapologetic focus on economic "empowerment" contrasts sharply with cause-oriented progressive organizations and traditional organizations. Economic livelihood organizations focus on harnessing financial management and savings skills and creating an investment-oriented, forward-looking mindset that sees migrant domestic work as a step toward achieving something more rather than as a survival job. Rather than questioning structural imbalances between states that led to labor migration in the first place or criticizing and lobbying for policy changes or even supporting charitable projects in the Philippines, these organizations see migrant domestic workers' economic interests as superseding other considerations. I was somewhat uncomfortable with Concepcion's occasional judgmental observations that migrant domestic workers should not "pick up gossip magazines" during their free time but should instead use their free time to work and to learn. It was a statement that reminded me of the Godmother Network's Marla Jose's statement that migrant domestic workers should work rather than "going to discos" (see chapter 2). These rationales, while well-meaning, appeared to take on a paternalistic veneer, with allies assuming that they know better than migrant care workers.

Nevertheless, I understood the rationale underpinning economic livelihood organizations' larger goals. Mesina's explanation of Enrich HK's mandate trenchantly underscores economic livelihood organizations' approach: "Because we always tell [migrant domestic workers], you have to have power and control over your finances. You have to own that. If you just leave it to the wind or have other people dictate how you will be spending your money, you'll have no control. But if you know it, and we will give you the tools to understand how to, you know, go about it, then you'll have much more control. And that's where power lies." Economic livelihood organizations in Hong Kong see their work as being geared toward helping migrant care workers achieve financial independence. Caring for migrant care workers entails giving them the tools to accomplish this.

There is a wide range of various organizations representing migrant care workers in Hong Kong. There was a reason why International Migrants Alliance (IMA), a transnational grassroots alliance of progressive migrants' organizations whose work I discuss in greater detail in chapter 3, was first established in Hong Kong. The desire to make Hong Kong a "world-class" city, coupled with the long history of migrant organizing, meant that such organizing was more visible in Hong Kong compared to any of the other sites that I visited. In addition, the urban density of Hong Kong and the concurrent absence of space for migrant care workers to hang out in on Sundays meant that migrant organizers have informally divided up entire areas of the city as "belonging" to certain advocates.

The presence of different types of migrant organizations, from progressive to traditional to economic livelihood organizations, shows the truth of the statement that Hong Kong serves as an exemplar for migrant organizing that other countries should follow. Progressive organizations, much like their counterparts in the Philippines and in Canada, wed their structural analysis and ongoing policy advocacy with the creation of communities of care for migrant care workers and their families. Traditional organizations do not make structural analyses a formal part of their work; rather, they emerge in support of migrant care workers' specific needs, whether for skills upgrading or for the provision of emergency relief funds for their hometowns. Economic livelihood organizations, in contrast, see their work as exclusively associated with economic empowerment. These ideological variations aside, all the care activists I spoke to respected the presence of different organizations. They recognize that there are different ways to show care for migrant care workers. They see value in having numerous organizations representing various migrant care workers.

The political upheavals occurring in Hong Kong had consequences for care activism. The increase in the number of protest actions organized by prodemocracy actors because of the proposed passage of the 2019 Extradition Bill affected migrant care workers.[8] Although there were migrant workers organizing in support of Hong Kong's prodemocracy protests, prodemocracy campaigns generally did not see the welfare of migrant workers as being part of their agendas, remaining "indifferent to the plight of migrant workers" (Li 2019). In fact, some migrant care worker activists noted that they did not feel that they could support how certain prodemocracy activists equated their cause with the United States and Donald Trump, who issued statements in support of the protesters (Bin 2020, 171). As one activist noted, "I understood most parts about the Hong Kong social movement last year till I saw protesters waving USA flags and Trump's photos while calling on Trump to liberate Hong Kong. . . . You know the Philippines was colonized by the United States before, right? For me, that's not liberation to Hong Kong. They're calling for colonization" (171).

Because of these concerns, prodemocracy activism and migrant activism both took place but generally did not overlap. As Sring Atin, the chairperson of the Indonesian Migrant Workers' Union, stated, "Our protest actions are not about extradition to China. They are about migrants' rights" (Joles and Chiu 2019).

Distinguishing between the two movements' goals allows migrant care worker activists to be clear about how the protests violated migrant care workers' labor rights. Some had employers who required that workers extend their working days or that they relinquish their days off so that the employers could participate in protests (Joles and Chiu 2019). Yet other workers had employers who fired them for returning to their houses after their designated curfew, refusing to accept migrant care workers' rationale that public transportation closures led to their late arrival (Joles and Chiu 2019). That prodemocracy activities took place in spaces normally occupied by migrant care workers during their days off affected the types of actions that activists could take, compelling them to find other venues for their protests (Zhao 2019).

The COVID-19 pandemic, which led to a lockdown across Hong Kong, further curtailed migrant care workers' labor rights (Vilog and Piocos 2021; Lui et al., 2021). Migrant care workers who got COVID-19 faced magnified risks of being evicted from their employers' households, leading to rising cases of migrant homelessness. COVID-19 additionally impeded migrant care workers' access to public spaces, which became dangerous for many, given the increase in surveillance and in policing taking place. One out of every four people who were fined for violating bans on public gatherings, in fact, are migrant care workers, "even though they are less than 5% of the population" (Sun, Servando, and E'Silva 2022).

As a result of migrant care workers' increased vulnerability during COVID-19, all migrant care worker organizations, regardless of their ideological affiliation, found that they needed to be more active. They drew attention to the challenges migrant care workers faced, granting interviews to the media to condemn migrant care workers' circumstances and using social media to publicize their concerns. Migrant care worker activists, in addition, deployed their resources to regularly have virtual *kamustahans* (check-ins), which they characterized as them doing their work as "second-liners," a term they used as a deliberate contrast to their work as "front-line" health care workers during the pandemic (Vilog and Piocos 2021, 189). Given that employers forbade some migrant care workers from using their mobile phones during the workday, migrant care worker activists had to schedule their check-ins and other virtual activist events at "strange times" (Bin 2020, 160).

Migrant care worker activists who run shelters for migrant workers without housing organize different "bonding activities," including "handicraft sessions, interfaith sessions, online mass services, exercises, yoga, Zumba, and cooking lessons," to make shelter residents feel like they are with "a family away from their own families" (Vilog and Piocos 2021, 191). Through checking in, migrant care worker activists deliberately carved virtual communities of care that enabled migrant care workers to feel less isolated during the pandemic. These spaces also functioned as a way to reach out to distressed migrant care workers who use these channels as a way to get advice and necessary resources for themselves and their families. They used these sessions, for instance, to coordinate the receipt of personal protective equipment (PPE), which some migrant care workers could not access, and even funds (Lui et al., 2021). Hence, during the pandemic, the "labor of care" enacted by migrant care worker activists gave migrant care workers reasons to keep persevering (Vilog and Piocos 2021, 191).

Singapore: Care Activism in a Closed Context

Singapore has rules prohibiting migrants from being part of political organizations. Migrants do not have the same labor rights as migrant workers in other countries. Migrant domestic workers, in particular, are subjected to regular and invasive pregnancy tests, chest X-rays to screen for tuberculosis, and HIV/ AIDS tests; a positive test result means immediate expulsion from the country. In addition, regulations in Singapore require all employers to pay the Singaporean government a "security bond" of $5,000; this will be refunded once the employment contract has ended or is cancelled and if there are no violations of the work permit (Su 2017, 40). These regulations have led Singapore's foreign domestic workers program to be compared to Arab states' *kafala* system, in which the well-being of migrant domestic workers is ultimately entrusted to their employers (Anjara et al., 2017). Researchers have found that employers fear losing this bond and so restrict the mobility rights of the migrant domestic workers whom they are employing (Huang and Yeoh 1996; Devashayam 2010). In fact, the relationship between migrant care workers and employers is described as one of "soft violence," where employers hide the power they hold over migrant care workers by developing a close, familiar relationship in order to "maximize labour" out of migrant care workers (Parrenas, Kantachote, and Silvey 2021).

In July 2017, upon entering Lucky Plaza in downtown Singapore, I immediately felt as though I was in a shopping mall in the Philippines. Inside Lucky Plaza, one can find money exchange booths, remittance centers, shops selling Filipino groceries and Filipino DVDs, and even a franchise of Jollibee, a popular Filipino fast food chain. On the top floor of Lucky Plaza are offices that provide services for migrant domestic workers. These offices include a medium-sized office space for the Humanitarian Organization for Migrant Economics (HOME), an organization founded by Sister Bridget Tan in 2004 that supports migrant domestic workers' "welfare, empowerment and advocacy" (HOME 2019).

When I entered HOME, Peaches immediately hugged me. Peaches was a longtime migrant domestic worker activist whom I first met in 2010 during the first year of deliberations on the creation of an ILO convention on domestic work. During the deliberations at the Palais des Nations, Peaches and I frequently sat together in the NGO and civil society observers' section. Peaches explained to me in 2010 that she had been living and working in Singapore for almost twenty years, supporting her parents, her siblings, and her nieces and nephews. She has been volunteering with HOME for a long time and in fact was one of the migrant domestic worker activists who was selected to go to Geneva to represent HOME. In 2010, when I first asked her what working in Singapore was like, Peaches laughed wryly and compared the Singaporean government to Voldemort, the villain in the Harry Potter book series. Elaborating, she mentioned that it was difficult for many migrant domestic workers to live in Singapore. For instance, she decried mandatory annual pregnancy and HIV/AIDs tests imposed on migrant domestic workers; restrictive policies that curtailed migrant domestic workers' mobility, such as prohibitions against migrant organizing; and the absence of worker rights that are standard in other countries such as Hong Kong, such as mandatory days off. The passage of legislation giving migrant domestic workers mandatory days off did not pass until 2012.

Peaches' observations in 2010 were apt. The overall belief among migrant domestic workers was that Singapore ranked in the middle in terms of workers' rights compared to other migrant-receiving countries. While the Singaporean government has passed policies to safeguard migrant care workers' well-being, succumbing to the pressures created by passage of the ILO convention and to the existence of stronger migrant domestic worker protections in neighboring countries such as Hong Kong (Koh et al., 2017), such policies have only incrementally improved migrant care workers' situations in Singapore. As Adela, a migrant caregiver activist who moved to Toronto in 2007, told me, "Canada is on top because there is the opportunity to apply for citizenship. Hong Kong would probably be in the middle because they offer some protections for migrant workers. Singapore would be below that. The wages aren't as high, and there are so many tests that you have to take. At the bottom would be countries in the Middle East, like Saudi."

Upon meeting again in 2017, Peaches and I sat down in a corner to catch up. The room was full of Filipina and Indonesian migrant domestic workers who were gathered for a financial training course. It was a warm environment. A few minutes after I arrived, one woman passed around *suman* (a glutinous rice cake wrapped in banana leaves), which we all ate contentedly. Peaches proudly discussed the programs that HOME sponsored, which included courses training migrant domestic workers in assorted skills such as cooking and financial literacy. I mentioned to Peaches that the previous day I noticed groups of women wearing HOME T-shirts sightseeing in the Botanic Gardens. Beaming, Peaches mentioned that HOME scheduled regular outings for migrant domestic workers, many of which are covered through donations. In these spaces, Peaches explained that the women form community by exchanging resources, sharing stories, and even discussing possibilities for what I have termed "microresistance" in this book.

After Peaches and I had spent an hour conversing, Glenda arrived at the HOME office. Glenda and I also met in Geneva in 2010, where she was another HOME representative. Like Peaches, Glenda had been working in Singapore for close to two decades, leaving the Philippines in order to support her children. Glenda and I left the HOME office soon thereafter to continue our conversation. Over dinner, Glenda shared her experiences with me. She noted that while she and her daughter were estranged, with her daughter being resentful that her mother was away working abroad, their relationship had in recent years become closer because her daughter began to understood the depth of her mother's sacrifice abroad. Glenda also shared with me the impacts that being part of HOME had on her, as well as her work with migrant church ministries.

When I asked her why it was important for her to be part of these organizations, Glenda said that they gave her life in Singapore a purpose: "It is hard to be a domestic worker in Singapore. I've been lucky in that I've had good employers, but many don't. So it is important for me to give back and to help when I can." The discourse of helping out, or "giving back," was more pervasive among the migrant domestic worker activists whom I met in Singapore. In contrast to Hong Kong, where space was provided for civil society organizing, migrant workers in Singapore were keenly aware that overt attempts to be political placed them at risk of being expelled from the state. Thus, unlike Hong Kong, there were no organizations that were "cause-oriented" such as UNIPHIL. Instead, the organizations that I observed included traditional organizations, ally-led organizations that gave migrant domestic workers access to social networks and provided support for them when they were in distress, and economic livelihood organizations. In the case of HOME, one of the organizations featured here, its activities encompassed support provision, policy lobbying, and economic livelihood programming. Significantly, aside from traditional organizations, the other two types of organizations were led not by migrant domestic workers but by allies. In what follows, I describe the different types of organizations that I observed in Singapore, tracing how having a different national context shaped migrant organizing.

Paula, a Filipina migrant domestic worker who is part of the Filipino Family Network, met me in front of a nondescript storefront in Little India. It was my first time meeting Paula, whom I was introduced to by a family friend who used to work as a migrant domestic worker in Singapore. We walked for a few minutes before entering a building where Paula ushered me into a room where other members of the Filipino Family Network were meeting for weekly computer classes.

I quietly sat at the back of the room and observed the class. All of the people in the room were women, and they were attentively listening to the teacher, who I presumed was a local Singaporean, go over how to use a word-processing program. After class, Paula and I debriefed. Paula explained to me that the Filipino Family Network was an ad-hoc, informal group that met for classes and that also served as a social gathering space. Consisting only of migrant workers, the Filipino Family Network provided Filipino migrant domestic workers with a social network that allowed them to exchange resources with their peers and find camaraderie with each other. "It is hard to be abroad, so you need to keep busy," Paula stated before describing the activities that the network supported, which had in the past included a dress-making course and, through a partnership with another organization, financial literacy classes. "The most important thing we do is give each other support and celebrate each other's achievements," Paula stressed. Paula then took out her phone to show me pictures of a recent graduation ceremony celebrating the women who finished a recent financial management course.

Like the Indonesian Family Network, which consisted of Indonesian migrant domestic workers and with whom the Filipino organization shared space, the Filipino Family Network also provided informal counseling for migrant domestic workers facing employment, health, immigration, and other problems. Paula was quick to note, however, that they were not an official organization. When approached by migrant domestic workers who needed legal advice, they referred women to Transient Workers Count Too (TWC2) or to HOME. Paula was aware that migrant organizing was explicitly prohibited by the Singaporean government and took pains to emphasize that what they were doing was not "political."

"Is it hard to be in Singapore compared to Hong Kong?" I asked Paula, who, prior to coming to Singapore, had worked and been active in organizations in Hong Kong. Paula shrugged and said, "Hong Kong was great because there were more organizations for migrant workers. Every week, there were so many cultural events, so many political events. Singapore is different because it's smaller than Hong Kong, and there aren't organizations for migrants that are allowed to exist. Despite [these restrictions], we find ways to get together. We may not be as visible in that you won't see us marching in the streets or meeting government officials, but we're still here, helping each other." She then emphasized the need to work closely with allies who provided migrant domestic workers with important support. "I see us [migrant domestic workers] as quiet partners, who give our allies such as TWC2 information on what's happening on the ground. Through them, we can support migrant workers."

My subsequent interviews with advocates in Singapore were with allies who were not migrant workers but who took it upon themselves to support migrant workers. When interviewing these advocates, I kept thinking of Flor Contemplacion. Contemplacion was a Filipina migrant domestic worker in Singapore who was accused of murdering a fellow Filipina migrant domestic worker, Delia Maga, and the child assigned to Maga's care. Contemplacion was later found guilty and sentenced to death by hanging in 1995. Even though I was only twelve years old when this happened, the pervasiveness of news coverage, the release of a popular film on the case, and, a few years later, my witnessing of the challenges migrant domestic workers faced in Hong Kong meant that her story made a lasting impression on me. Hearing firsthand accounts from Migrante leaders on how Contemplacion's story catalyzed their political consciousness strengthened my awareness of Contemplacion's impacts.

I remembered Contemplacion when conversing with John Gee, one of the founding members of and a current volunteer with TWC2, after he disclosed that TWC2 was founded following the death of a migrant domestic worker. TWC2 provided migrant workers in distress with a crucial source of support in Singapore. Such support services include assistance for migrant workers who are facing labor abuse (e.g., disputes over salary or over workplace injuries) and a food voucher program that gave migrant workers access to subsidized meals in participating restaurants. Because of rules against migrant organizing and labor unions' reluctance to take up the cause of migrant workers, TWC2 and HOME became important organizations advocating on behalf of migrant workers.

Gee emphasized that TWC2's work deliberately tried not to focus only on "exceptional" cases of migrant death or extreme instances of migrant abuse, because such cases were rare. As the first organization to explicitly advocate on behalf of migrant workers, TWC2 saw the importance of shifting its discourses and policies toward migrant work. Gee was matter-of-fact when describing Singaporean society's attitude toward migrant workers: "I think in Singapore society there's this abusive behavior that's tolerable and there's abusive behavior that is intolerable. You can be insulting to domestic workers, and people will shrug their shoulders. Start beating them, that's a no-no. But it's the lower-level kind of abuses—not paying someone, making them work ridiculously long hours, or underfeeding them. Those things still go on and tend not to be seen as so, so serious by most people." One of TWC2's tasks was to attempt to shift societal attitudes toward migrant workers in Singapore and improve policies. Although Gee acknowledged that notions of "human rights" in Singapore were seen as "Western" concepts and not as persuasive to older generations, "arguments that seem more practical will often have greater traction." Echoing Chiu Yee Koh and colleagues' (2017) observations that, ultimately, pragmatic arguments grounded in the "long-term economic interests" of Singaporean society led to the passage of policies giving migrant workers days off, Gee observed that justifying improvements to migrant workers' situations by referring to the monetary benefits of doing so were crucial. He noted too, though, that "another one which we do use without so much referring directly to rights is just to appeal to people's basic sense of justice, which is often more persuasive than a more explicit rights approach. So, you know, you remind them about what their expectations are for their own families, for example. Or ask how they would feel in the same situation."

TWC2's campaigns to achieve a "more enlightened regulatory framework" for migrants were grounded in the same justice-oriented approach. For Gee, an "enlightened" approach necessitated thinking of migrant workers' welfare. This meant, then, that policies needed to place at the center migrant workers' secu-rity. For instance, TWC2 advocated that migrant workers should be allowed to work while waiting for the outcome of their cases against abusive employers so that they could support themselves. According to Gee, current policies, which barred migrant workers with pending cases from paid employment, expected "migrant workers to survive on air" and were thus inhumane. An enlightened framework would also prohibit employers from firing and deporting workers at will. Although Singapore's policies provided a check on employers' ability to arbitrarily terminate workers by allowing migrant workers to declare to Min-istry of Manpower officials at the airport that they have a complaint against their employers, thereby delaying their deportation, the balance of power was so skewed in favor of employers that migrant workers rarely did so.

I met Jolovan Wham, the former executive director of HOME, at a shelter for distressed migrant workers. During our conversation, I noted that he mostly agreed with Gee's observations. He agreed that Singapore took a pragmatic approach to change, though he believed that rights-based arguments reso-nated with Singaporeans provided they were "basic" entitlements, which he described as the "right to a salary, your right not to be abused, not to be hit, not to be sexually assaulted." Getting support for other rights, such as the right to a weekly day off or overtime pay or even introducing the concept of maternity leave, was more difficult. To combat these assumptions, HOME organizers made it a point to issue frequent press releases and provide media interviews to present alternate discourses on migrant workers. Wham admitted that it was challenging to combat assumptions about migrant domestic workers in Singapore because of what he described as the abundance of "horror stories" about thieving and lazy "maids" from Singaporean employers. Ensuring that there existed alternative depictions of migrant domestic workers as deserving fair treatment, he argued, might lead to improved treatment: "We think it's important to have a counternarrative, because this can also be a pressure point for change."

Wham observed that a vital part of HOME's work, aside from shifting dis-courses and lobbying policy officials, was providing distressed migrant domes-tic workers with shelter. Although the Philippine and Indonesian embassies also provided migrant workers with shelter while their cases against their employ-ers were pending, those who took shelter in embassies were forbidden from ever leaving the embassies, thereby restricting their mobility. HOME's shelter provided migrant domestic workers with a less restrictive space.

In addition, HOME raised migrant workers' consciousness of their rights and their entitlements. Responding to my question about the level of involvement that migrant domestic workers themselves have in organizations such as HOME and TWC2, Wham admitted the following:

> One of our weaknesses is that we have these platforms, we have these groups, but it hasn't turned into something political yet. . . . That's why we haven't been able to harness this energy and this solidarity and community bonding into something that can have a direct impact on policies and laws and effect structural change, right. So we haven't been able to do that successfully because . . . any hint of these workers getting involved will endanger their job. So we don't want to do that. But we have been able to at least harness that energy in terms of raising consciousness, getting them more aware of their rights.

Affirming Paula's observations that migrant domestic workers are a "silent partner" to migrant advocacy, Wham discussed how migrant domestic workers actively provided feedback to HOME on how Singapore's and sending states' policies and programs affected them, therefore influencing HOME's policy recommendations and the type of advocacy that HOME pursued. While migrant domestic workers could not be directly linked to overt types of activism, allies' efforts in ensuring that migrant domestic workers' experiences were reflected in their advocacy efforts enabled migrant domestic workers to attain some form of representation in Singapore.

Traditional organizations in Singapore, similar to traditional organizations in Hong Kong, provide support for migrant workers' everyday needs, be they English classes and counseling. In contrast to policy and social welfare organizations, traditional organizations operate more as grassroots organizations that do not, as Paula notes, engage in any policy advocacy activities. In contrast, social welfare and policy organizations in Singapore were the only organizations that were officially permitted to represent migrant workers' needs and interests by officially providing programming to support migrant workers and issuing policy recommendations. Yet unlike organizations in Canada and Hong Kong, where civil society organizing is permitted and migrant organizing flourishes, directly issuing criticisms of the government through overt political actions such as rallies was forbidden in Singapore.[9] Hence, describing HOME's and TWC2's work as involving policy advocacy and social welfare renders their activities acceptable in Singapore. Given prohibitions against migrant organizing in the country, this means that the face of these organizations is Singapore residents. Yet the involvement of migrant workers in the everyday activities of these organizations, primarily through their establishment of communities of care that can scale up and provide the basis for more covert forms of solidarity building, show that they are an integral part of these groups.

According to Wham, HOME started its economic livelihood classes for migrant domestic workers in 2007, with current enrollment amounting to a thousand students. As Peaches, who had participated in and led a number of HOME programs, affirmed, HOME's programs provided migrant domestic workers with an opportunity to form a community and learn new skills.

Aside from HOME, other organizations provided migrant domestic workers with economic livelihood training. One such organization was AIDHA, which was considered a "sister" organization to Enrich HK. AIDHA's name refers to the Sanskrit word for "that to which we aspire." When I asked Marjanne Van der Helm, AIDHA's program manager, about the reason why AIDHA was started, she responded that it emerged from a seed project funded by UNIFEM Singapore on financial management for migrant domestic workers. Eventually, in 2007 AIDHA became an independent organization led by former president Sarah Mavrinac, who initially taught classes on financial management to a group of twenty-five migrant domestic workers in her condominium. Van der Helm argued that Mavrinac was motivated by the desire to "lift migrant domestic workers out of poverty through sustainable wealth creation." As AIDHA's programs began to attract an increasing number of migrant domestic workers, it developed a "holistic approach" to teaching, which meant that students did not take classes separately but were made to take them simultaneously. By offering classes on savings and financial management, computer literacy, communications, confidence building, and entrepreneurship, AIDHA aimed to provide migrant domestic workers with a well-rounded education that they could then channel toward their futures. A key lesson that AIDHA taught migrant domestic workers in all of these various modules was the necessity of prioritizing long-term planning even when doing so might run counter to their family members' expectations:

> [Migrant domestic workers] are obliged to send everything home. We're saying, maybe you don't need to send everything home. And don't make your family too reliant only on your support. So that requires negotiation, right? With the family back home, it may take courage to say, I'm not gonna—I'm gonna save some part of this for myself but also maybe for you, like sort of a safety net or maybe from like investment in education in the house. So it's not only just saying no but also taking [your family] along in the savings journey and investment journey. Migrant domestic workers have to learn to communicate and also to see themselves, right. To take their family with them in that dream story.

When asked about the success rates of these programs, Van der Helm pointed to cases of migrant domestic workers who were able to start small-scale businesses such as money-lending companies, *sari-sari* (convenience) stores, and junkyards. One of AIDHA's most successful alumni, a migrant domestic worker from Sri Lanka, succeeded in setting up an online tea shop, an experience that she discussed in a TED talk. An established alumni network and corporate mentors provided assistance to migrant domestic workers.

Economic livelihood organizations such as AIDHA in Singapore and its counterparts in Hong Kong and Canada see migrant domestic workers' needs as being best represented through economic empowerment. Although I continue to wonder whether migrant care workers could truly achieve economic independence, given that they are still operating within a colonial economic structure that imposes demands on developing countries and that offers very little protection to people whose livelihoods are affected by economic and social upheavals, I understood the power of seizing one's autonomy. Because migrant domestic workers and their families undergo the sacrifice of living apart in order to carve out more sustainable futures, the leaders of these organizations believe that long-term economic planning is key to meeting migrant domestic workers' needs and even to ending the cycle of labor migration.

Compared to other countries in my study, care activism in Singapore is more constrained. The national context in Singapore remained hostile to overt forms of organizing. In fact, the rules that migrant care workers are subjected to significantly impede migrant care workers' physical autonomy. Regular HIV/AIDS tests and pregnancy tests impede migrant workers' reproductive autonomy, presenting an ever-present reminder that the Singaporean state views them not only as sources of contagion but also as "just workers" whose "sole purpose . . . is to contribute reproductive labour for the host community" (Constable 2020, 3492). While Hong Kong has similar restrictions on migrants' reproductive rights, with policies prohibiting migrant workers from living with their families and barring migrant workers from acquiring permanent residency, Singapore is unique in that migrant workers who fail their pregnancy tests immediately get deported, and migrant workers who wish to marry are required to get permission from the government first (3492). Hence, along with its policies against migrant organizing, Singapore arguably presents more impediments to migrant organizing compared to Canada, the Philippines, and Hong Kong.

Yet care activism in Singapore exists. While such care activism is more covert than care activism in Canada, the Philippines, and Hong Kong, what struck me when I was in Singapore was witnessing workers' collective efforts to create robust communities for each other. Traditional organizations, which provide support for migrant care workers who need direct counseling advice, language classes, and the like, flourish. They provide a space for migrant care workers to gather and just be. Social welfare and policy advocacy organizations and economic livelihood organizations are both helmed by Singaporean nationals, yet the major drivers of their everyday programming are migrant care workers. The time I spent at the HOME offices at Lucky Plaza, for instance, made clear to me that migrant care workers drive the types of programming being promoted by the organization. Despite the covert and oftentimes hidden nature of care activism in Singapore, the organizations here similarly understand the importance of creating communities of care for migrant care workers.

During COVID-19, the situation of migrant care workers worsened. While migrant care workers were exempted from the Singaporean government's requirement that migrant workers live in migrant dormitories, where there were numerous cases of COVID-19 outbreaks (Hancock 2022), they nevertheless faced intensified surveillance over their activities. Living with their employers meant restrictions on workers' mobility, longer working hours, and even cases of violence (Antona 2020).

These increased challenges led to the concurrent increase in care activism. Heightened policy restrictions, all undertaken in the name of pandemic containment but which effectively meant further regulations on migrant workers' activities, led to higher instances of migrant worker abuse. As a result, HOME and TWC2 ramped up their policy campaigns. They submitted a joint report to the Office of the High Commissioner of Human Rights at the United Nations that outlined the deteriorating conditions of migrant workers during the pandemic and their recommendations, which mentioned the need for domestic work to be included in the Employment Act and for COVID-19 regulations to be "applied in a non-discriminatory way and not in a blanket way based on immigration or accommodation status" (HOME and TWC2 2020, 13).

Both organizations also experienced an increase in demands for their services. HOME reported a 25 percent increase in the number of phone calls it received from migrant care workers facing distress (Antona 2020). Because of these increased demands, HOME organized a fundraising drive that would allow it to expand its programming (HOME 2022). These organizations, together with the Filipino Family Network and the Indonesian Family Network, continued to organize events for migrant care workers to facilitate the creation of communities of care. Because of restrictions on large gatherings, HOME, TWC2, the FFN, and the Indonesian Family Network held a small carnival with photo booths, arcade games, and stations where organization representatives could talk to migrant workers about their rights (GAATW 2022).

As in the Philippines and in Hong Kong, COVID-19 did not cause care activism to slow down; instead, care activism continued. As they had in prepandemic times, migrant care worker activists saw the importance of advocating for and connecting with migrant care workers.

Conclusion

There are many faces to care activism. By examining care activism in the Philippines as a migrant-sending state and in Hong Kong and Singapore, both of which are migrant-receiving states, I explored whether and how national contexts affected migrant organizing.

Migrant organizing in the Philippines focuses on exerting pressure on the Philippine state to improve its policies toward Filipino migrant workers and their families. Rather than seeing migration as a given, organizations seek policies that would benefit migrant workers and their families. Yet these organizations differ in their normative visions and their tactics. Progressive organizations draw linkages between the phenomenon of labor migration and larger structural issues, ultimately seeking the realization of national democratization in the country. In contrast, mainstream organizations focus on migrant workers' immediate needs by working with the Philippine government and with bilateral and transnational institutions to improve policies and programs and by providing support for economic development projects.

Migrant organizing in Hong Kong and Singapore was conducted from the perspective of migrant care workers who were currently living temporarily in a receiving state. Migrant care workers sought improvements in the situations of migrant care workers in these locations, creating communities of care for migrant workers who were living apart from their families. Migrant organizers also sought better policies for migrant workers in Hong Kong and in Singapore.

However, care activism in Hong Kong was more vibrant compared to Singapore and even compared to Canada. Hong Kong's political environment provides ample space for a range of migrant organizing, enabling migrant domestic workers to assume key leadership roles within organizations. The dynamism of migrant organizing in Hong Kong, in fact, serves as a model for organizers in other locations. Different types of migrant organizations coexist in Hong Kong, ranging from progressive "cause-oriented" organizations to traditional organizations to economic livelihood organizations.

In contrast to that in Hong Kong, migrant organizing in Singapore is more constrained. Because of strict prohibitions against migrant organizing, organizations cannot be too overt in their political actions. The organizations that are present include traditional organizations led by migrant workers that provide spaces for migrant workers to gather and that organize workshops as well as social welfare and policy advocacy organizations and economic livelihood organizations run by allies. What is interesting, though, is that despite the many restrictions facing migrant domestic workers in Singapore, the very formation of communities of care meant that the politics from below, while less visible, still exists. While seemingly mundane and apolitical, the bonds of friendship that form during cooking and computer literacy classes allow migrant domestic workers to have a space that is truly theirs. In addition, the ability of allies to be the public face of migrant advocacy enables migrant domestic workers to act as "silent partners" within these organizations.

Differences in national context, however, do not mean that there are no commonalities between the various care activist sites that I examined. Regardless of the different types of migrant organizing found in each location, a common thread uniting migrant care worker activists is a desire to care for each other, for the larger communities of migrant care workers, and for migrant care workers' families. Ultimately, care activism entailed forming a community of care with fellow migrant care workers. The differences that exist are rooted in distinct understandings of how best to show care. Progressive organizations in the Philippines and in Hong Kong, for example, believe that care activism necessitates political education: to care for migrant care workers means raising their political consciousness and fighting for structural changes. Economic livelihood organizations in Hong Kong and in Singapore, to use another example, believe that caring for migrant care workers means guaranteeing their economic security. Yet for all of these organizations, establishing communities of care was a crucial part of their work. This was especially true during times of political and social upheaval, specifically during heightened periods of political turmoil in the Philippines during Duterte's presidency and in Hong Kong during the prodemocracy protests and the COVID-19 pandemic. When all is said and done, care activism—whether in Canada, the Philippines, Hong Kong, Singapore, or elsewhere—is about providing migrant care workers with a community that can help them bear witness to each other's journeys and that can provide the sense that they are not alone.

Chapter 5

Everyday Care Activism

ADELA: It is so hard for me to continue working as a caregiver. I was a trained nurse, and the absence of employment opportunities in the Philippines meant I had to go abroad. The minute I gave birth to my child, I had to leave. There was no way to support her. We are in close contact over text messaging and Skype, and I try to show my love by being both the mother and the father. It's been a hard journey. In Canada, only Canadian families matter. What about our family?

HOST OF MISS CAREGIVER 2017: What is the greatest challenge facing you as a caregiver?

MISS CAREGIVER BEAUTY PAGEANT CONTESTANT: Nothing is more challenging than being a mother separated from her children. . . . We take care of other children while not being able to put our own kids to bed. We are unable to sing lullabies for our children. It is good that we have technology. Thank you to Canada for the Caregiver Program and giving us the promise of reuniting with our families in the future.

ELY: My employers are OK. Sometimes they try to get you to do things that aren't covered in your contract, so I have to watch out. When that happens, I try not to say no outright, because employers don't like that. So I find a way out. For example, when they asked me to clean their swimming pool, I pretended that the chemicals made me dizzy. Then they felt bad. From then on, they never asked me to clean the pool. You just have to be strategic.

Between 2007 and 2017, migrant care workers shared with me their stories of everyday life. Such stories include the complex navigations of having to maintain the family across borders, as in the accounts shared by Adela and the Miss Caregiver contestant above. They also include workplace conundrums, as in Ely's story.

What these stories show me is that care activism does not only take place within the realm of migrant organizations. Rather, care activism also takes place in the intimate spaces of the family and the home, at work, and in individual encounters in public spaces. As such, the central question I explore in this chapter is, simply, What does care activism look like in migrant care workers' daily lives? To answer this question, I turn to the interviews that I had with migrant care worker activists who, over the course of my research on care activism, shared with me their experiences with their transnational families, at work, and in public spaces. Although I had initially approached migrant care worker activists to ask them about their *organizational* agendas as migrant activists, I soon realized that their motivations behind becoming activists were deeply personal. Emotions were at the heart of their actions, including anger about the injustices that they experienced, vicarious trauma when bearing witness to the struggles their fellow care workers faced, embarrassment over their experiences of deskilling, sadness and grief for the losses that they encountered (including temporal loss, or time lost waiting for the processing of papers), joy when hearing about family members' achievements, exhilaration when being in community with other care workers, and hope for what the future brings (de Leon 2018; Ticar 2018; R. Brown 2016; Nasol and Francisco-Menchavez 2021). Care activism is as much about policy and structural changes as it is about validating the *affective* dimensions of each other's experiences. It is about validating migrant care workers' own needs and desires (Tuck 2009).

Care activism was also about resisting, oftentimes in covert ways, the challenging circumstances wrought by workers' realities of family separation and their challenging encounters at work and in public. In order to fight back against these challenges, migrant care workers use various tactics, from creating new norms, taking part in covert workplace microrebellions, and shifting discourses on migrant care work to illuminate its complexities. Everyday care activism enables migrant care workers to show their agency while living with the constant and ongoing challenges of migrant care work. It is about carving out spaces away from "labor time," or time spent fulfilling one's work contract (Isaac 2022, 13). These spaces result from global capital's imperatives to export labor, but they are ultimately spaces that belong to migrant care workers in that they are "excluded" from capital's reaches (14). Ultimately, everyday care activism is a way for migrant care workers to seize back power for themselves, for their families, and for larger communities of migrant care workers and their networks. Taken as a whole, these individual moments of resistance show the combined power of migrant care workers' conviction that they—and their work and their *lives*—are important.

Grounding my discussion of everyday care activism is the recognition of the vital role played by migrants' imaginations in allowing them to envision possibilities within and beyond their everyday realities. Here, I draw from the concept of "cognitive processes" that underpins much of migrants' everyday resistance (Mahler and Pessar 2001). We can witness such cognitive processes when we consider, for example, Alisha Ticku's (2017) vivid ethnography of expatriate and migrant workers' "Dubai dreamscapes." In this work, Ticku argues that thinking of "dreamscapes" allows migrants—whether they work for multinational corporations, construction sites, or other families as domestic workers—to feel "the freest when they are imagining worlds beyond their own mundane realities" (53). Instead of seeing dreams as only residing in people's subconscious, Ticku shows that "dreams have real, lived consequences in our daily lives" (53). I also draw from the concept of "critical hope" (Zembylas 2014; Grain 2022), which sees hope as a crucial praxis that allows migrant care workers to look beyond their current realities and to move toward a better future. "Critical hope" can also be understood as alternative temporal spaces where migrant care workers harness their "creative and life-making" capacities (Isaac 2022, 21). Whether they are dreaming of a brighter future for themselves, their children, and their imagined community of migrant care workers, imagining the possibilities of different presents and futures in their engagement with pageants and artistic performances, or interpreting their actions through the lens of empowerment and agency, dreaming is a crucial part of workers' everyday care activism.[1]

In this chapter, I first address the challenges of migrant care work. The racialized and gendered nature of the work additionally creates barriers for migrant care workers to gain recognition for their labor contributions. More significantly, the requirement that migrant care workers live where they work blurs the boundaries between work and home and, in fact, between worker and household member. Then I look at everyday care activism through practices of what I call "transnational hypermaternalism," covert workplace rebellions and participation in public events that endeavor to shift negative stereotypes of migrant care work.

Migrant Care Work

Recognizing migrant care workers' engagement in everyday care activism first requires acknowledging how exploitation is built into the very structure of migrant care and domestic work. Understanding this context might help explain the motivations behind everyday care activism. A receiving state such as Canada ties migrant care workers' work permits to their employers, which means that migrant care workers' ability to continue living and working in Canada is dependent on their employers. This component of the Live-In Caregiver Program (LCP) and the Caregiver Program (CP)—and, in fact, of Canada's different temporary labor migration programs—is at the root of worker exploitation. Having tied work permits means that migrant domestic workers are *captive labor*: workers are reliant on their employers' goodwill to stay in Canada. All of the migrant care workers I have spoken to seek Canadian permanent residency for themselves and their families. Because Canada's LCP and CP require that workers complete a two-year work contract with their employers before they can apply for Canadian permanent residency, employers' power over migrant care workers is magnified.

In instances of employer abuse, the labor protections enshrined by Canadian federal and provincial governments that mandate safe working environments and that create a "bad employer" blacklist are ineffective because migrant domestic workers risk jeopardizing their ability to stay in Canada if they report their employers after immigrating since their employment status is tied to their employers. Reporting workplace abuse may even result in their deportation if they are unable to find new employment. Although migrant care workers can switch employers, many are reluctant to do so, because finding a new employer is not easy. Many employers are hesitant to assume the costs of filing the sponsorship fees with the federal government. In fact, migrant care workers have told me that they have offered to pay their employers directly for these sponsorship costs just so they can transfer employment and consequently meet the requirements for permanent residency. Relatedly, another barrier preventing migrant care workers from seeking better working conditions is the reality that leaving their employers will prolong the permanent residency application process.[2]

Workers who were initially hired through recruitment agencies are especially susceptible to abuse (Larois et al., 2020). There have been cases of migrant care workers who, upon coming to Canada, found themselves "released upon arrival"; that is, they found that they had no employers when they came to Canada because recruitment agencies had fabricated the names of these employers or had listed themselves as employers with no intention of hiring these workers. When put in this situation, migrant care workers found themselves having to work for the agencies' clients, sometimes doing so for free, because recruitment agencies claimed that prospective employers wanted to see if the workers were a good fit first. Recruitment agencies take advantage of migrant care workers' financial need and their desire to attain Canadian permanent residency (Larois et al., 2020).

Indeed, sending and receiving states, employment agents, and employers are complicit in encouraging the dehumanization of migrant care and domestic workers. Not only is the job difficult, demanding, and poorly compensated, but these stakeholders bolster the belief that they are entitled to have control over migrant care and domestic workers' *personhood*. From sending states such as the Philippines' deliberate marketing of its nationals as being efficient yet loving "supernannies," to receiving states' invasive policies requiring potential migrant care and domestic workers to pass multiple medical tests, to agencies and employers using arbitrary criteria such as age, skin color, and physical appearance when sifting through applications (Bakan and Stasiulis 2005; Chin 1998), migrant care and domestic workers find themselves objectified to the point where their individual qualifications as workers become moot.

Moreover, since care and domestic work are so intimate and breed close familiarity with the personal details of people's daily lives, many employers feel the need to employ not just a worker but someone who can be "part of the family," thereby obscuring the line between employers and workers. Being seen as a family member does not necessarily translate into better treatment. As Abigail Bakan and Daiva Stasiulis (1997, 11) note, migrant domestic workers are asked to "take on many stressful 'family responsibilities' and burdens of a family that is not their own" while being unable to enjoy the benefits adult family members receive. Migrant domestic workers are frequently infantilized in the workplace in ways that adult family members frequently do not have to experience. They oftentimes live in a state of hypersurveillance, during which employers monitor workers' appearance, their food choices, their schedules, and even their activities during their days off (Pratt 1997; Constable 1997; Bakan and Stasiulis 2005; Tungohan et al., 2015). They have to perform a great deal of "emotional labor," as Premilla Nadasen, citing sociologist Arlie Hochschild, observes: domestic workers "were evaluated by their ability to be cheerful, caring, and compassionate.... [T]hey were expected to listen to and comfort employers, nurture children, and project an upbeat yet deferential personality" (2016, 91).

In addition, many scholars have pointed to the arduous nature of migrant care and domestic work. The boundaries between work and home are blurred. Even when migrant care workers were done with work for the day, they were, in practice, expected to continue working because they were still in their places of employment. The absence of privacy makes it hard for migrant domestic workers to feel at ease even during their time off. Cases of sexual harassment are pervasive and difficult to escape, because migrant domestic workers are compelled to live and work in their employers' households. Migrant domestic workers who differ from their employers on the basis of their religion and their culture may find that they have to hide both. Some employers, for example, asked that migrant domestic workers not cook specific Filipino dishes because the employers did not like the way the food smelled or looked (Tungohan et al., 2015). Because migrant domestic workers are constantly hungry as a result of these restrictions, the communal act of eating and sharing food, which I discuss later, becomes a revolutionary act.

The multiple responsibilities that migrant domestic workers have to juggle go beyond providing care for their charges. Although the terms of the LCP and the CP in Canada specify that domestic workers are only supposed to undertake domestic tasks that are related to their caregiving responsibilities, such as "light" housekeeping and "cooking," in practice, migrant domestic workers are expected to do the majority of the housework (Bakan and Stasiulis 2005). I participated in a research study that included thirty-two focus groups with domestic workers across Canada. My research collaborators and I discovered that migrant caregivers were being asked to work in their employers' restaurants, clean their employers' family members' houses, and undertake tasks that were not specified in their employment contracts (Tungohan et al., 2015). They suffer from societal perceptions that care work and domestic work are not "real" work, which may be a reason why some employers ask that workers do additional work. A common observation among the women I interviewed, for instance, was how employers "requested" that they do other tasks while they are "watching" their charges. As Adela, who came to Toronto under the LCP in 2007 and has lived apart from her children for ten years, stated, "My employer always asks me to do things like polish her silver or scrub the floors or even clean her chandeliers. 'Since you're just watching [my mom], why don't you go ahead and do this?' And I can't say no. How can I? I need to get along with her because I live with her."

The reality that migrant care work and domestic work are stigmatized for being low-status racialized and gendered labor presents an additional challenge. Although discrimination against migrant care workers is arguably more visible in locations such as Hong Kong, where local residents resent the "colonization of public spaces" during domestic workers' days off and have occasionally fought to ban domestic workers from certain public spaces (Tillu 2011), the same stigma certainly exists in Canada (Tungohan et al., 2015). For instance, one woman who participated in the research study cited above talked about how the lack of access to public space led her to aimlessly walk around the city for hours, eventually finding refuge in a bus shelter (Tungohan et al., 2015). And even though there are no public spaces where migrant domestic workers are explicitly banned, subtle manifestations of discrimination against Filipino migrant workers enhance feelings of discomfort. Luisa, who came to Vancouver under the LCP in 2008, discussed why she decided to rent a room in an apartment with a friend on Sundays: "Canadians are supposed to be 'nice,' but you can tell when people are treating you differently because they think you're a nanny. It's tiring to always be on your guard. Sometimes, you just want to relax. So we decided to rent this room so we have time to be by ourselves without anyone watching us."

Because most of the women in the LCP and the CP have college and university degrees, with many having previously worked in white-collar professions in the Philippines (Kelly et al., 2009; Banerjee et al., 2018), migrant domestic workers contend with experiences of deskilling and deprofessionalization. Such experiences are exacerbated by the fact that the Canadian government does not permit current domestic workers to take courses from community colleges that would have allowed them to maintain or upgrade their professional skills and that would also have helped them transition out of care work once they are done with the LCP and the CP. "I was a nurse in the Philippines and then a nurse in Saudi," Luisa said to me. "And now I am a nanny. Is this why I went to school and worked for so many years?"

Everyday Forms of Care Activism

Migrant domestic workers counteract the challenges they face daily by engaging in the politics of the everyday. Rather than accepting their living and working conditions and the negative discourses that accompany migrant care and domestic work, using everyday acts of resistance enables migrant domestic workers to fight back, even in ways that may not be immediately obvious. Although migrant domestic workers engage in the politics of the everyday in multiple ways, I now focus on three actions: practices of transnational hyper-maternalism, individual workplace rebellions, and participation in public events that enable migrant domestic workers to take up space and counter negative perceptions of migrant care work.

On a Sunday afternoon in the early fall of 2010, Luisa and I sat at the food court of a mall in a Vancouver suburb trying to get a Wi-Fi signal. Luisa was about to call her fourteen-year-old daughter, Tina, who lived with her grandmother in a rapidly developing beach town two hours away from Manila. (Her eighteen-year-old son, Patrick, was away at university, and Luisa would try to reach him later.) Luisa left the Philippines to work as a nurse in Saudi Arabia, where she worked for three years, after which she received the opportunity to come to Vancouver as a caregiver for an elderly woman. She left the Philippines in 2005, arrived in Vancouver in 2008, and was now two years into the LCP. Tina was ten years old in 2008, while Patrick was fourteen. According to Luisa, both were old enough to understand why their mother had to leave. Being a single mother, Luisa felt that she had to go abroad in order to support her children. The three were in constant contact. They texted each other several times a day and had a standing date to Skype every Sunday.

When Luisa finally was able to get a Wi-Fi signal, I met Tina, a gangly teenager who eagerly waved hello when Luisa introduced me. Luisa and Tina immediately launched into a conversation that they had started via text message, discussing what to do about Tina's upcoming dance performance at a school talent show. After going over Tina's outfit and how she would wear her hair, Luisa asked Tina to perform her entire piece in front of both of us. Periodically, Luisa would ask Tina to stop dancing and offer suggestions on choreography. "Don't turn around so quickly! Try to turn around a bit more slowly," Luisa gently advised.

I left briefly to get coffee for Luisa and myself. When I returned, Luisa's mother, Lola Nene, had joined Tina. Lola Nene was in the midst of telling Luisa the difficulties she was facing when procuring rental money from the new tenants renting one of the units in the apartment building that Luisa had bought in their hometown using her savings. Luisa told her mother that she would ask her brother to look into it and then inquired about whether Lola Nene was able to get the medication she needed for her glaucoma. "Just spend the money I sent you last week," Luisa counselled. "Don't worry, I'll send more."

After Luisa hung up, I asked her how it felt to be so far away from her children and her mother. "It is hard, but what can I do?" Luisa shrugged.

Working abroad and supporting my family make me feel good. Before, I relied on other people to take care of everything. I had to keep borrowing money from my parents and my siblings so I can pay for food and rent and my children's tuition fees. Instead of relying on them for support, now they rely on me. I'm paying for my parents' medical bills and also paying for the schooling of my children as well as my nieces and nephews. I'm not just the one who takes care of people. Now I'm the one who sends money and who cares. I'm both the father and the mother.

Luisa's experience was commonplace among the migrant domestic workers I met. For many of the women, the need to support their families was the primary reason why they opted to leave the Philippines in the first place. An absence of economic opportunities in the Philippines led them to go abroad, with some working in other countries first before coming to Canada and others coming to Canada directly. Due to gender norms that see women as being natural domestic workers, most women participate in "global care chains" (Hochschild 2014) by entrusting the care of their children to female relatives such as their mothers or their sisters or to a female domestic worker while taking care of other people's family members abroad. As a result, an "international transfer of caretaking" transpires (Parrenas 2000).

Yet not inhabiting the same space as their children does not mean that migrant women are absent from their children's lives. As this vignette shows, intensive forms of mothering occur through close contact and through surveillance techniques using new technologies. I describe such intensive forms of mothering as "transnational hypermaternalism," which opened the opportunity for migrant mothers to reshape the boundaries of parent-child relationships. I define transnational hypermaternalism as the way migrant women exhibit maternal care through financial support and surveillance techniques that enable close communication across borders. By showing that migrant women are present in the lives of their children even though they are not physically there, transnational hypermaternalism allows migrant women to reconstruct the discourse of maternal absenteeism into a discourse of maternal involvement.

The availability of Skype, Facebook, WhatsApp, Signal, and other forms of communication enabled Luisa and all of the migrant mothers I interviewed to practice transnational hypermaternalism. Tessa, a live-in caregiver whom I met in Toronto in 2010 and who reunited with her family in Canada in 2012, talked about how she was so grateful for free and quick modes of communication that allowed her to keep abreast of her family's activities. Interestingly, Tessa was a child of a domestic worker herself. Her mother lived and worked in Spain for decades, only returning to the Philippines when Tessa already had her own family. "Back then, in the 1980s, we relied on letters and the occasional phone call. I remember being so excited when Mama sent me a telegram for my high school graduation," Tessa recounts. "And now, it's so different. It's better. I know more about my children's lives than my mother knew about mine."

Even when mothers and children are in different countries, the women I spoke to were able to supervise aspects of their children's lives. Luisa was able to give Tina instructions on her dance performance. Tessa was able to participate in different family gatherings, such as Christmas Eve and New Year's, by having her husband place a computer on the dinner table where her family members were gathered. Another woman, Christina, a live-in caregiver who came to Vancouver in 2006, told me that she sometimes texted her son's teachers to keep abreast of his performance in school. Christina explained how she felt she was able to maintain this level of surveillance in Canada, unlike when she was physically present in the Philippines, where she had too many other responsibilities that took time away from her ability to parent.

Of course, the daily acts of care that children require mean that the women have to find a relative to care for their children. Although some of the women I interviewed questioned gender norms and entrusted the care of their children to their husbands, most of the women I spoke to entrusted their children to the care of a female relative while also paying someone else—usually another woman—in their community to provide other forms of domestic work. Half of the migrant women I spoke to who at the time of our interviews were still under the LCP were either single or were separated from their husbands, which may be a reason why many women did not have the option of asking their husbands to care for their children. Yet many also justified leaving the care of their children with extended family members by emphasizing that the notion of the family in the Philippines was different from that in Canada (and in other Western countries). Rather than abiding by a strict nuclear family model, seeing "family" as encompassing one's siblings, parents, aunts, uncles, and cousins meant that—at least theoretically—children should have multiple guardians.

Valerie Francisco-Menchavez's (2018) multisited ethnography with Filipina domestic workers in Queens, New York, and with their families in Manila, Philippines, powerfully illustrates how the "labour of care" involves multiple family members and is multidirectional. That is to say, migrant domestic workers' husbands, parents, siblings, and children in the Philippines provide care for each other while workers are away. Family members in the Philippines maintain close contact with migrant domestic workers in the United States to ensure that family members abroad remain part of the family.

As Patricia, a caregiver who came to Montreal in 2005 and left her children under the care of her husband and with the support of his brothers and their wives, said, "Our [extended] family lived in one compound: next to us was my husband's brother, and next to him was another brother, and next to them was another brother's house. I left thinking that my sons will be OK because they had so many aunties around them. In the compound, they'll never be alone. And they are good at keeping me involved about everything going on. We text and Skype and post on our family's Facebook group multiple times a day." Instead of seeing her departure as an unbearably sad occasion, Patricia rationalized it by adding that "[extended] families are a source of strength."

By insisting that her children are loved, Patricia challenges the stereotypes of migrant families as facing a problem (R. Brown 2016) and the "perception that the separated family is abnormal" (Catungal 2017, 30). In doing so, Patricia questions why "particular forms of family"—specifically, heterosexual families "with a proper caring mother . . . in close proximity to her husband and children"—are seen as being normal (30).

Interestingly, some of the migrant women I observed entered into queer partnerships during their time abroad, thereby disrupting nuclear family models. Luisa even introduced her partner to her children over Skype as a *tita* (auntie), which she said went well. Scholars argue that the prevalence of queer partnerships among migrant women abroad shows migrant women's flouting of heteronormative cultural constraints and their explicit rejection of the way their bodies are policed and scrutinized in ways mentioned above (Constable 2000; Sim 2010). Scrutinizing the "micro-politics of their daily life" (Constable 2000, 240) through their queer partnerships therefore highlights subtle yet potent forms of transgression.

Despite migrant domestic workers' rejection of normative, heterosexual family arrangements and the creative ways that they have adapted to their circumstances, the migrant domestic workers in my study were sad about being apart from their children. As Francisco-Menchavez notes, "The very conditions that pull migrants and their families to be creative in keeping their families together are the same conditions that count on their separation for national profit for the Philippines" (2018, 149). Even though innovations in information technology allow workers and their families to keep in contact, living apart from their families and, in particular, their children was not easy. The sadness of living away from each other and not having the intimacy of daily, physical contact undergirds their experiences.

For example, while Patricia expressed gratitude that her children were well taken care of, there were occasions when she felt an insurmountable sense of longing to witness their daily routines and to be physically present. "Sometimes I just want to hug my kids. I want to smell them. I want to just touch them," Patricia shared. She also admitted to feeling tremendous pressure to show her children that she thought about them constantly. Despite being fortunate in having a large extended family to support her sons, Patricia felt that she still had to shoulder a lot of maternal responsibility. Deeply entrenched gendered norms meant that children felt the absence of their mothers more than they felt the absence of their fathers (Parrenas 2005; Battistella and Conaco 1998), which also likely placed added pressure on migrant women to show evidence of their love across borders. In fact, every single migrant caregiver whom I spoke to said that the hardest part about being a caregiver had to do with the pain of leaving behind their families, especially their children, echoing research showing the depths of migrant women's emotional pain when being separated from their families (Parrenas 2001; Pratt 2012; Francisco-Mechavez 2018; de Leon 2018).

Many of my conversations with migrant domestic workers included discussions about their children and their plans for the future. Because the terms of the LCP and the CP allow migrant domestic workers to reunite with their families in Canada, migrant domestic workers like Luisa pinned their hopes on the prospect of having a successful and happy life in the country. Luisa, for example, planned extensively for her children's arrival. She asked friends about the school system, started collecting clothes and other miscellaneous items that she felt that Tina and Patrick needed, and researched college-level courses that Patrick might be eligible to take. Luisa once described herself as leading a bifurcated life, saying that "my body is in Canada, but my heart is in the Philippines." Luisa and her fellow migrant mothers were counting down the days until they could be reunited with their children and were actively making plans for their children. The promise of Canada—the "Canadian Dream"—persuaded the women I spoke to that their sacrifices were not for naught.

Although no one I talked to would ever say that their situations were ideal, the migrant mothers I spoke to saw family separation as a situation to be lived with rather than a case of unrelenting tragedy. I join Martin Manalansan (2008) and others in offering an alternative interpretation of migrant care worker narratives, one grounded in workers' expressions of agency and their push back against being seen as passive victims. Rather than succumbing to defeatist, anti-woman, and antimother discourses, the migrant mothers whom I encountered used transnational hypermaternalism as a way to resist the aforementioned "narratives of tragic linearity" that are associated with migrant domestic workers' lives (Manalansan 2008). They recognized the Philippine government's complicated and contradictory discourses that see them as economic heroes, on the one hand, and "bad" mothers, on the other hand, and how this placed them in an impossible situation. The coexistence of both discourses leads to contradictory policies in sending states. On the one hand, entire government apparatuses are dedicated to facilitating labor migration because it is a crucial source of economic growth. On the other hand, policymakers decry the "breakdown" of the family due to absentee mothers and ask migrant women to return. Social ills are blamed on the absence of the mother. From Poland, where "Euro-orphans" describe the children of migrant mothers who went to western European countries to work, to the Philippines and Sri Lanka, which once considered a law stating that only single women without children could work abroad, migrant mothers are scapegoated for the harms their families face in their absence (Parrenas 2013, 196–97). Hence, reframing these portrayals by seeing themselves as good mothers and as economic heroes allowed workers to feel empowered.

Although most of my interviews were with migrant mothers, I also had the opportunity to meet the children of migrant care workers who became activists because of their experiences with family separation and family reunification. These interviews illuminate how migrant care worker activists also include the children of migrant care workers who have lived with the realities of family separation and family reunification and who fight against it. Like their mothers, the children understood the necessity of keeping in contact when living apart, and they do their part to ensure that their mothers' sacrifices were not in vain by accomplishing milestones, as Francisco-Menchavez demonstrates (2018). Yet unlike their mothers, migrant youth activists who are part of the migrant care workers' movement were more motivated to make sure that migrant youth, like them, did not have to go through similar experiences.

One of these activists, Wilma, was a member of a migrant youth organization. I met Wilma in 2016 at a workshop that I had organized in Toronto and then later again in Vancouver when I attended a migrant workers' conference that Wilma's organization helped organize. Wilma and I met for coffee a few weeks after the conference, during which Wilma talked about how she and her siblings were left behind with members of her mother's extended family while her mother was a caregiver. Wilma was abused by one of her relatives, which her mother did not know about. Because this was in the 1990s, when advances in information technology had not yet occurred, Wilma and her mother relied on letters and the occasional phone call to keep in touch. This made it hard to have fraught conversations. When they were reunited in Canada after ten years apart, Wilma recounted her mother's surprise at seeing her and her siblings so grown-up. The winter clothes that her mother bought did not fit her and her siblings. The last time they had seen each other, Wilma was still a child, and now she was a teenager. It took a while for Wilma, her siblings, and her mother to feel close, with Wilma admitting that her first years in Vancouver were difficult. She had to adjust to a completely new educational environment where she faced bullying and to a new living environment that appeared wasteful, with Wilma observing that there are "things that are taken for granted here like food and electricity. We have blackouts in Philippines so many times [that] even those kind of things give you a cultural shock. And then you ask, How is my country so poor? How is Canada so wasteful when it comes to cars, electricity, water

... These make you really realize that there's a big social gap in the world. It's beyond cultural shock."

Wilma also had to adjust to living with her mother. She was frequently told by her relatives and by her mother that she should be happy and grateful to be in Canada and that she should recognize that her mother's sacrifices meant that she could have a better future. This in turn made it difficult for her to express constant feelings of loss:

> There's like homesickness, but then there's more than homesickness. There is also like—you feel like you're living and always feeling lost. From a very young age there are too many good-byes. It feels like there is a part of you that is taken away big time. First, you lost your parents, then you lost your home country, and then you lost your relatives there, and then when you come here, you lose your parents again because you never see them. You lose them first because of all of the waves of migration, and then when you're reunited, it's hard to be together.

It was the recognition that migrant youth's issues need affirmation that drove Wilma to become an activist: "The thing about being a migrant youth is that you don't have control. Things are decided for you." Hence, for Wilma, giving the children of migrant domestic workers the space to acknowledge their experiences and to talk about their feelings was important: "I want the community to know that it is possible for us to be really vocal about our issues. I want them to get out of their fear that they cannot talk about it or we cannot change our situation." That the children of domestic workers are oftentimes left out of conversations about the impacts of labor export programs was tragic for Wilma because it led children to feel that their needs did not merit attention. Hence, being a caregiver activist and drawing attention to experiences of migrant families, specifically to migrant children's experiences of trauma, was important.

Similarly, Clara, whose mother came to Canada as a caregiver after working in Hong Kong as a domestic worker, became involved in migrant advocacy because of her mother's harrowing experience and her own experiences with family separation and reunification. Describing her mother's experience, Clara noted:

> My mom had a lot of problems in Hong Kong, where she was being abused. Her Chinese employer locked the refrigerator so she could not eat anything while the kids are at school. My mom still gets emotional when talking about the time she was a caregiver because she feels a lot of guilt, you know? Having to leave her kids and looking after other people's kids. Of course, when we immigrated there was also other kinds of issues that came with the family.

I was twenty-one when we reunited with her, but she still treated us like we were fourteen years old. So I understand the issues very well. I feel for families that are separated and certainly feel for people who are not getting the right to permanent status because I also went through that. So I think those things that happened to my family prompted me to get involved and to fight for domestic workers and their children.

For migrant mothers and, especially, for migrant youth, being able to "make it work" does not mean that they condoned family separation. For them, their experiences drove them to become care activists: they wanted to ensure that current and future communities of migrant care workers and their families did not have to undergo the same hardships. As I explored in the preceding chapters, the fundamental desire to *care* for each other and for an imagined community of migrant care workers compelled their advocacy work.

Migrant care workers' tied work permits inhibit their ability to ask their employers to respect workers' labor rights. The live-in requirement that was in effect until 2014 prevented migrant domestic workers from being forthcoming with their employers. For many migrant domestic workers, following the Tagalog adage of *pakikisama*, or "getting along well with others," made the most sense. As Tessa said matter-of-factly, "I see my employers every day. They're not just my employers, but they are also my housemates. So maintaining peace in the household is important." When asked whether *pakikisama* was a point of pride for her, Tessa explained how the ability to get along with different types of people was one of the reasons Filipinas made good care workers, which she saw as a point of pride: "Filipinos are good at adapting and getting along with different folks. They prioritize *pakikisama*, which makes us good workers."

Yet migrant care workers also engage in covert acts of workplace microrebellions in order to protect their interests. Among the myriad strategies migrant care workers employ, the women discussed "playing dumb" when their employers give them a difficult time about their supposed responsibilities. For example, Luisa pretended that she was allergic to dogs when her employers initially asked her to walk their three dogs as part of her daily duties. Migrant care workers also described going above their duties to perform tasks that their employers did not expect in order to ensure that they remain in their employers' good books. For instance, Patricia told me that she once alphabetized her employer's library without being asked to do so to curry favor with her employer. In other cases, workers described feigning incompetence and/or poor health to get out of doing certain tasks. For instance, Ely, a migrant caregiver who worked in Toronto and whom I interviewed in 2009, described how she pretended to be dizzy when her employers asked her to clean their swimming pool.

While one could see these actions as proof that workers are not being straightforward and, at least in the first and third cases, that they are shirking their responsibilities, further analysis shows that these women were finding creative ways to ensure that their interests are protected. Luisa and Ely were aware that the tasks they were being asked to undertake were not part of their contracts, which specified that live-in domestic workers are only meant to undertake "light housekeeping" (and even then, live-in domestic workers are only supposed to do household tasks related to care work, such as cooking food for their charges). They were reluctant to confront their employers directly about the fact that they were being asked to undertake tasks unrelated to their contracts because they did not want to potentially jeopardize their working relationships and thus make themselves vulnerable to being terminated before they finished the LCP's required two-year live-in requirement. Patricia was aware that it would be in her interests to make her employer grateful for her hard work, which to her also meant that her employer would be willing to treat her better. Patricia also discussed how taking a keen interest in her employer's life and providing emotional support was a way for her to ensure her job security. Even though performing acts of emotional labor added to her workload, Patricia felt that this was not too onerous. "By making myself indispensable, I make sure that I continue working," she reasoned.

Migrant care workers also use workplace microrebellions when facing hostile work situations. Because they were reluctant to confront their employers directly, workplace microrebellions are an opportunity for migrant caregivers to seize a bit of agency in situations that would otherwise feel unbearable. Tessa's first employer refused to pay her overtime pay and demanded that she clean the houses of her employer's relatives, which were clear violations of her employment contract. Tessa did not want to complain and risk prolonging the time she was separated from her family. Instead, she opted to covertly show her opposition to the way she was being treated through her use of humor. "In Tagalog, my employer's first name sounds very close to *aswang* [vampire], so I call her *aswang*, and she thinks I am just calling her name." Tessa admitted to me that this was petty, but having the ability to laugh at her employer made her feel empowered.

Adela also covertly resisted her employer's occasionally inappropriate labor demands using humor. Adela was a prominent member of the migrant caregiver activist community and was assertive. She was keenly aware when her employer was violating the terms of her labor contract, which clearly specified that her only responsibilities pertained to care work and not housework. Yet her employer expected her to do the entire household's laundry, made frequent requests that she "just watch" the employer's child (without pay) when she needed to "step out" of the house when Adela was off the clock, and did not pay Adela overtime wages. "I believe in justice," Adela joked, "but I also believe in *just tiis*." Putting a humorous spin on "justice" by combining the words "just" and the Tagalog word *tiis*, which, loosely translated, means "withstanding tough situations," Adela described what was an arduous work environment humorously and ironically, thereby making it more bearable.

When I asked her why she did not just ask her employer to stick to the contract, Adela responded that she was not going to risk alienating her employer and getting fired. "You can't just fight all the time. You have to accept your situation. And you have to laugh at it. If you can still laugh at it—and at them—then you're still OK," Adela explained. The subversive use of humor is similar to Francisco-Menchavez's (2018, 25) observations of how migrant domestic workers in New York ironically discussed their job responsibilities as involving "paper work," that is, the literal use of toilet paper to clean their charges and paper towels to wipe floors, scrub toilet seats, and other household tasks, and as being "CEOs," that is, responsible for cleaning, *ebak*-wiping (*ebak* is Tagalog for "poop"), and organizing their wards' day-to-day needs.

Not only did these darkly humorous interpretations of their jobs allow migrant care workers to covertly reverse the power hierarchy between themselves and their employers, they also strengthened the bonds that migrant care workers had with each other. Narrating these stories and sharing jokes allow migrant domestic workers who are also experiencing the same challenging work environments to bond with each other. Through shared humor about work, specifically about instances of workplace microrebellions, situations become bearable. In fact, after witnessing and taking part in countless hours of shared jokes about ways that migrant workers secretly defied their employers, I see these shared moments of cathartic joy as the glue binding together communities of care. The migrant women who celebrate and commiserate with each other become dissident friends, witnessing, affirming, and uplifting each other. These moments allow migrant care workers to recuperate their dignity after facing dehumanizing workplace situations.

Through workplace microrebellions, migrant care workers carve out spaces to strategically resist their working environments. Such microrebellions include currying favor with their employers to ensure better future treatment, "playing dumb," feigning sickness, and engaging in dark humor. Through these tactics, migrant care workers show care for themselves. Rather than accepting as given their current situations, they fight back in subtle ways. Sharing these stories with each other, including jokes, also enables stronger bonds of community with fellow migrant care workers. Collective feelings of catharsis allow migrant care workers to feel more empowered.

Everyday care activism involves making visible migrant care work on migrant care workers' own terms. As I mentioned in the introduction, migrant care workers are placed in a paradoxical situation of invisibility and hypervisibility. They are invisible in that their labor largely remains unrecognized. That they remain out of the public eye because they work in private households heightens their invisibility. Yet migrant care workers are also hypervisible. Stereotypical depictions of "nannies" abound. For instance, existing media coverage of migrant care workers has fixated on notions of migrant care worker distress and abjection. There are also stereotypes of nannies as greedy husband-stealers.

To counteract these competing imperatives of being both invisible and hypervisible, migrant care worker activists seize back narratives of migrant care work. By depicting the complexities of their lives as migrant care workers, they add nuance to existing portrayals of migrant care workers. More importantly, their knowing participation in these actions engenders feelings of care and solidarity with other communities of migrant care workers. These actions thus become a vital part of everyday care activism.

On July 15, 2017, while I sat in the audience at the Miss Caregiver 2017 beauty pageant, I took note of the excited buzz of friends, family members, and migrant domestic workers around me. With most of the audience members dressing up for the occasion, the atmosphere was festive. Many were taking group selfies. A few groups were carrying bouquets of flowers to present to the contestants afterward. I overheard a few people in the crowd—some of whom were conspicuous because they were some of the few non-Filipinos present—introduce themselves as employers of some of the contestants who wanted to show support.

While sitting there, I too was excited. I eagerly awaited the beginning of the show. Having previously watched three Miss Caregiver beauty pageants, I was familiar with the proceedings. The candidates would be introduced, and then there would be different competitions, such as the costume, evening gown, talent, and sportswear (in lieu of swimwear), followed by a question-and-answer portion. Whereas the first Miss Caregiver beauty pageant in 2006 was held in a modest assembly hall, Miss Caregiver 2017 was held in the cavernous and brightly lit auditorium of a private, all-boys Catholic school in midtown Toronto. And whereas the first Miss Caregiver was given a modest crown, Miss Caregiver 2017 and the other finalists were bedecked in shiny tiaras, capes, and sashes. Miss Caregiver had become an established event, accruing more sponsors and more contestants over the years.

At 6:33 p.m., the lights dimmed and a video began. Immediately, the room became silent in anticipation. The structure of the video was similar to those shown in other beauty pageants: the contestants posed, smiled, and talked to the camera to introduce themselves. The difference here was that all of the contestants highlighted their migration journeys to Canada.

"I am a single mother of three kids. I first went to Kuwait to work as a domestic worker, and then I came to Canada. I joined Miss Caregiver because I wanted to widen my social circle and meet other domestic workers. When you're a caregiver, you don't really have time during the week to develop your skills and have fun," declared contestant number 3.

"Because the proceeds of Miss Caregiver will go toward a charity in the Philippines, I decided to join the pageant. I want to give back to the Philippines. Miss Caregiver is great because it allows domestic workers to be part of the Philippines even when living far away. I also want Canada to know how loving and how wonderful domestic workers are—I want to show Canadians that we give back to our community. Before coming to Canada, I was an OFW [overseas foreign worker] in Hong Kong. It was hard, but God was with me the entire time," stated contestant number 6. She went on to say, "My family used to own a big business back home, but then because of economic problems, our business shut down. I had to become the breadwinner, so I became a caregiver. I am proud that I am a caregiver and that I can support my family. I joined Miss Caregiver to be a role model to other domestic workers. I also want to support other domestic workers."

After these introductions and the singing of both the Canadian and Philippine national anthems—performances of nationalism that are commonplace in many Filipino migrant community events that I have attended—a noted Filipino pastor and migrant community activist took the stage. During his remarks, he spoke about the caregiver program as a "nation-building program" and emphasized that domestic workers, as "community activists and as heroes," should be proud of their contributions to Canada. "Domestic workers are a part of Canada," he intoned. "Thank you to Canada for allowing us to come here."

Following the pastor's remarks, each of the different portions of the beauty pageant proceeded as usual. The theme for Miss Caregiver 2017 was global warming, which gave the contestants creative license to make sure that their costumes adhered to the theme. Bedecked in gowns made out of recycled paper and boxes, brightly painted in hues of red and green, and, in some cases, shaped to resemble melting snow (to represent melting polar ice caps), birds, and plants, the contestants—to thunderous applause from the audience—strutted up and down the stage. The sportswear portion saw many contestants wearing sporting gear bearing the logos of Canadian sports teams. One contestant, wearing a Blue Jays jersey, enthusiastically swung a bat back and forth to roars of approval from the crowd. I noted that no one wore sportswear that bore the logos of Philippine sports teams. This portion of the beauty pageant seemed designed to show how thoroughly the contestants had adapted to Canadian cultural norms, of which loyalty to Canadian sports teams was an important part.

It was, however, the talent and question-and-answer portions that elicited the most emotional reactions from the audience. During the talent portion, contestant number 1 did an interpretive dance that was meant to symbolize love, longing, and sacrifice. Behind her, the projector flashed pictures of Filipino migrant workers at the airport carrying their luggage, a migrant woman kissing her baby farewell before going through airport security, and a painting of different migrant workers—including a woman pushing a wheelchair—standing in front of the Philippine flag. The poignant song lyrics included the following refrain: "Hold on . . . put your trust in God . . . follow your dreams . . . dream, just dream."

Contestant number 6 used colored sand to create a picture of a flower, which she described upon finishing as representing the ambition, beauty, and strength of domestic workers. "Love," she stated, "is not what we do for ourselves but what we do for others." Similarly, during the question-and-answer portion, the contestants drew attention to migrant domestic workers' strengths. One contestant, for example, talked about how domestic workers always "gave back" to their communities. By invoking domestic workers' ambitions, the love that they showed to their families in the Philippines and their employers' families in Canada, and their contributions to their communities, the contestants gave public tribute to what they saw as migrant domestic workers' positive attributes.

At the end of the pageant, the winners were announced, with all of the contestants receiving an award. Aside from Miss Caregiver and first and second runner-up, the organizers bestowed awards for Miss Leadership, Miss Charity, and Miss Serenity. While these awards—which have, in the past, included Miss Obedience and Miss Congeniality—may be criticized for invoking gendered stereotypes of "good" female traits, it was important for the organizers to ensure that everyone won something. The goal of the pageant, after all, was to uplift migrant domestic workers.

That the Miss Caregiver beauty pageant has in the span of eleven years become an established event among certain communities of migrant domestic workers was impressive. Founded by the Fil-Core Support Group in 2006, Miss Caregiver was not only intended to be a one-time event for its contestants but also meant to create leaders within the community. As Fil-Core Support Group's founder, Judith Gonzales, stated when talking about the history of the beauty pageant during the event, "We wanted domestic workers to realize their power and to be agents of change." Because contestants for Miss Caregiver had to undergo weeks of leadership training, the hope was that all contestants, not just the winner of the beauty pageant, would be equipped with important advocacy skills.

When the Conservative government was in power in Canada, the Fil-Core Support Group was able to award the winner of the beauty pageant a trip to Ottawa, where they got a personal tour of the House of Commons and a one-on-one meeting with former immigration minister Jason Kenney, during which they had the opportunity to discuss issues facing migrant domestic workers. For instance, one of the judges for the 2017 beauty pageant was Miss Caregiver 2010, who used her platform to campaign to clear the backlog in permanent residency applications.

The winner of Miss Caregiver had an important platform to represent community issues not only to different Filipino and migrant community members in different community events but also in an official capacity with senior government officials. At Miss Caregiver 2017, members of Parliament and a Filipino Canadian senator were present during the proceedings. When they were addressing the domestic workers present, these politicians praised not only their commitment to their jobs and to Canada but also their ability to support each other.

In addition, Miss Caregiver was a fundraising event for the Fil-Core Support Group. Unlike other migrant caregiver beauty pageants, which required migrant domestic workers to pay a hefty entrance fee, Miss Caregiver was free for contestants.[3] Contestants were only asked to help sell tickets, the proceeds of which went either to a charitable organization in the Philippines or directly to a caregiver needing funds to pay for medical care.

Other migrant caregiver organizations in Canada have helmed beauty pageants. In 2011, for instance, Migrante-Canada's chapter organizations in Toronto organized a Mother-of-the-Year beauty pageant. Unlike the Fil-Core Support Group, Migrante-Canada is a militant grassroots organization that does not shy away from overt political actions. While I addressed these ideological divisions between organizations in chapter 4, it is important to note here that the types of activities that organizations engage in to shift harmful discourses on migrant domestic work depend on their ideologies. Hence, Mother-of-the-Year, in contrast to Miss Caregiver, was more overtly political. There were no politicians invited, nor were there migrant community activists who were part of Conservative organizations. No platitudes were given to Canada for being generous in opening its doors to domestic workers. The audience members consisted almost exclusively of migrant domestic workers, migrant activists, and their allies. The judges did not consist of community "dignitaries" and politicians but included migrant activists and allies, all of whom were women.[4]

Though Mother-of-the-Year had the same beauty pageant events, minus the swimwear/sportswear portion, the talent and question-and-answer portions showcased the contestants' more political mindsets. One of the contestants, for example, performed a skit showing her taking care of her charge in Canada while attempting to communicate to her children in the Philippines. During her performance, she showed how hard it was to be forthcoming with her children about the realities that she was facing, instead answering that she was "fine" when asked. Based on the emotional audience response, it was clear that this performance touched migrant domestic workers who could perhaps relate to the need to "protect" their families from the hardships of their circumstances abroad. The answers to the questions presented the contestants' more critical standpoints compared to those of Miss Caregiver contestants. The contestants shared the same narratives of family sacrifice and caregiver resilience as the Miss Caregiver contestants but also tied their situations to the ongoing problems of economic strife in the Philippines and to neoliberal capitalist structures that created labor export programs in the first place.

Despite these ideological differences, the Miss Caregiver and Mother-of-the-Year pageants showed that the bonds of community that domestic workers form with each other and with the audience members of primarily fellow migrant domestic workers made these beauty pageants cathartic events. Echoing Alisha Ticku's (2017) and Sarah Mahler and Patricia Pessar's (2001) observations regarding the power of dreams, ambitions, and cognitive processes, migrant beauty pageants give migrant domestic workers the opportunity to dream about life beyond the mundane. At least for an evening, domestic workers are given the chance to shine in a glamorous setting, to showcase their talents, and, more crucially, to share with other contestants and the audience of domestic workers their struggles and their triumphs while living abroad.

During the question-and-answer portion of these pageants, it is common for contestants to describe their experiences of family separation, their resilience and heroism in experiencing and overcoming adversity while living abroad, and their ambitions for the future. These answers resonate deeply with the audience of domestic workers. Having a public expression of their private challenges validates their experiences and can even legitimate their decision to work abroad.

In fact, the use of beauty pageants as a tool for community building and caregiver empowerment is pervasive in other countries. When I was in Hong Kong in July 2017, my respondents told me that there were several beauty pageants focused on migrant domestic workers in the city. One of them was Hot Mommies 2017, which my respondent told me was a way to recognize the sacrifice of migrant mothers living apart from their families while also drawing attention to their beauty. My respondent also told me that the sexualized name of the beauty pageant was also deliberately tongue-in-cheek. The documentary *Sunday Beauty Queen*, which follows a character named Chairman Leo, a queer domestic worker who organizes beauty pageants for Filipino domestic workers in Hong Kong, as well as three of its contestants, highlights how pageantry became an antidote to the frequent drudgery of care and domestic work. By presenting positive representations of migrant domestic workers, migrant beauty pageants present migrant care work in a more empowering light.

An inadvertent consequence of such positive representations may also result in migrant domestic workers flouting immigrant communities' class biases. For example, class divisions exist between more established members of the Filipino diaspora in Canada who arrived in the 1970s as permanent immigrants and Filipino immigrants who arrived in later waves in the 1990s and 2000s and who came, in part, as migrant domestic workers (see, e.g., Eric 2012). Hence, there are Filipino community members in the first group who are ashamed of the way migrant care work is associated with Filipinos; consequently, beauty pageants that draw public attention to Filipino migrant domestic workers are shameful.[5] In a telling exchange in a Filipino message board on Facebook, one community member made fun of Miss Caregiver. "What will be next? Mr. Custodian?" he scoffed. Beauty pageants for migrant domestic workers have become part of the public landscape, enabling migrant domestic workers to make their experiences visible and public. Pageants offer a way for migrant domestic workers to disavow classist mindsets. As queer theorists who discuss the profound impacts of queer beauty pageants and pride parades show, finding ways to celebrate identities that have historically been marginalized is a way of taking back control of mainstream narratives that malign these identities.

On an unseasonably warm spring day in March 2018, a group of women from Gabriela-Ontario, Anakbayan-Toronto, and Migrante-Ontario unfolded their banners at the gathering space for International Women's Day marchers. They placed a loudspeaker at the corner, stood in formation, and started dancing. One woman in the middle led the group behind her in a series of simple steps while members of these organizations who were not dancing talked to passersby about what was happening. I, too, helped distribute flyers. "This is for One Billion Rising," I explained to one passerby. "It is about drawing awareness to gender violence." In the middle of clapping and cheering, we spoke about why migrant domestic workers are particularly vulnerable to gender violence. Other passersby laughed, clapped, and even followed along to the dance steps. At the end of the dance, the women laughed and hugged each other. One Billion Rising, which started in 2012 with the explicit purpose of "linking the struggle of women in the fight against global capitalist structures" through flash dances (One Billion Rising 2016), also had the additional benefit of offering a space where migrant domestic workers could have fun, feel empowered, and be *seen*. Migrant care workers use flash dances to get the public engaged in their concerns.

Another flash dance that I observed took place on October 18, 2017, at the University of Toronto–Mississauga as part of the Carework as Choreography event. A group of migrant domestic workers, including members of the Care Workers Connections, Education and Support Organization (CCESO), formed a circle and, following the lead of activist-artist Marisa Moran Jahn, started a series of dance moves that were meant to replicate the daily tasks that migrant domestic workers undertake. Marisa, who was from the United States, was in Toronto that week. Her project, the CareForce dialogues, involved driving across the United States and holding one-on-one conversations with different migrant domestic workers. "Now we are getting the *lancha* [iron]," Marisa exhorted. "Let us iron, iron, iron," she encouraged. "And now we are getting El Windex! Then we are sweeping!" After a few steps—which, to everyone's amusement, also involved pushing a wheelchair and dusting—the dance ended with Marisa exhorting everyone to strike a "superhero pose." Although there were one or two people standing at the sidelines and watching, nearly everyone in the room—both migrant domestic workers and members of the public, which included students and professors—participated in the flash dance. Following this dance was another dance, with steps that involved "reaching out and rising up," "crossing the border," and "taking power and sharing power."

While trying to keep up with the dance moves, I remember exchanging a glance with Penny, a migrant caregiver in Toronto who lost legal status recently after her permanent residency application was rejected. Canadian immigration officials had deemed that her son, who has a disability, would cause "excessive demand" on the Canadian welfare system. "This is exhausting," I panted at her. Penny smiled. "Ha! Try doing all of this every day." Marisa led the entire group through three additional dances. Afterward, everyone cheered. The migrant domestic workers gathered for a group picture, with Marisa in the middle, and donned CareForce Disco paper glasses, which prominently displayed the CareForce hashtag (#CareForce).

"That was fun," I said to Penny afterward. "It is good to escape from my problems," Penny agreed. Almost as an afterthought, Penny added, "I also think it's good for us to have fun and for people to see us having fun." Enabling migrant domestic workers to escape from their worries, even for a brief moment, makes flash dances a crucial source of respite.

Other artistic endeavors that I have observed migrant domestic workers taking part in included migrant caregiver organizations' use of a flash dance on Mother's Day 2018 to draw attention to migrant mothers' ongoing separation from their children, Caregiver Action Center's Art to Unite workshops, Migrante-BC's artist-led painting workshops for migrant domestic workers (the paintings were later sold), and CCESO's and Gabriela-Ontario's drama classes. According to Martha Ocampo, CCESO, in fact, has regularly put on theatrical productions featuring domestic workers. Their first play, held in 1983, was entitled *Carding* and was based on a dramatic workshop that they organized called "A Life of an Immigrant," during which domestic workers shared their experiences. They also performed another play, *Home Sweet Home*, which dealt with domestic violence, and yet another play, *If My Mother Could See Me Now*, which was performed entirely in Tagalog. The latter was first performed in Toronto and then later performed in Vancouver, Winnipeg, and small towns in British Columbia. Ocampo described the play as showing "how hard it is for domestic workers, how waiting to become landed is such a struggle, and their loneliness. In the play, we showed how one caregiver actually committed suicide, which actually happened. We workshopped the play for a long, long time, and they are all domestic workers who attested to these issues."

Another notable endeavor that migrant domestic workers actively took part in was the comic-book workshops led by the group Kwentong Bayan, which loosely translates as "stories of the people." Consisting of two Filipina artists, Jo SiMalaya Alcampo and Althea Balmes, Kwentong Bayan, alongside CCESO, convened regular meetings with domestic workers who were interested in creating a "collaborative, community-based comic book" based on their stories. When asked how they encouraged migrant domestic workers to share their experiences, Alcampo said, "They would kind of just naturally talk about their own experiences and say, yeah, my employer was hard, and they would list all of their struggles."

Stories of their families also emerged that affirmed the difficulties of family separation and reunification and that discussed the realities of transnational family life. Many migrant domestic workers, for example, bonded over the logistical difficulties of coordinating family meetings online when family members are dispersed across three different countries. Alcampo reflected further that seeing the commonalities of migrant domestic workers' experiences was affirming for everyone in the group because these stories showed that they were not alone. Yet Alcampo cautioned that when migrant domestic workers were asked to talk about their lives, they inevitably fought back against tropes of caregiver suffering: "They would always end in a very positive way of how they survived that and how they created a life with their community and having their family here."

The very act of sharing stories also became a way for the migrant domestic workers to give voice to experiences that remain hidden within the Filipino community, such as being part of a same-sex partnership and having to "prove" that their relationship is "real" to Canadian immigration authorities. Speaking openly about the homophobia inherent among many Filipino community members was important for queer migrant domestic workers because it recognized their specific hardships; that members of the group later organized a "queer migrant domestic workers" float for the Pride Parade in Toronto was in fact a sign of the community's love, acceptance, and insistence on visibility.

In addition, having such a space enabled migrant domestic workers to reflect on the histories of caregiving in Canada. As Balmes explained, "Decolonizing migrant domestic workers' mindsets was a crucial part of our work." She reflected further, "I think we talk about how we've been so divided and kind of like paired against each other. We look at the history of caregiving here, it used to be, in the very beginning it used to be um English nannies, and then it turned into Indigenous women and then Black women from the Caribbean, and . . . now it's more Filipinos. So there's sort of like even within the caregiving community, caregiver history is not really talked about." By sharing stories in a supportive community setting, making visible "hidden" experiences, and even decolonizing migrant domestic workers' mindsets, Kwentong Bayan's gatherings were about more than creating comic books. As Alcampo described it, "It's bonding and socialization. It's so important for the community. . . . It's not just about mental health but also physical, spiritual, um emotional, psychological health. [Being together] allows us to endure all the oppressions, whether there [are] microaggressions, or huge kind of systemic things, um filling out forms, misinformation, how you deal with all those challenges is you need to have, like, folks you can trust."

Religious rituals were also repurposed to raise awareness about migrants' issues. Erie Maestro from Migrante-BC cited the example of migrants' Stations of the Cross, held every Lent in a church in downtown Vancouver, during which organizers argued that Jesus himself was a migrant and thus ensured that "each Station of the Cross was represented by a migrant. There was the passport, the suitcase, the experiences of abuse, there was migrant rallying." In partnership with Latino migrants, this annual event made visible the plight of migrant workers, thereby encouraging churchgoers to develop compassion toward them.

To be clear, it is the very act of making migrant domestic workers *visible on their own terms* that makes the aforementioned artistic and theatrical performances a compelling part of everyday care activism. The phrase "make care work visible," in fact, appeared at the end of the CareForce pamphlet explaining the different dance moves. The bulk of care work involves staying behind closed doors. Migrant care workers, in fact, are only really visible in public spaces in cities in Canada during the weekdays when they are taking their charges for walks in the park, picking them up from school, and the like. In Canada, the contrasts between the visibly racialized migrant women taking care of primarily white children were trenchantly depicted in *Brown Women, Blond Babies* (Boti and Bautista 1992), a documentary that followed Filipina migrant domestic workers in Canada and their challenges. Hence, taking up space through flash dances, drawing public attention to workers' presence, and showing the joy that they experience in doing so defeat the stereotype of migrant care workers as being uniformly abject and tragic (as per Manalansan's arguments concerning the tendency to depict migrant domestic workers as following "narratives of tragic linearity"). Forming community with each other, whether through pageantry, theater, comic books, or dance, enables a sense of collective togetherness and strength. Being public about the joy, the sorrows, and the emotional complexities that define migrant domestic workers' lives in Canada is thus a form of resistance. Knowing that other migrant care workers can take strength from these depictions shows how these actions are fundamentally rooted in caring for migrant care workers.

Conclusion

At a planning meeting on possible actions that migrant and labor organizations can support to advocate for possible changes to the Live-In Caregiver Program in the fall of 2014 in Toronto, a migrant caregiver discussed why it was important to organize an event that celebrated domestic workers. She introduced the idea of migrant caregiver beauty pageants as an example of a way to empower domestic workers; events like these, she stated, could be used to bring migrant domestic workers into further advocacy.

Immediately, one of the other migrant activists who, as a labor activist, was there as an ally refuted her suggestion. According to him, beauty pageants diminished the larger cause of migrant activism. They trivialized the struggle of migrant domestic workers by making it appear as though migrant domestic workers' situations were actually not that serious. A more direct form of action, such as holding a rally in front of government offices or finding the immigration minister's speaking schedule and disrupting the event, may be more effective in garnering public attention. The actual process of individually empowering migrant domestic workers through everyday care activism did not seem as important to him as advocacy tactics that can help bolster the larger cause of migrant justice. What was the point of beauty pageants when they did not "scale up" and lead to policy and structural changes?

The migrant caregiver who spoke became silent, and the meeting continued with other suggestions of more conventional types of political action. When I later thought about this interaction, I realized why it is so important for there to be organizations that are led by and for migrant care workers—which I address throughout the book—and why reversing the discourse on migrant care work by making migrant care work visible in migrant care workers' own terms was so revolutionary. When we consider the way some migrant and labor activists condemn creative modes of organizing for not meeting their criteria for what constitutes appropriate forms of resistance, we admire migrant care workers' persistence in taking part in these events in spite of such opposition even more. Care activism, after all, is about more than just pushing for policy and structural changes. What this chapter shows by focusing on everyday care activism is that care activism is also about the affective, the intimate, and the personal. It is about migrant care workers' own desires—their desires to be good mothers, to escape the drudgery of care work through pageantry and through art, and to subvert expectations of what care work looks like.

Echoing queer theorists' discussions of the significance of events such as pride marches and feminist thinkers' appreciation of covert forms of resistance, my discussion in this chapter draws attention to how everyday care activism enables oppressed communities to seize moments of resistance in otherwise debilitating arrangements, to subvert expectations of what families and care work and motherhood look like, to use cognitive processes such as dreaming and imagining, to find joy in community, and to strategically make aspects of their lives visible to reverse deeply embedded stereotypes (Dyer and Mecija 2019; Ticku 2017; Mahler and Pessar 2001).

By acknowledging migrant care workers' own desires, these assorted acts of care activism recognize migrant care workers' "complex personhood" (Tuck

2009, 420). These acts acknowledge that migrant care workers, like all people, "reproduce, resist, are complicit in, rage against, throw up hands/fists/towels, and withdraw and participate in uneven social structures" (419). Using a desire-based framework that centers migrant care workers' humanity therefore enables a way outside the false binary between "reproduction" and "resistance" (419) or between structure and agency where people are assumed to be ensnared in structures of power that make reproducing inequity inevitable or, conversely, where they are seen as active agents fighting against such inequities.

In some cases, as in the example of migrant caregiver beauty pageants, migrant and labor activists may even find these actions irrelevant, if not out-right harmful. Yet migrant care workers found meaning in directly challenging harmful stereotypes of absentee migrant mothers through transnational hypermaternalism, covertly undermining their employers through workplace microrebellions, ironically reimagining their debilitating working environments through humor, and making visible previously hidden experiences of migrant domestic work through participation in beauty pageants, flash dances, and other artistic projects. By constructing themselves as empowered women with the agency to redefine themselves away from harmful stereotypes, migrant care workers take ownership over their situations and prove to themselves that they are *agents* with the capacity to act. Embedded in these assertions of agency are their critiques of systemic and structural harms. More importantly, these actions allow them to knowingly show care to other migrant care workers by providing affirmation of and catharsis for their own experiences.

Conclusion

Toward a Politics of Critical Hope and Care

AIMEE BEBOSO (MIGRANTE-OTTAWA, RESPONDING TO 2019 POLICY CHANGES TO THE CAREGIVER PROGRAM): It is an important win after years and years of organizing. I stand on the shoulders of women who've been organizing in support of this not temporary program and these not temporary needs. If they are able to bring their families, this is a huge win for organizers, their families, and their children. . . . But what we're concerned about is that this is still a temporary program, this is still a pilot program. The campaign continues for landed status because the need for childcare and elderly care in Canada is not temporary.

LUISA (RESPONDING TO THE QUESTION OF HOW HER AND HER DAUGHTER TINA ARE ADJUSTING UPON BEING REUNIFIED IN 2016): I am so happy that after years apart, Tina and I are finally together. It's been a hard journey, though. I left Tina when she was a kid, and now she is a teenager with her own agenda. And Tina misses home. She misses her family. And we've had fights. You know what's great, though? We have a community here, for me and for her. She has gotten to know other nannies' kids. And they are helping her adjust. It's getting better. Whereas before, she was ashamed that, unlike the other kids she is meeting, her mom is a nanny, now, after talking to other migrant youth, she is realizing that there's no shame in her journey.

Amid much excitement and relief, migrant care workers and their allies gathered to listen to former immigration minister Ahmed Hussen announce changes to the Caregiver Program in 2019. When Hussen announced that a new pilot program would be created that would enable domestic workers to bring their families with them and give domestic workers permits that are not tied to their employers, thereby making it easier for workers to leave abusive employers, some women gasped. "Finally," one of them whispered to me, "we're getting somewhere."

Such enthusiasm was tempered by the realization that these changes fell short of activists' calls for landed status on arrival. More importantly, as a pilot program, this meant that the policies were only going to be implemented on a temporary basis.[1] In addition, the government placed annual quotas limiting the number of domestic workers who could apply for permanent residency annually and created language and licensing requirements that made it harder for domestic workers to qualify for permanent residency. The government also left unanswered the question of what would happen to undocumented domestic workers. Caregiver activists in Quebec were also furious because the new policy mentioned that domestic workers in the province would have to prove their intention of residing outside Quebec in order for their permanent residency applications to be successful.[2] "This means that the Filipino community is effectively going to die in Quebec," bemoaned a caregiver activist to me after hearing about this change. Nevertheless, despite these restrictions, the prevailing sentiment among many was one of cautious optimism. Taking the time to celebrate victories and gearing up for the next fight, after all, are crucial activist lessons that migrant care workers and their allies have learned well.

Of course, it is important not to interpret the "success" of the movement primarily in terms of policy changes. Luisa's narrative, included above, highlights how the impacts of the migrant care workers' movement transcend policy changes. Its impacts can also be felt in the realm of the everyday through the provision of networks of support for migrant domestic workers and their children and, more crucially, through the discursive and representational shifts that encourage new ways of understanding one's situations. That Tina, Luisa's daughter, no longer felt embarrassed for being the "nanny's kid" but instead began to see that there was no shame in her and her mother's immigration trajectory illustrates the powerful impacts of migrant domestic workers' activism in shaping people's cognitive processes.

In this book, I have attempted to show that movement successes cannot and should not be measured solely through the lens of policy changes, movement "growth" and uptake, and other such measurements of movement activity. To do so is to ignore the impacts of migrant care worker movements. Instead, I argue that to truly understand migrant care worker activism, we have to use the lens of care activism. Care activism deliberately centers the affective dimensions of activism by outlining the manifold ways that migrant care worker activists care for each other and for an imagined community of past, present, and future migrant care workers. Their advocacy in various spaces—ranging from the national to the transnational and taking place in the realm of the everyday—is motivated by a praxis of care.

Seeing that care is at the heart of advocacy work illuminates why migrant care worker activists, despite facing their own challenges (not the least of which includes temporary migration status), keep going. Feeling a sense of "shared fate" with fellow migrant care workers emboldens the women whose narratives are at the heart of this book. They understand, all too well, just how excruciating migrant care work can be, along with the ongoing challenges of family separation, immigration-related stresses, and near-daily experiences of being both invisibilized and hypervisibilized. By forming communities of care with each other and with an imagined community of other migrant care workers, migrant care worker activists thus bear witness to one another's journeys. They become *kasamas*.

The chapters in this book traced the varied contours of care activism, all of which show how care motivates these actions. There are different scales to care activism. I assess the ebbs and flows of migrant care activism within Canada (chapter 1), the internal dynamics of individual migrant care worker organizations (chapter 2), and migrant care worker organizations' participation in the transnational fora of the mainstream International Labour Organization and the grassroots International Migrants Alliance (chapter 3). I then shift my analysis away from migrant care worker organizations in Canada to consider migrant care worker organizing in the Philippines, Hong Kong, and Singapore (chapter 4). I conclude my analysis of care activism by examining care activism in the realm of the everyday, where I unearth individual and community forms of resistance (chapter 5). In analyzing different scales of care activism, however, I did not intend to portray these as being discrete categories. Instead, the forms of care activism in each scale are inextricably interlinked, with activists simultaneously participating in different scales. Threading together these disparate and multiscalar types of care activism illuminates how a desire-based framework (Tuck 2009) that places at the center migrant care workers' dreams, desires, and priorities is key to understanding migrant activism, with migrant care workers motivated by the need to care for themselves, for each other, and for the larger community of previous, present, and future migrant care workers and their families.

As I conclude this project, there remains the looming question of whether migrant care workers' activism is sufficient to redress injustice or whether their activism merely offers band-aid solutions to the more fundamental problem of global economic, political, and social inequalities. Labor migration is so deeply embedded in the practices of both receiving states like Canada and sending states like the Philippines that it becomes difficult to envisage alternatives.

On the one hand, in Canada, the absence of a national child and elderly care program and the scarcity of childcare spaces mean that programs such as the Caregiver Program become attractive options for families. There is the endemic belief that temporary foreign workers such as migrant domestic workers are a cheaper and a more efficient labor force. When families calculate the costs of how much they would pay in daycare fees, which roughly amounts to $1,600 (CDN) per child monthly in urban centers like Toronto, versus the costs of hiring a caregiver at or near minimum wage, which amounts to $14 (CDN) an hour in Ontario, it makes financial sense to hire domestic workers, especially when one has multiple children. For families who need to provide care for elderly parents and grandparents and for disabled family members, the high costs of assisted living facilities also make the Caregiver Program an attractive option. These economic realities, coupled with the belief embedded in Canadian policymaking circles from the 1990s until the present day that immigration into the country should enhance Canada's economic competitiveness by prioritizing "high-skilled" and not "low-skilled" migration (Abu-Laban and Gabriel 2002), mean that there is hardly any political will to change policies.

On the other hand, sending states like the Philippines have tied their economic growth so closely with the remittances sent by migrant workers that they have become labor brokerage states. The Philippine Statistics Authority's latest figures, taken during a survey of overseas foreign workers (OFWs) from April to September 2017, showed that during this time period, there were 2.3 million OFWs, with a higher proportion of female OFWs (53.4 percent) compared to male OFWs (46.3 percent) (PSA 2018). Most OFWs (37.6 percent) worked in "elementary professions," which encompass care and domestic work. During this time period, Filipino OFWs sent roughly US$4 billion (205.2 billion pesos) in remittances (PSA 2018). Although there have been nascent efforts by previous Philippine government officials to curb the tide of abuse against migrant workers by, for instance, banning the labor migration of its nationals to countries with high incidents of migrant abuse, these attempts were soon abandoned after it became clear that some workers were driven by economic desperation and still found their way into these countries without documentation. The Philippine government also sponsors "migrant reintegration programs," which attempt to provide returning migrants a foothold into the Philippine economy so they will not need to migrate again. These programs notwithstanding, labor export programs remain intact. In fact, as a "model" sending country that frequently deploys its officials on exchange missions to other sending states, the Philippines reaps so many benefits from labor migration that there will likely not be any serious attempts to find alternatives to labor migration.

In what follows, I address one standing issue related to the question of lasting change and visions for the future. I discuss attempts by migrant domestic worker activists and their allies to envisage ways to move beyond the existing status quo. Here, I tease out the possibilities offered by the concept of "critical hope" (Zembylas 2014), which I argue can scale up and may even catalyze the possibilities for collective action that subverts the status quo. I end this book by emphasizing how sites of resistance encompass collective cognitive processes such as dreaming, imagining, and strategizing. Through cognitive processes, migrant care worker organizations envisage alternate realities, thinking about what the world can and should look like while never losing sight of important structural critiques. As part of this vision and particularly in the wake of COVID-19 and the 2022 election of Bongbong Marcos, the son of Philippine dictator Ferdinand Marcos, whose rule led migrant activists to go into exile and come to Canada, imagining what a world centered around hope and care would look like becomes key.

Care activism takes place in communities, in nation-states, and even in transnational fora. Care activists are driven by caring for migrant care workers and their families. Their "imagined community" includes previous, present-day, and future migrant care workers. They wish to honor the legacy of the migrant care workers whose sacrifices and whose activism preceded theirs and feel accountable to current and future migrant care workers. Fundamentally, their hope for a better world drives their work. In fact, my discussion of care activism highlights the importance of cognitive processes—of dreaming, imagining, and strategizing—that compel migrant care worker activists to dream of futures that are radically different from the present day. Dreaming and imagining a world where migrant care workers and their families are not separated, where labor migration is not an inevitable reality, and where structures of neoliberalism, imperialism, settler colonialism, militarism, and white supremacy are finally abolished fuel care activism.

Such cognitive processes include everyday care activism. Dreaming in a way that transcends the mundane (Ticku 2017) enabled women to exercise subversive forms of humor, to make visible domestic work in public spaces, and even to withstand current realities because of what the future could offer. Indeed, in other research projects, I encountered migrant workers who were part of Canada's low-skilled Temporary Foreign Workers Program (TFWP)—some undocumented—and witnessed how they seized agency in otherwise debilitating circumstances. Their use of cognitive processes, in fact, allowed them to "mentally claim rights for themselves" (Tungohan 2018, 2). This meant that, contrary to stereotypes of abject and exploited migrant workers lacking in agency, the people whom I met deliberately envisioned alternative life paths that allowed them to think beyond their everyday circumstances. The ability to dream of what could be was an important part of everyday care activism.

The question I now turn to is whether cognitive processes, which for me encompass dreaming, imagining (i.e., dreaming of possible life paths), and strategizing (i.e., preparing responses to different scenarios and calculating how to get ahead) (see also Tungohan 2018, 2), can be used by social movements in their work. Specifically, how can hope be used collectively in the politics from below?

There are examples of marginalized groups' use of hope. Sarah Wright (2008) discusses how small-scale subsistence farmers in the Philippines formed an organization called Masipag ("hard-working" in Tagalog) that made hoping a deliberate part of their work. Rather than accepting as given existing practices of economic dependence, whereby farmers are placed in a cycle of debt bondage by requiring them to borrow funds for farming equipment and to purchase seeds, which they would have to harvest and sell in an environment of "capitalist, corporatized agriculture" (Wright 2008, 226), Masipag uses a "decentralized" structure that allows farmers "locally adapted, sustainable farming systems using farmer-bred and farmer-selected seeds" (225). By placing farmers' knowledge at the center of the project, Masipag actively harnesses their agency in determining farming processes and how to make their livelihoods. In short, by using hope, which "draws on connections and on the work of creating and recreating solidarities through the very act of living . . . [farmers] reinvent themselves as fully formed, active agents able to imagine and bring into being new futures" (225).

Similarly, Sasha Courville and Nicola Piper (2004) discuss how NGOs use hope in their everyday practices. Using the case study of Philippine-based migrants' rights NGOs, they show the linkages between agency, hope, and empowerment, highlighting how these NGOs contest the harmful processes of globalization by "attempting to construct alternatives that are based on the actual activities and experiences of the grassroots" (Courville and Piper 2004, 51). By tracing the activities of migrants' rights NGOs from service provision to providing "advocacy and empowerment programs" to seeking "broader solutions to migrant problems," the authors cogently illustrate how migrant organizations' perspectives of their roles evolve over time. They show that many migrant activists eventually realize that for their work to have widespread impact, it is important to think about long-term changes. When doing so, they use hope, which they argue has "value [that] is not measured alone but is a necessary active ingredient in any social-change process" (56). Courville and Piper note that hope can "sustain a movement until the timing is right to enforce change" (57). Wright's and Courville and Piper's accounts of organizations' use of hope provide fertile ground for better understanding grassroots and NGO resistance. These examples of hope as organizational strategies provide evidence of how hope is a conscious and a deliberate practice, one that migrant care worker organizations cultivate. For example, the economic livelihood organizations mentioned here—from the Godmother Network in Canada to organizations in the Philippines, Hong Kong, and Singapore—are rooted in hoping for a more economically sustainable future. What remains unanswered, however, are our questions concerning lasting change and ongoing structural critique.

I believe that there are possibilities offered by critical hope, which I see as being more closely interlinked with the cognitive processes discussed above and as being tied to the active and ongoing praxis of critique. As a pedagogical practice, it entails an "acknowledgment of the unjust and unequal societies where we live" and "requires an analysis of how historical and material conditions have led us to our present positions" (Bozalek, Carolissen, and Leibowitz 2014, 40). Distinct from "naïve hope," which is characterized by a lack of reflexivity, an unwillingness to confront existing inequities, and a "blind faith that things will get better" (Zembylas 2014, 13), practicing critical hope necessitates "a critical analysis of power relations and how they constitute one's emotional ways of being in the world, while attempting to construct, imaginatively and materially, a different lifeworld" (13). It can therefore scale up and lead to "transformative action" (Bozalek, Carolissen, and Leibowitz 2014, 40). In a way, practicing critical hope characterizes migrant activists' pursuit of both "contingent possibilities" (i.e., advocacy pursuits that can be realized in the world as it is) and "possibilia" (i.e., dreaming of what the world can possibly be) because these contradictory practices are fueled by the realization that the future holds potential despite the limitations of the present. As Harald Bauder argues, such critical approaches necessitate an acceptance of the "contradictions between the material world and abstract ideas, and between actual circumstances and what is possible" (2017, 125).

Are there spaces within care activism that encourage the use of critical hope? In answer to this question, I tentatively say yes, with the caveat that the issue of migrant domestic workers' use of critical hope necessitates further research. Ethnographic research of migrant domestic worker movements underscores the way critical hope harnesses possibilities for a future that allows migrant domestic workers and their families the ability to pursue their dreams and that also eliminates structural inequities. Earlier, I discussed various events associated with the International Migrants Alliance (IMA) where the emphasis was placed on imagining alternate futures. Rather than taking as given the inevitability of labor migration, the conference provided space for migrant workers to criticize the effects of structural inequities while also grounding these critiques with a recognition of individual and community ambitions. It seems to me that while hope underpins care activism, critical hope is most frequently harnessed by progressive organizations.

Subsequent research shows the relevance that critical hope plays in these encounters. In August 2014 I had the opportunity to speak with Justicia for Migrant Workers' Chris Ramsaroop in Toronto, whose advocacy work on behalf of seasonal agricultural workers has led to important victories such as public awareness of the plight of female migrant farmworkers who were being sexually harassed by their employers, the occupational health and safety hazards migrant farmworkers faced, the many instances of death and forcible "medical" repatriation that migrant farmworkers were subjected to, and employer abuse. Justicia's campaigns, such as the establishment of a migrant caravan that saw migrant farmworkers and their allies travel from southern Ontario (where most of the farms were located) to Ottawa (Canada's capital city), drew even more public awareness to migrant farmworkers' plight. When Ramsaroop and I spoke, the political environment against all migrant workers—be they low-skilled temporary foreign workers, migrant domestic workers, or seasonal agricultural workers—was particularly fraught. The Canadian economy was plummeting, and there was a vitriolic nativist discourse reigning that blamed temporary foreign workers for economic ills, specifically for their supposed theft of Canadian jobs for Canadians.

Ramsaroop and I discussed advocacy tactics when facing widespread xenophobia. His discussion of the need to build bridges between different workers was inspirational. He addressed how Justicia organized a dialogue between temporary foreign workers and Canadian workers. It was initially a fraught encounter, because Canadian workers were, at that point, encountering the "enemy," whom they saw as stealing jobs. Yet the dialogue continued. Eventually, both groups of workers saw the commonalities in their respective experiences of precariousness. Both parties faced poor working conditions and substandard wages, and both were perpetually worried about making ends meet. They also conceded that other workers were not the enemy. Rather, multinational corporations that ran the corporate farms and the establishments where they worked, apathetic government institutions that did not see the need for publicly funded daycare, and global power structures that placed the bulk of profits into the hands of a select few were the culprits.

Ramsaroop also talked about how Justicia activists would present Canadian passersby with pieces of fruit, asking them where they thought the fruit that they ate came from. Some passersby were receptive to this dialogue and seemed at least willing to discuss ethical farming practices and the working conditions that migrant farmworkers faced. These encounters were not easy. In fact, they were completely challenging. But through these moments, bonds of solidarity were forged (if tentatively). Hearing Ramsaroop discuss these tactics and others, it struck me that there was a politics of critical hope that was being created here. Rather than only seeking better treatment for migrant workers, these encounters engendered the building of solidarities across different groups, solidarities that were grounded in an ongoing structural critique.

In December 2016 I attended and spoke at Migrante-BC's first-ever conference on temporary foreign work, held in New Westminster, British Columbia. Entitled "Building and Strengthening Workers' Solidarity," the conference brought together migrant activists, migrant workers, migrant children, policymakers, union leaders, immigration lawyers, and interested community members. There were many panels that strove to instill awareness of the plight of different groups of migrant workers. For instance, stories of migrant adversity and resilience were featured in a panel that included Avelina Vasquez and Cholo Sales, temporary foreign workers who successfully won a case against Denny's; Hessed Torres, who discussed her experiences of labor abuse under the LCP; Mildred Germain, who disclosed the hardships of family separation and reunification under the LCP; and Gabriel Allahdua, a seasonal agricultural worker who addressed the challenges of migrant farmwork. There were also panels that actively strategized on how to meet the short-term needs of migrant workers. For example, during a panel on the Canadian Border Service Agency's Project Guardian, which encouraged the public to anonymously snitch on migrant domestic workers whom they suspected of immigration violations, everyone brainstormed on ways to provide support for migrant workers and to fight against policies. More importantly, though, the conference provided a space to ruminate on the importance of retaining critical hope when living in a contemporary political environment where xenophobia and antimigrant sentiments were a common part of everyday discourse. Community activist Elsie Dean, union activist Marion Pollack, and community activist Harsha Walia all spoke on a panel on the importance of recognizing the interconnectedness of various struggles, of looking historically at advocacy losses and successes as a way of finding the path forward, and of retaining one's vision of what social justice can and should look like in the long term. I heard in these speakers' narratives deliberate practices of critical hope that gave space for fighting against immediate struggles and for imagining more socially just futures, all of which is sustained by an ongoing and unceasing practice of caring and generative critique.

In a meeting with members of Anakbayan, a migrant youth organization in Toronto, in March 2019, I was impressed when listening to young migrant activists share their experiences with activism with a Migrante activist from the United States. They paired hopeful visions of the future with an understanding of the structural changes necessary to make these hopeful visions a reality. Rather than only seeking the end of labor export, which many criticized because of the effects such policies had on their respective families, many saw the interlinkages between various social movement struggles. Migrant activism for them cannot exist without acknowledging and working in alliance with other movements such as Indigenous movements, environmental movements, and movements for Black lives. By unpacking the connections between various struggles, they encouraged recognition of how intersecting structures of power—namely, white supremacy, settler colonialism, imperialism, and neoliberalism—led to the marginalization of intersectionally disadvantaged groups; in turn, identifying the roots of the problem can engender new advocacy strategies grounded in expressions of solidarity across different groups and can even lead to new visions of the future.

Can solidarity take place during a global health pandemic, when the inequities facing migrants and citizens, Indigenous, Black, and racialized community members, women, and other equity-seeking groups have increased? As I reflect on the realities of COVID-19 and how the pandemic has placed many of the migrant care workers in a dire situation, I think immediately of just how much harder migrant care workers' lives have become. As racialized women from the Global South with temporary migration status, the pandemic has heightened their vulnerability. A project that I am currently pursuing in partnership with Migrant Resource Centre Canada and Gabriela-Ontario examines the experiences of Filipina care workers during the pandemic. Through *kuwentuhan* (talk-story) sessions (Francisco-Menchavez 2018) over Zoom, we discussed what their lives were like. Our results are grim: migrant care workers have been tasked with keeping society going through their social reproductive labor. With only minimal and temporary increases in salary and with uneven access to personal protective equipment, many migrant care workers were afraid. Border closures meant that the time it would take for them to be reunited with their families had been indefinitely prolonged. How, then, could they keep going?

Nevertheless, despite these dire situations, what struck me in our conversations was how critical hope still resonated. The migrant care workers were well aware that lip-service declarations that migrant care workers are "heroes" did not concretely translate to robust protections. Yet moments of dark humor and of catharsis abounded. Significantly, many of the women we spoke to saw the necessity of communities of care during the pandemic. Those who were part of migrant care worker organizations continued to be active. Interestingly, those who were not part of such organizations became interested in being part of these communities.

In fact, the pandemic did not lead to decreased care activism. On the contrary, care activism merely adapted to the current reality and in fact took on added urgency. Migrant care workers whom I spoke to expressed amazement that they were witnessing a rise in the number of people who wanted to join them. As a result, care activism intensified. Migrante-Canada, Gabriela-Ontario, and other progressive organizations organized a food drive campaign called Kapit Bisig (the literal translation is "linked arms"), which brought groceries and other essential goods to migrant households that were lacking them. The Migrant Resource Centre Canada (MRCC), which many progressive organizations support, organized a CARE project that provided counseling services for migrant workers facing labor and immigration problems, online resources, and care packages.

In 2020 and 2021 I also observed how care activism expanded and worked in solidarity with other movements for social change. The truth that we are currently living in a necrocapitalist and a necropolitical society (Tyner 2019; Mbembe 2011) where some lives are simply deemed more valuable than others became especially clear. Indeed, for many migrant care worker activists, it was harrowing to witness the effects of the pandemic and racially motivated violence. The latter included Black deaths in the hands of the police (namely, in 2020 George Floyd in Minneapolis and Regina Korchinsky-Paquet and Andrew Loku in Toronto); the shooting of Asian women at a massage parlor in Atlanta; the anti-Muslim murder of a Muslim family in London, Ontario; and, more recently, the discovery of the unmarked graves of Indigenous children across Canada. Migrant care worker organizations convened Zoom-based webinars and rallies in alliance with Indigenous and Black organizations, with labor organizations, and with other migrant groups such as migrant sex worker organizations, organizations representing international students, and organizations representing various racial and religious minority communities. The conversations during these webinars and rallies started tackling issues that were previously deemed irrelevant to different communities' specific concerns. Speakers and audience members drew connections between different communities, seeing commonalities in their experiences.

More crucially, migrant care worker activists also started understanding their own complicity in perpetuating unequal power structures. For instance, during a webinar that Gabriela-Ontario and Migrant Resource Centre Canada organized entitled "Building Solidarities across the Filipinx Community: The Impacts of COVID-19, Anti-Black Racism and Activism," held on July 2020, speakers and audience members addressed the pervasiveness of anti-Black racism within the Filipinx community and the limitations of respectability politics (i.e., the amassing of credentials, achieving career advances). I have also seen migrant activists hold webinars on settler colonialism, teaching migrant activist elders, including migrant care worker activists, the importance of supporting Indigenous movements. In these webinars, connections were drawn between colonial systems that push labor migrants out of countries like the Philippines due to the Philippines' continued dependency on affluent states for economic survival and that concurrently push Indigenous groups in Canada, such as the Wet'suwet'en Indigenous community, to take back their land.

These conversations also began to plant the seeds for considering abolitionist futures. In 2020, when discussions about police brutality took place within migrant advocacy spaces, for instance, demands to abolish the police and abolish prisons sometimes came up. It was frequently hard and uncomfortable to hold these conversations, especially given the defensive reactions some have, which tended to revolve around practicalities. ("Who will protect us if we're robbed?" is a common question, as is "where would the bad guys go?") Surprisingly for me, however, the tenor of these conversations remained respectful. When existing ways of life are upended due to COVID-19 and when the ugly realities of anti-Black and anti-Asian racism, anti-indigeneity, and Islamophobia became too conspicuous to ignore, conversational openings were created. Migrant care worker communities, including those I would have characterized as being more conservative, appeared receptive to the idea of radical change.

These tentative attempts to build solidarities with Black and Indigenous communities and with other migrant communities embody the practice of critical hope and perhaps even enable an expansion of care activism. Since a central contention of this book is that migrant care workers become advocates because they care for fellow migrant care workers and their families, perhaps the work of building solidarities with other communities can widen what "care" looks like. The failures of democracy, as seen in Bongbong Marcos's election, signified to migrant activists even more forcefully that they cannot rely on states to protect them—to care for them—but that they needed to rely on their larger communities, communities that by necessity have to also include other communities. I consequently see coalitions being built not only because building them is a pragmatic exercise or because joining forces makes it more likely for policies to be passed and for power brokers to listen but also out of a genuine belief in shared fate and in relationality. As Harsha Walia notes, "We can weave solidarities through the lens of abundance, rather than scarcity, and celebrate the interdependence of the particularities of our humanities" (2021, 215).

The building of coalitions across various movements, across different nation-state borders, and across different generations that are united by practices of critical hope seems to be the next step for migrant care worker organizing specifically and migrant organizing more generally. Can there be new power structures that cease the indebtedness of Global South countries on Global North countries and that stop cycles of dependency? Are there alternatives to labor migration? Are there alternatives to practices of forced migration and family separation? Are there alternatives to practices of border control and border policing? Can care activism be extended not only to caring for one's real and imagined community of human beings but also to nonhuman kin and the planet? Through these coalitions, I am hopeful that alternatives to existing arrangements can be envisioned.

I end this book by returning to the words that Wilma, a migrant youth activist, shared with me when we were discussing what keeps her going with her advocacy work:

> I have a lot of hope for the future even when it all looks like terrible right now. I look back to the people and believe that there is a lot of love that bind us. Our generation—and previous generations—are built on love and struggle. We were under oppression [because of] colonialism for how many hundreds of years, and we still made it to today! I want our children to know we didn't allow the oppression to happen; there's a group of people who stood up against oppression. We try to unite even though we come from different backgrounds and places, yet we still find each other. When we're together, no one can deny your experiences as a community. We become each other's witnesses. Let's keep talking about the interconnections between

our experiences of oppression, let's keep fighting for what's better, but let's also keep hoping and dreaming.

I believe that migrant care workers can sustain the coalitions that they have formed between themselves and with diverse movements to oppose and find alternatives to inequitable structures, institutions, policies, and everyday practices, all while practicing a politics of critical hope and care.

Notes

Introduction. Care Activism and Communities of Care

1. I also refer to them as migrant care workers and as migrant domestic workers throughout the text in a conscious and deliberate attempt to use the various terminologies that workers use to describe their work.

2. This time period coincided with my doctoral research and follow-up research I conducted as an assistant professor.

3. While I recognize that religious organizations have been a crucial source of support for migrant care workers, I was interested in examining organizations that are led by migrant care workers and so opted to exclude church-based domestic worker organizations. As the analysis I present shows, though, many of the migrant care worker organizations still retained religious beliefs.

Chapter 1. Contextualizing Care Activism

1. A fascinating and in-depth account of Finnish immigrant women's experiences in domestic service and their attempts to change their workplace conditions can be found in Varpu Lindström-Best's (1988) *Defiant Sisters: A Social History of Finnish Immigrant Women in Canada*. Lindström-Best discusses how the Finnish immigrant women who came to Canada in the late nineteenth century to early twentieth century were primarily from rural, working-class backgrounds and were single. Because domestic service was one of the few industries where they found gainful employment, Finnish women, through their networks, dominated care work. Lindström-Best discusses in detail the hardships

they faced as care workers, most of which resembled conditions today, and additionally disclosed how Finnish women, much like the Filipina migrant care workers in this study, participated in microrebellions to contest their living and working conditions and also participated in organizations such as different socialist organizations to improve their collective situations. The crucial difference, of course, is that Finnish women, unlike women who entered Canada's migrant care worker programs, were already Canadian permanent residents and thus did not face the risk of expulsion.

2. Much less is known about the Chinese and Japanese men working as domestic servants and as "coolies" (Ty 2004, 21–22) or about the Caribbean women who worked as servants but were later sent back to their countries (Calliste 1989) from the late 1800s to the mid-1900s. The only information that is really known about Chinese and Japanese "coolies" is derived from historical records showing that these men originally came to Canada to work as laborers for the Canadian Pacific Railway and for the agricultural industry but later sought work in domestic service, probably as a result of endemic discrimination preventing them from working in other professions. Aside from a few Chinese women who were sold from rural communities in China and subsequently brought to British Columbia as "slave girls" (Barber 1991, 14), Asian men, not Asian women, were the ones who undertook paid domestic work.

3. According to Marilyn Barber, when asked by the government, employers described the Caribbean migrant care workers they hired as being a "little slow but clean, polite, obedient, docile and moral, definitely preferable to the Canadian domestics who, one employer complained, wanted to be the mistress of the house" (1991, 14).

4. That this "temporary" stream has, for certain migrant groups such as seasonal agricultural workers, continued unabated is ironic. Recent changes to Canada's caregiver program, which will be discussed later in the chapter, have gone into effect supposedly on a temporary (read: "pilot") basis but have been renewed since 2013.

5. That Caribbean countries later signed agreements to export migrant farmworkers through seasonal agricultural workers programs, which almost exclusively consisted of male migrants, shows the value these countries saw in labor export.

6. Solicitation letter, March 11, 1980, Frances Gregory Personal Correspondence, Intercede Collection (0-001-S1-F1222), Canadian Women's Movement Archives, University of Ottawa.

7. "Upgrading the Status of Domestic Workers in Ontario: Recommendations for Legislative Change," 1983, 6, Intercede Policy Recommendations, Intercede Collection (0-001-S1-F1222), Canadian Women's Movement Archives, University of Ottawa.

8. Meeting minutes, May 14, 1980, Intercede Collection (0-001-S1-F1222), Canadian Women's Movement Archives, University of Ottawa.

9. Solicitation letter, March 11, 1980.

10. Interview conducted in Toronto, Ontario, May 17, 2011.

11. Solicitation letter, March 11, 1980.

12. "Upgrading the Status."

13. In 2018 WCDWA changed its name to the Migrant Workers Resource Centre.

14. Pura Velasco, "An Open Letter to the Minister of Employment and Immigration," 1992, Intercede Collection (0-001-S1-F1222), Canadian Women's Movement Archives, University of Ottawa.

15. To be more specific, the AAFQ sees the LCP as a program whose success is contingent on ensuring the continued presence of a steady supply of racialized migrant women who lack privacy, mobility, and access to their families (AAFQ 1998). Sexual violence occurs frequently, and labor abuse is almost a given. Extending their analysis beyond Canada, the LCP, like other migrant care worker programs, is also unfeminist in that it enshrines "global care chains," whereby women from developing countries are being asked to leave their families and their children behind in order to take care of other women's families and children. Through these programs, then, women from developing countries fare badly; while it is true that working abroad allows them to economically support their families and their children, the very fact that they are able to ensure the "liberation" of women in the developed world from care work by allowing these women to access the public sphere of paid employment shows the blatant discrepancies between the situations of migrant care workers and their female employers. On these grounds, then, the AAFQ believes that, ideally, programs like the LCP should not exist.

16. In drawing attention to these two cases, my intention is not to say that caregiver activism solely focused on these two events. In fact, conversations with other migrant care worker activists during which I explained my analysis of the role played by these key events in inspiring migrant care worker activism have led to spirited disagreements. These were not the only cases, they argued; in fact, there are many other cases and many other campaigns. The Jeffrey Riodica case (the murder of Riodica, a Filipino teenager, at the hands of the police) similarly galvanized the Filipino community. My interpretation of the decisive impacts of the cases, however, rested in their focus on the specific precarities facing migrant care workers. In contrast to other cases, these two cases—more than others I have examined—led to a widespread social movement campaign.

17. Shifting leadership structures meant that CAC would later ally with the Migrante and Gabriela networks. The formation of the Migrant Workers Alliance for Change (MWAC), which evolved from the Coalition for Change, later encompassed Migrante and Gabriela.

18. The CP was a bit better than the Conservative government's proposal to tie the Caregiver Program into its Express Entry program, which would have placed domestic workers into a common pool with all other immigration applicants and would have likely disqualified domestic workers from permanent residency because they would not be able to earn the same number of points as other, more skilled immigrants.

19. See Carens (2013) for a discussion of how the ongoing presence of immigrants, including migrant workers, as opposed to jus soli and jus sanguinis, justifies the acquisition of citizenship.

Chapter 2. Care Activism within Migrant Advocacy Organizations

1. I previously discussed sections of my analysis of Migrante's work in an article entitled "Intersectionality and Social Justice: Assessing Activists' Use of Intersectionality through

Grassroots Migrants' Organizations in Canada," which was published in *Politics, Groups, and Identities* (see Tungohan 2016).

2. The word *magkasama*, a verb, means "being with someone." The idea behind being *kasamas* is grounded in the same sentiment.

3. Bayan Canada's name is a play on the Filipino word *bayan*, which means "nation."

4. These are the organizations that, as of the time of writing in 2022, form part of the Magkaisa Centre, according to its website. The Philippine Women Centre Network is comprised of the following organizations: National Alliance of Philippine Women in Canada, Philippine Women Centre, SIKLAB-Canada, Filipino-Canadian Youth Alliance, Filipino Nurses Support Group, Kabataang Montreal, Philippine Canada Task Force on Human Rights, and Sinag Bayan Cultural Arts Collective.

5. Cecilia Diocson, untitled speech presented at the PWC International Women's Day Celebration, March 5, 2011, Toronto, ON.

Chapter 3. Scaling Up Care Activism in Transnational Spaces

1. The material for parts of this chapter was previously published as a chapter entitled "International Approaches to Governing Temporary Labour Migrants," in *International Approaches to Governing Ethnic Diversity*, edited by Jane Boulden and Will Kymlicka and published in 2015. This chapter was reproduced by permission of Oxford University Press: https://global.oup.com/academic/product/international-approaches-to-governing -ethnic-diversity-9780199676583?cc=de&lang=en&.

2. This song has its origins among domestic workers in South Africa. When President Myrtle Witbooi was elected as the president of the International Domestic Workers Federation during the IDWF Congress in 2013, she led the community in singing this song (IDWFED 2013).

3. During breaks between sessions, NGOs organized separate meetings held on the grounds of the UN itself that were open to everyone and that discussed further their specific agendas, their interests in ratifying the convention, the experiences of migrant domestic workers in their countries, and the research they have undertaken that illustrated further the situation facing migrant domestic workers, among many topics.

Chapter 4. Care Activism in the Philippines, Hong Kong, and Singapore

1. Of course, while the Philippines is a democracy, former president Rodrigo Duterte's deliberate targeting (known as "red-tagging") of progressive, left-leaning civil society organizations, including those tied with migrant organizing, has created a negative impact on organizing. Duterte officials have arrested and charged progressive advocates with terrorism (Robertson 2021). Since holding the conversations with migrant activists in 2017, I have observed the intensification of red-tagging among activists, including some of the migrant activists whom I spoke to for this research. Of considerable concern to me is how some of these activists have sought asylum in other countries because they feared being targeted by Duterte. Furthermore, some of those who are active in Canada even

informed me that they were advised against returning to the Philippines while Duterte was in power.

2. I classified these organizations under these two categories based on the descriptions provided by my respondents. Another way to classify these organizations under the same groupings is to call progressive organizations "people's organizations" and mainstream organizations "civil society organizations." Under this mode of classification, there is a clear distinction being drawn between grassroots social justice movements and NGOs. I opted not to classify organizations in this way, however, because I did not want to leave the impression that grassroots organizations are not part of civil society.

3. Of course, spaces for civil society organizing look different for Hong Kong residents in the wake of the passage of the National Security Law in 2020 and, before that, the protests that took place in opposition to draconian limits to freedom of expression. As foreign nationals, migrant workers were not subjected to the same limitations. Nevertheless, it is interesting to note that some migrant organizations were also part of the Hong Kong protests. Some migrant care workers recognized the common links between the Philippine government's practice of red-tagging to quell dissent and the Chinese government's extradition policies to limit Hong Kong residents' protest actions (Beltran 2019).

4. Villanueva and I first met in Geneva in June 2011, during the ILO Convention on Domestic Work discussions, and connected again in July that year during the International Migrants Alliance (IMA) meetings in Quezon City, Philippines.

5. Much like migrant domestic workers in Canada, most migrant domestic workers in Hong Kong do not wish to stay in their employers' households during their days off and so gather in spaces around the city where they can run errands, send remittances, meet friends, and, if they are activists, organize.

6. It should be noted that there were also specific church ministries that were devoted to migrant workers.

7. *Sunday Beauty Queen* followed a group of Filipina migrant care workers' beauty queen ambitions. It showed how pageantry allowed the women to experience glamour in their lives and to form communities of care with fellow pageant winners. Of course, the downside to such involvement, as the film illustrates, is the financial costs of being part of these pageants.

8. The passage of this bill would have allowed the chief executive of Hong Kong to decide on requests to extradite individuals suspected of criminal activity to their home countries even when Hong Kong does not have formal extradition agreements with these countries. Prodemocracy protesters claim that this is in violation of the "one country, two systems" arrangement put into place in Hong Kong following the 1997 handover of Hong Kong to China. They feared that dissidents in Hong Kong who were critical of the Chinese regime would be sent to China, where they would face trial in an authoritarian legal system (Mayberry 2019).

9. Progressive advocates such as Jolovan Wham, whom I interviewed, who flouted regulations found themselves arrested and detained. According to Amnesty International

(2021), the Singaporean government used Wham as an example of what could happen to human rights activists if they decided to protest.

Chapter 5. Everyday Care Activism

1. The crucial role played by cognitive processes in activism is of course not unique to migrant care workers. Other social movements have consciously harnessed the role of dreaming in resistance movements. For example, Grace Simbulan (2020) writes about how Indigenous leaders who are part of the Obo-Manobo community in the Philippines see dreams as "crucial forms of resistance," drawing linkages between present-day and ancestral dreams for the Obo-Manobo "people-and-land." Dreaming also forms an important part of the Black radical tradition, with Robin D. G. Kelley (2002) writing about the significance of "Freedom Dreams" in fueling movement imaginations. Kelley in fact eviscerates the tendency to evaluate social movements on the basis of "successes," seeing these as erroneously focusing on outcomes. Studying social movements thus needs to focus on the "merits and powers of the visions" and how these "inspire new generations to continue to struggle for change" (Kelley 2002, 11).

2. As chapter 2 shows, one of migrant caregiver activists' successes actually pertains to giving migrant domestic workers more time to finish the LCP's requirements in order to make allowances for migrant domestic workers who left their employers.

3. These practices have drawn gentle criticisms from academics such as Ju-Chen Chen (2015, 46), whose research on migrant caregiver beauty pageants arose out of her curiosity about why migrant domestic workers were willing to pay as much as one-third to two-thirds of their monthly income in order to participate.

4. I should note that, due to a last-minute cancellation, I was asked to be one of the judges.

5. This bias against domestic workers, which community members construe as a low-status profession, is commonplace. Chapter 1, for example, pointed to how Caribbean domestic workers under the Caribbean Domestics Scheme faced stigma from members of their community for being domestic workers.

Conclusion. Toward a Politics of Critical Hope and Care

1. Indeed, the changes that Hussen announced at that time ended up forming part of the "Interim Pathway for Caregivers," which only took effect for eight months, from January 2019 until October 2019. I discuss this Interim Pathway in chapter 1.

2. In Canada, Quebec, as a subnational government, exercises autonomy in establishing immigration policies. As a result, Quebec was able to institute changes to the Caregiver Program that were distinct from federal legislation. In this case, the Quebec government opted to shut down care worker pathways.

References

Abu-Laban, Yasmeen, and Christina Gabriel. 2002. *Selling Diversity: Immigration, Multiculturalism, Employment Equity, and Globalization*. Toronto, ON: University of Toronto Press.

Agojo, Kevin. 2021. "Policing a Pandemic: Understanding the State and Political Instrumentalization of the Coercive Apparatus in Duterte's Philippines." *Journal of Developing Societies* 37 (3): 363–86.

Alcaraz, Nellie, Liza Lorenzetti, Sarah Thomas, and Rita Dhungel. 2021. "Breaking Isolation: Social Work in Solidarity with Migrant Workers through and beyond COVID-19." *Social Work* 67 (1): 48–57.

Allen, Juliet, Daniella Jenkins, and Marilyn Howard. 2020. "Crises Collide: Capitalism, Care and COVID-19." *Feminist Studies* 46 (3): 583–95.

Amnesty International. 2021. "Singapore: Quash Conviction and Sentence of Human Rights Defender Jolovan Wham." *Amnesty International Press Release*. https://www.amnesty.org/en/latest/press-release/2021/02/singapore-quash-conviction-and-sentence-of-human-rights-defender-jolovan-wham/.

Anderson, Benedict. 1983. *Imagined Communities*. New York: Verso.

Anderson, Bridget. 2010. "Mobilizing Migrants, Making Citizens: Migrant Domestic Workers as Political Agents." *Ethnic and Racial Studies* 33 (1): 60–74.

Anjara, Sabrina, Laura Nellums, Chiara Bonetto, and Tine Van Bortel. 2017. "Stress, Health, and Quality of Life of Female Migrant Domestic Workers in Singapore." *BMC Women's Health* 17 (98): 1–13.

Antona, Laura. 2020. "The New Normal or Same Old? The Impacts of the COVID-19 Pandemic on Live-In Migrant Domestic Workers in Singapore." *LSE Southeast Asia Blog*, November 4. https://blogs.lse.ac.uk/seac/2020/11/04/the-new-normal-or-same

-old-the-impacts-of-the-covid-19-pandemic-on-live-in-migrant-domestic-workers-in
-singapore/.

Arat-Koc, Sedef. 1997. "From 'Mothers of the Nation' to Migrant Workers." In *Not One of the Family: Foreign Domestic Workers in Canada*, edited by Daiva Stasiulis and Abigail Bakan, 53–80. Toronto, ON: University of Toronto Press.

Asis, Maruja. 2020. "Repatriating Filipino Migrant Workers in the Time of the Pandemic." International Organization for Migration, Migration Research Series No. 63. https:// publications.iom.int/books/mrs-no-63-repatriating-filipino-migrant-workers-time -pandemic.

Astorga-Garcia, Mila. 2007. *The Road to Empowerment in Toronto's Filipino Community: Moving from Crisis to Community Capacity Building*. Toronto, ON: CERIS.

Auethavornpipat, Ruji, and Maria Tanyag. 2009. "Caregiver Power." *Philippine Reporter Community News and Features*. April 2.

———. 2021. "Protests and Pandemics: Civil Society Mobilisation in Thailand and the Philippines." Policy Briefing SEARBO2. Sydney, Australia: New Mandala—New Perspectives on Southeast Asia. https://openresearch-repository.anu.edu.au/bitstream /1885/238577/2/SEARBO-Report-Auethavornpipat-and-Tanyag.pdf.

Bakan, Abigail, and Daiva Stasiulis. 1994. "Foreign Domestic Worker Policy in Canada and the Social Boundaries of Modern Citizenship." *Science and Society* 58 (1): 7–55.

———. 1995. "Making the Match: Domestic Placement Agencies and the Racialization of Women's Household Work." *Signs* 20 (2): 303–35.

———, eds. 1997. Introduction to *Not One of the Family: Foreign Domestic Workers in Canada*, edited by Abigail Bakan and Daiva Stasiulis, 3–28. Toronto, ON: University of Toronto Press.

———. 2005. *Negotiating Citizenship: Migrant Women in Canada and the Global System*. Toronto, ON: University of Toronto Press.

Banerjee, Rupa, Philip Kelly, Ethel Tungohan, Petronila Cleto, Conely de Leon, Mila Garcia, Marco Luciano, Cynthia Palmaria, and Christopher Sorio. 2018. "From 'Migrant' to 'Citizen': Labor Market Integration of Former Live-In Caregivers to Canada." *ILR Review* 71 (4): 908–36.

Bapat, Sheila. 2014. *Part of the Family: Nannies, Housekeepers, Caregivers, and the Battle for Domestic Workers' Rights*. New York: iG Publishing.

Barber, Marilyn. 1991. *Immigrant Domestic Servants in Canada*. Ottawa, ON: Canadian Historical Society.

Battistela, Graziano, and Cecilia Conaco. 1998. "The Impact of Labour Migration on Children Left Behind." *Sojourn* 13 (2): 220–41.

Bauder, Harald. 2017. *Migration, Borders, Freedom*. New York: Routledge.

Beltran, Michael. 2019. "Why Are Migrant Workers Joining the Hong Kong Protests?" *The Diplomat*. https://thediplomat.com/2019/07/why-are-migrant-workers-joining -the-hong-kong-protests.

Bin, Novia. 2020. *The Non-ordinary Residents: Voices from Migrant Domestic Workers amid COVID-19*. Self-published.

Blackett, Adelle. 2019. *Everyday Transgressions: Domestic Workers' Transnational Challenge to International Labor Law*. Ithaca, NY: Cornell University Press.

Boris, Eileen. 2019. *Making the Woman Worker: Precarious Labor and the Fight for Global Standards, 1919–2019*. Oxford: Oxford University Press.

Boris, Eileen, and Jennifer Fish. 2014. "'Slaves No More': Making Global Labor Standards for Domestic Workers." *Feminist Studies* 40 (2): 411–43.

Boti, Mari, and Fiorchita Bautista, directors. 1992. *Brown Women, Blond Babies* (documentary). Montreal: Productions Multi-Monde.

Bozalek, Vivienne, Ronelle Carolissen, and Brenda Leibowitz. 2014. "A Pedagogy of Critical Hope in South African Higher Education." In *Discerning Critical Hope in Educational Practices*, edited by Vivienne Bozalek, Brenda Leibowitz, Ronelle Carolissen, and Megan Boler, 40–54. New York: Routledge.

Brown, Michael P. 1997. *RePlacing Citizenship: AIDS Activism and Radical Democracy*. New York: Guildford Press.

Brown, Rachel H. 2016. "Re-examining the Transnational Nanny: Migrant Carework beyond the Chain." *International Journal of Feminist Politics* 18 (2): 210–29.

CAC (Caregivers Action Centre). 2012. "About Us." http://caregiversactioncentre.org /about-us/.

———. 2018. "About Us." https://caregiversactioncentre.org/about-us/.

CAC (Caregivers Action Centre), CCDWR (Vancouver Committee for Caregivers and Domestic Workers Rights), MWAC (Migrant Workers Alliance for Change), and CCESO (Care Workers Connections, Education and Support Organization). 2020. *Behind Closed Doors: Exposing Migrant Care Worker Exploitation During COVID-19*. https://migrantrights.ca/wp-content/uploads/2020/10/Behind-Closed-Doors _Exposing-Migrant-Care-Worker-Exploitation-During-COVID19.pdf.

CADIW (Committee Against the Deportation of Immigrant Women). 1977. Position Paper. CADIW position papers, box 10-001-S1-F629, Canadian Women's Movement Archives, University of Ottawa.

———. 1978. Letter of Solicitation. CADIW personal correspondence, box 10-001-S1-F629, Canadian Women's Movement Archives, University of Ottawa.

Calliste, Agnes. 1989. "Canada's Immigration Policy and Domestics from the Caribbean: The Second Domestics Scheme." In *Race, Class, Gender: Bonds and Barriers*, edited by Jesse Vorst, 131–48. Toronto, ON: Between the Lines.

———. 1992. "Women of 'Exceptional Merit': Immigration of Caribbean Nurses to Canada." *Canadian Journal of Women and the Law* 6:85–102.

Canada Manpower and Immigration. 1966. *White Paper on Immigration*. Ottawa: Queens Printer.

Carens, Joseph. 2013. *The Ethics of Immigration*. Oxford: Oxford University Press.

Catungal, John Paul. 2017. "Toward Queer(er) Futures: Proliferating the 'Sexual' in Filipinx Canadian Studies." In *Diasporic Intimacies: Queer Filipinos and Canadian Imaginaries*, edited by Robert Diaz, Marissa Largo, and Fritz Pino, 23–40. Evanston, IL: Northwestern University Press.

Change.org. 2021. "Filipina Careworkers Deserve Rights, Protection and Dignity During and Beyond COVID-19." https://www.change.org/p/filipina-care-workers-deserve -right-protection-and-dignity-during-and-beyond-covid-19?utm_source=share _petition&utm_medium=custom_url&recruited_by_id=47864c00–2c67–11ec-8dfb -f98bf5d41c5d.

Chavez, Karma. 2013. *Queer Migration Politics: Activist Politics and Coalitional Possibilities.* Urbana: University of Illinois Press.

Chen, Ju-Chen. 2015. "Sunday Catwalk: The Self-Making of Filipino Migrant Women in Hong Kong." In *The Age of Asian Migration: Continuity, Diversity and Susceptibility,* vol. 2, edited by Yuk Wah Chan, Heidi Fung, and Grazyna Szymanska-Matusiewicz, 44–66. Newcastle upon Tyne: Cambridge Scholars Publishing.

Chin, Christine. 1998. *In Service and Servitude: Foreign Domestic Workers and the Malaysian "Modernity" Project.* New York: Columbia University Press.

Cho, Jennifer, Kimberlé Crenshaw, and Leslie McCall. 2013. "Toward a Field of Intersectionality Studies: Theory, Applications, and Praxis." *Signs* 38 (4): 785–810.

Chowdhury, Elora Halim, and Liz Philipose. 2016. Introduction to *Dissident Friendships: Feminism, Imperialism, and Transnational Solidarity,* edited by Elora Halim Chowdhury and Liz Philipose, 1–10. Urbana: University of Illinois Press.

City News. 2007. "Suspect in Mississauga Maid Murder Was Just Days Away from Leaving the Country." December 18. https://toronto.citynews.ca/2007/12/18/suspect -in-mississauga-maid-murder-was-just-days-away-from-leaving-the-country/.

Cleto, Petronilla. 2011. "A New and Groundbreaking Force: Binnadang-Migrante First General Assembly." *Philippine Reporter Community Opinion and Analysis,* November 11.

Coloma, Roland. 2008. "Border Crossing Subjectivities and Research: Through the Prisms of Feminists of Color." *Race, Ethnicity, Education* 11 (1): 11–27.

Coloma, Roland, Bonnie McElhinny, Ethel Tungohan, John Paul Catungal, and Lisa Davidson, eds. 2012. *Filipinos in Canada: Disturbing Invisibility.* Toronto, ON: University of Toronto Press.

Combahee River Collective. 1983. "The Combahee River Collective Statement." In *Home Girls: A Black Feminist Anthology,* edited by Barbara Smith, 264–74. New Brunswick, NJ: Rutgers University Press.

Constable, Nicole. 1997. *Maid to Order in Hong Kong: Stories of Filipina Migrant Workers.* Ithaca, NY: Cornell University Press.

———. 2000. "Dolls, T-Birds, and Ideal Workers." In *Home and Hegemony: Domestic Service and Identity Politics in South and Southeast Asia,* edited by Kathleen M. Adams and Sara Dickey, 221–48. Ann Arbor: University of Michigan Press.

———. 2009. "Migrant Workers and the Many States of Protest in Hong Kong." *Critical Asian Studies* 41 (1): 143–64.

———. 2014. *Born out of Place: Migrant Mothers and the Politics of International Labour.* Berkeley: University of California Press.

———. 2020. "Tales of Two Cities: Legislating Pregnancy and Marriage among Foreign Domestic Workers in Singapore and Hong Kong." *Journal of Ethnic and Migration Studies* 46 (10): 3491–507.

Courville, Sasha, and Nicola Piper. 2004. "Harnessing Hope through NGO Activism." *Annals of the American Academy of Political and Social Science* 592 (1): 39–61.

Cusipag, Ruben, and Maria Corazon Buenafe. 1993. *Portrait of Filipino Canadians in Ontario (1960–1990)*. Etobicoke, ON: Kalayaan Media.

Daenzar, Patricia M. 1997. "An Affair between Nations: International Relations and the Movement of Household Service Workers." In *Not One of the Family: Foreign Domestic Workers in Canada*, edited by Abigail Bakan and Daiva Stasiulis, 89–118. Toronto, ON: University of Toronto Press.

de Leon, Conely. 2013. "Family Separation and Reunification among Former Filipina Migrant Mothers and Their Two Daughters in Two Canadian Cities." In *When Care Work Goes Global: Locating the Social Relations of Domestic Work*, edited by Wenona Giles, Valerie Preston, and Mary Romero, 139–58. London: Routledge.

———. 2018. "Exhaustion, Blood and Sweat: Transnational Practices of Care and Emotional Labor among Filipino Kin Networks." PhD dissertation, York University. https://yorkspace.library.edu.

Devashayam, Theresa. 2010. "Placement and/or Protection? Singapore's Labor Policies and Practices for Temporary Women Migrant Workers." *Journal of the Asia-Pacific Economy* 15 (1): 45–58.

Dilts, Andrew, and Harsha Walia. 2016. "Dismantle and Transform: On Abolition, Decolonization and Insurgent Politics." *Abolition Journal*, May 22. https://abolitionjournal.org/dismantle-and-transform/.

Doolittle, Robyn, and Jim Wilkes. 2007. "Slain Maid Had Safety Fears." *Toronto Star,* October 4. https://www.thestar.com/news/gta/2007/10/04/slain_maid_had_safety_fears.html.

Dyer, Hannah, and Casey Mecija. 2019. "Leaving to Love: Filipina Caregivers and the Queer Kinship of Transnational Childcare." *World Futures* 74 (7–8): 542–58.

England, Kim. 2017. "Home, Domestic Work and the State: The Spatial Politics of Domestic Workers Activism." *Critical Social Policy* 37 (3): 367–85.

Epstein, Rachel. 1980. "'I Thought There Was No More Slavery in Canada': West Indian Domestic Workers on Employment Visas." *Canadian Women's Studies* 2 (1): 1–14.

Eric, Josephine. 2012. "The Rites of Passage of Filipinos in Canada: Two Migration Cohorts." In *Filipinos in Canada: Disturbing Invisibility*, edited by Roland Coloma, Bonnie McElhinny, Ethel Tungohan, John Paul Catungal, and Lisa Davidson, 123–41. Toronto, ON: University of Toronto Press.

Fabregas, Rafael. 2010. "Remember Juana Tejada: 1969–2009." *Philippine Daily Inquirer*. March 16. http://opinion.inquirer.net/inquireropinion/letterstotheeditor/view/20100316-258959/Remembering-Juana-Tejada-1969–2009.

Fine, Michael, and Joan Tronto. 2020. "Care Goes Viral: Care Theory and Research Confront the Global COVID-19 Pandemic." *International Journal of Care and Caring* 4 (3): 301–9.

Fish, Jennifer. 2017. *Domestic Workers of the World Unite! A Global Movement for Dignity and Human Rights*. New York: NYU Press.

Francisco-Menchavez, Valerie. 2018. *The Labour of Care: Filipina Migrants and Transnational Families in the Digital Age*. Urbana: University of Illinois Press.

Fresnoza-Flot, Asuncion. 2010. "The Catholic Church in the Lives of Irregular Migrants in Italy: Identity Formation, Empowerment, and Social Control." *Asia Pacific Journal of Anthropology* 11 (3–4): 345–61.

Fudge, Judy. 1997. "Little Victories and Big Defeats: The Rise and Fall of Collective Bargaining Rights for Domestic Workers in Ontario." In *Not One of the Family: Foreign Domestic Workers in Canada,* edited by Abigail Bakan and Daiva Stasiulis, 119–46. Toronto, ON: University of Toronto Press.

Fujii, Lee Ann. 2018. *Interviewing in Social Science Research: A Relational Approach.* London: Routledge.

GAATW (Global Alliance Against Traffic in Women). 2022. "TWC2 Celebrates International Migrants Day." Global Alliance Against Traffic in Women E-Bulletin. January 17. https://www.gaatw.org/resources/e-bulletin/1137-twc2-celebrates-international-migrants-day.

Gabriela-ON. 2021. Filipina Caregivers during COVID-19 Policy Brief. https://drive.google.com/file/d/15HtdiWHJQCDcouYiHBNSo-iCvvHAL-L4/view.

Gilligan, Carol. 1982. *In a Different Voice.* Cambridge, MA: Harvard University Press.

Gilliland, Julia. 2008. "Permanent Worker, Temporary Resident: Media Representations of Canada's Live-in Caregiver Program." MA thesis, University of Victoria. https://dspace.library.uvic.ca.

Goli, Maximilian. 2009. "The Philippine Women of Canada's Live-In Caregiver Program." MA thesis, Simon Fraser University. https://summit.sfu.ca/item/9542.

Grain, Kari. 2022. *Critical Hope: How to Grapple with Complexity, Lead with Purpose, and Cultivate Transformative Social Change.* Berkeley, CA: North Atlantic Books.

Green, Joyce. 2017. "The Impossibility of Citizenship Liberation for Indigenous People." In *Citizenship in Transnational Perspective: Australia, Canada, New Zealand,* edited by Jatinder Mann, 175–88. New York: Palgrave.

Guevarra, Anna. 2010. *Marketing Dreams, Manufacturing Heroes: The Transnational Labor Brokering of Filipino Workers.* New Brunswick, NJ: Rutgers University Press.

Hancock, Adam. 2022. "Singapore Migrant Workers Labour under COVID Curbs." *Al Jazeera,* January 30. https://www.aljazeera.com/news/2022/1/30/singapore-migrant-workers-covid-curbs.

Hapal, Karl. 2021. "The Philippines' COVID-19 Response: Securitizing the Pandemic and Disciplining the Pasaway." *Journal of Current Southeast Asian Affairs* 40 (2): 224–44.

Harding, Sandra. 1987. "Introduction: Is There a Feminist Method?" In *Feminism and Methodology: Social Science Issues,* edited by Sandra Harding, 1–14. Bloomington: Indiana University Press.

Henry, Annette. 1998. *Taking Back Control: African Canadian Women Teachers' Lives and Practices.* Albany: State University of New York Press.

Henry, Frances. 1968. "The West Indian Domestic Scheme in Canada." *Social and Economic Studies* 17 (1): 83–91.

Hochreuther, Eva-Maria. 2019. "Resistance under Repression: The Political Mobilization of Female Migrant Domestic Workers in Lebanon." Master's thesis, Malmö University. http://urn.kb.se/resolve?urn=urn:nbn:se:mau:diva-22868.

Hochschild, Arlie. 2014. "Global Care Chains and Emotional Surplus Value." In *Justice, Politics, and the Family*, edited by Daniel Engster and Tamara Metz, 249–61. New York: Routledge.

HOME (Humanitarian Organization for Migrant Economics). 2019. "About Us." https://www.home.org.sg/about-us.

———. 2022. "Support Migrant Workers in Crisis." https://www.giving.sg/humani tarian-organisation-for-migration-economics/continued_support_for_migrant _community/.

HOME and TWC2 (Transient Workers Count Too). 2020. "Universal Periodic Review of Singapore, 3rd Cycle, 2021." October 12. https://twc2.org.sg/wp-content/uploads /2020/10/Joint_UPR_shadow_report_HOME-TWC2_2020_v3.pdf.

Hong Kong Government. 2022. "Foreign Domestic Helpers: General Policy." September 30. https://www.fdh.labour.gov.hk/en/general_policy.html.

Howlett, Michael. 2000. "Managing the Hollow State: Procedural Policy Instruments and Modern Governance." *Canadian Public Administration* 43 (4): 412–31.

Huang, Shirlena, and Brenda Yeoh. 1996. "Ties That Bind: State Policy and Migrant Female Domestic Workers in Singapore." *GeoForum* 27 (4): 479–96.

Hussen, Ahmed. 2018. "There is and always will be a pathway to permanent residency for domestic workers under our government. Our government will not be shutting down opportunities for domestic workers to become permanent residents." Twitter post, February 15.

Iacovetta, Franca. 1992. *Such Hardworking People: Italian Immigrants in Post-war Toronto*. Kingston, ON: McGill-Queen's University Press.

IDWFED (International Domestic Workers Federation). 2013. "IDWF Congress: Our New Federation Is Born!" *International Domestic Workers Federation News*, October 28. https://idwfed.org/en/activities/idwf-congress-our-new-federation-is-born.

ILO (International Labour Organization). 2011. "C189—Domestic Workers Convention, 2011 (No. 189)." https://www.ilo.org/dyn/normlex/en/f?p=NORMLEXPUB:12100 :0::NO::P12100_ILO_CODE:C189.

———. 2016. "Decent Work for Migrant Domestic Workers: Moving the Agenda Forward." https://www.ilo.org/wcmsp5/groups/public/---ed_protect/---protrav/--- migrant/documents/publication/wcms_535596.pdf.

ILPS (International League of Peoples' Struggles). 2022. "About ILPS." https://ilps.info /en/about-us/.

IMA (International Migrants Alliance). 2008. "About." https://www.wearemigrants.net/.

Intercede. 1992. "Higher Educated 'Caregivers' from Poor Countries Can Come to Canada as Domestics." Press release. Canadian Women's Movement Archives. University of Ottawa.

———. 1994. "Intercede Protests Recommendations to Abolish LCP and Close Canada's Doors to Domestic Workers." *Domestics' Cross-Cultural News: Monthly Newsletter of the Toronto Organization for Domestic Workers' Rights*, October 1994, 1–3. https:// riseuparchive.wpenginepowered.com/wp-content/uploads/2015/09/DCCN-OCT -1994.pdf. Toronto, ON: Intercede.

———. 1999. "Now You Can Call Us from Outside Toronto." *Domestics' Cross-Cultural News: Monthly Newsletter of the Toronto Organization for Domestic Workers' Rights*, November 1999, 2–4. Toronto, ON: Intercede.

Isaac, Allan Punzalan. 2022. *Filipino Time: Affective Worlds and Contracted Labour*. New York: Fordham University Press.

IWworkers. 2011. "In Memory of Peter Leibovitch." *Philippine Reporter Community News and Features*, October 28.

Jacubowski, Lisa Marie. 2003. "Managing Canadian Immigration: Racism, Ethnic Selectivity, and the Law." In *Locating Law: Race, Class, Gender Connections*, edited by Elizabeth Comack, 98–124. Halifax, NS: Fernwood.

Jiang, Zhe, and Marek Korczynski. 2016. "When the 'Unorganizable' Organize: The Collective Mobilization of Migrant Domestic Workers in London." *Human Relations* 69 (3): 813–38.

Joles, Betsy, and Jaime Chiu. 2019. "Domestic Workers Search for Rights amid Pro-democracy Protests." *Al Jazeera*, October 21. https://www.aljazeera.com/features/2019/10/21/domestic-workers-search-for-rights-amid-pro-democracy-protests.

Kelley, Robin D. G. 2002. *Freedom Dreams: The Black Radical Imagination*. Boston: Beacon Press.

Kelly, Philip, Mila Garcia, Enrico Esguerra, and the Community Alliance for Social Justice. 2009. *Explaining the Deprofessionalized Filipino: Why Filipino Immigrants Get Low-Paying Jobs in Toronto*. Toronto, ON: CERIS—The Metropolis Centre.

Kenney, Jason. 2011. "Letter of Support." Caregivers Today Communication Links. FOACC, St. Catharine's, ON.

Keung, Nicholas. 2017a. "Committee Urges Federal Government to Repeal Law That Bans Disabled Immigrants." *Toronto Star*, December 13. https://www.thestar.com/news/immigration/2017/12/13/committee-urges-federal-government-to-repeal-law-that-bans-disabled-immigrants.html.

———. 2017b. "Immigration Backlog Keeps Live-In Caregivers from Their Families Back Home." *Toronto Star*, July 20. https://www.thestar.com/news/immigration/2017/07/20/immigration-backlog-keeps-live-in-caregivers-from-their-families-back-home.html.

———. 2018. "Ottawa Relaxes Restrictions on Immigration Applicants with Disabilities." *Toronto Star*, April 16. https://www.thestar.com/news/immigration/2018/04/16/ottawa-to-relax-restrictions-on-immigration-applicants-with-disabilities.html.

Khan, Sabaa. 2009. "From Labour of Love to Decent Work: Protecting the Human Rights of Caregivers in Canada." *Canadian Journal of Law and Society* 24 (1): 23–44.

Koh, Chiu Yee, Charmian Goh, Kellyn Wee, and Brenda Yeoh. 2017. "Drivers of Migration Policy Reform: The Day Off Policy for Migrant Domestic Workers in Hong Kong." *Global Social Policy* 17 (2): 188–205.

KWFCA (Kitchener-Waterloo Filipino Domestic Workers Association). 2012. "KWFCA." http://kwfca.blogspot.ca/.

Larmour, Sheila. 1993. "Canada Leaves Third World Domestic Workers out in the Cold." *Match News: News about Women and Development*, Spring 1993. Ottawa, ON: Match International Centre.

Larois, Lindsay, Jill Hanley, Manuel Cardona Salamanca, Mostafa Henaway, Nuha Dwaikat Shaer, and Sonia Ben Soltane. 2020. "Engaging Migrant Careworkers: Examining Cases of Exploitation by Recruitment Agencies in Quebec, Canada." *Migration and Border Studies* 6 (1–2): 138–57.

Lawson, Erica. 2013. "The Gendered Working Lives of Seven Jamaican Women in Canada: A Story of 'Here' and 'There.'" *Feminist Formations* 25 (1): 138–56.

Lestari, Eni, and Promise Li. 2019. "Fighting for Migrant Workers in Hong Kong." *Monthly Review: An Independent Socialist Magazine.* https://monthlyreview.org/2019/02/01/fighting-for-migrant-workers-in-hong-kong/.

Li, Promise. 2019. "Hong Kong's Protest Movement Must Stop Ignoring Migrant Workers." Open Democracy. https://www.opendemocracy.net/en/hong-kongs-protest-movement-must-stop-ignoring-migrant-workers/.

Lindio-McGovern, Ligaya. 2007. "Neo-liberal Globalization in the Philippines: Its Impact on Filipino Women and Their Forms of Resistance." *Journal of Developing Societies* 23 (1): 15–35.

———. 2013. *Globalization, Labour Export, and Resistance: A Study of Filipino Domestic Workers in Global Cities.* New York: Routledge.

Lindström-Best, Varpu. 1988. *Defiant Sisters: A Social History of Finnish Immigrant Women in Canada.* Toronto, ON: Multicultural History Society of Ontario.

Lui, Ingrid, Nimisha Vandan, Sara E. Davies, Sophie Harman, Rosemary Morgan, Julia Smith, Clare Wenham, and Karen Ann Grepin. 2021. "'We Also Deserve Help during the Pandemic': The Effect of the COVID-19 Pandemic on Foreign Domestic Workers in Hong Kong." *Journal of Migration and Health* 3. https://doi.org/10.1016/j.jmh.2021.100037.

Macklin, Audrey. 1992. "Foreign Domestic Workers: Surrogate Wives or Mail Order Servant?" *McGill Law Journal* 37:681–760.

Magkaisa Centre. 2021. "Cancel Canada Day." National statement, July 1. https://magkaisacentre.org/2021/07/01/cancel-canada-day/.

Magsumbol, Dani. 2018. "A Peculiar Infrastructure: Privacy in Homes Employing Live-In Care and Domestic Workers." *Society + Space.* https://www.societyandspace.org/articles/a-peculiar-infrastructure-privacy-in-homes-employing-live-in-care-and-domestic-workers.

Mahler, Sarah, and Patricia Pessar. 2001. "Gendered Geographies of Power: Analyzing Gender across Transnational Spaces." *Identities* 7 (4): 441–59.

Mahmood, Saba. 2005. *Politics of Piety: The Islamic Revival and the Feminist Subject.* Princeton, NJ: Princeton University Press.

Manalansan, Martin. 2008. "Queering the Chain of Care Paradigm." *Scholar and Feminist Online* 6 (3): http://www.barnard.edu/sfonline/immigration/manalansan_02.htm.

Matatag. 2021. "Open Letter." https://filipinacareworkers.com/open-letter.html.

Mayberry, Kate. 2019. "Hong Kong's Controversial Extradition Bill Explained." *Al Jazeera*, June 11. https://www.aljazeera.com/news/2019/6/11/hong-kongs-controversial -extradition-bill-explained.

Mbembe, Achille. 2011. *Necropolitics*. Durham, NC: Duke University Press.

McAdam, Doug, and William Sewell. 2001. "Temporality in the Study of Social Movements and Revolution." In *Silence and Voice in the Study of Contentious Politics*, edited by Ron Aminzade et al., 89–125. Cambridge: Cambridge University Press.

McElhinny, Bonnie, Lisa Davidson, John Paul Catungal, Ethel Tungohan, and Roland Coloma. 2012. "Spectres of Invisibility: Filipina/o Labour, Culture, and Youth in Canada." In *Filipinos in Canada: Disturbing Invisibility*, edited by Roland Coloma, Bonnie McElhinny, Ethel Tungohan, John Paul Catungal, and Lisa Davidson, 5–45. Toronto, ON: University of Toronto Press.

Migrante. 2012. "History." http://migranteinternational.org/?page_id=7.

Migrante-Ontario. 2008. *Justice for Juana Tejada*. Toronto, ON: Migrante-Ontario.

Mingol, Irene Comins. 2013. "Philosophical Perspectives on Caring Citizenship." *Peace Review* 25 (3): 406–13.

Miranda, Susana. 2007. "Exploring Themes in the Scholarship on Twentieth Century Domestic Work in Canada and the US." *Left History* 12 (2): 113–29.

Moeran, Brian. 2009. "From Participant Observation to Observant Participation." In *Organizational Ethnography*, edited by Sierk Ybema, Dvora Yanow, Harry Wels, and Frans H. Kamsteeg, 139–55. London: Sage.

Mohanty, Chandra. 1991. "Under Western Eyes: Feminist Scholarship and Colonial Discourses." In *Third World Women and the Politics of Feminism*, edited by Chandra Mohanty, Ann Russo, and Lourdes Torres, 51–80. Bloomington: Indiana University Press.

Moors, Annelies. 2003. "Migrant Domestic Workers: Debating Transnationalism, Identity Politics and Family Relations—a Review Essay." *Comparative Studies in Society and History* 45 (2): 386–94.

Moyal, Henry. 2010. "Key Changes to the LCP as of April 1, 2010." Balita. http://www .balita.ca/2010/04/key-changes-to-the-live-in-caregiver-program-as-of-april-12010/.

Nadasen, Premilla. 2016. *Household Workers Unite: The Untold Story of African American Women Who Built a Movement*. Boston: Beacon Press.

NAPWC-BC (National Alliance of Philippine Women in Canada–British Columbia). 2016. Sinigang Sundays Study Series. https://pwcofbc.wordpress.com/2016/06/29 /study-series/.

NAPWC-ON (National Alliance of Philippine Women in Canada-Ontario). 2008. Conference, "Filipino Community and Beyond: Towards Full Participation in a Multicultural and Multi-ethnic Canada." University of Toronto.

Nasol, Katherine, and Valerie Francisco-Menchavez. 2021. "Filipino Home Care Workers: Invisible Frontline Workers in the COVID-19 Crisis in the United States." *American Behavioural Scientist* 65 (10): 1365–83.

Nedelsky, Jennifer. 2011. *Law's Relations: A Relational Theory of Self, Autonomy, and Law.* Oxford: Oxford University Press.

Olayta, Terry. 2009. "Caregiver Resource Centre." Bill 210: Employment Protection for Foreign Nationals Act (Live-In Caregivers and Others). December 2, 2009. Standing Committee on the Legislative Assembly, Ottawa, ON. https://www.ola.org/en/legislative-business/committees/legislative-assembly/parliament-39/transcripts/committee-transcript-2009-dec-02#P530_123377.

One Billion Rising. 2016. "One Billion Rising Philippines 2017 Launches." https://www.onebillionrising.org/37719/one-billion-rising-philippines-2017-launches/.

Ong, Aihwa. 2009. "A Bio-cartography: Maids, Neo-slavery, and NGOs." In *Migrations and Mobilities: Citizenship, Borders, and Gender,* edited by Seyla Benhabib and Judith Resnick, 157–86. New York: New York University Press.

———. 2011. "Translating Gender Justice in Southeast Asia: Situated Ethics, NGOs, and Bio-welfare." *Journal of Women in the Middle East and the Islamic World* 9:26–48.

Parrenas, Rhacel. 2000. "Migrant Filipina Domestic Workers and the International Division of Reproductive Labour." *Gender & Society* 14 (4): 560–80.

———. 2001. *Servants of Globalization: Women, Migration and Domestic Work.* Stanford, CA: Stanford University Press.

———. 2005. *Children of Global Migration: Transnational Families and Gendered Woes.* Stanford, CA: Stanford University Press.

———. 2013. "The Gender Revolution in the Philippines: Migrant Mothering and Social Transformations." In *How Immigrants Impact Their Homelands,* edited by Susan Eckstein and Adil Najam, 191–212. Durham, NC: Duke University Press.

———. 2021. "The Mobility Pathways of Domestic Workers." *Journal of Ethnic and Migration Studies* 47 (1): 3–24.

Parrenas, Rhacel, Krittya Kantachote, and Rachel Silvey. 2021. "Soft Violence: Migrant Domestic Worker Precarity and the Management of Unfree Labour in Singapore." *Journal of Ethnic and Migration Studies* 47 (20): 4671–87.

Perez, Nancy. 2017. "Migrant Domestic Workers and Shifting Strategies of Organizing." *Sociology Compass* 11 (6): 1–9.

Pero, Davide, and John Solomos. 2010. "Introduction to Migrant Politics and Mobilization: Exclusions, Engagement, and Incorporation." *Ethnic and Racial Studies* 33 (1): 1–18.

Perry, Adele. 1997. "'Fair Ones of a Purer Caste': White Women and Colonialism in Nineteenth-Century British Columbia." *Feminist Studies* 23 (3): 501–24.

Philippine Reporter. 2008a. "Caregivers Want Landed Status." Community News and Features, February 1.

———. 2008b. "Heat's on Ottawa: Philippine Solons Ask Canada to Help End Human Rights Abuses in RP." Community News and Features, April 16.

———. 2009. "Juana Tejada's Courage Inspired Us All." Community News and Features, March 11.

Piper, Nicola. 2005. "Rights of Foreign Domestic Workers: Emergence of Transnational and Transregional Solidarity?" *Asian and Pacific Migration Journal* 14 (1–2): 97–119.

———. 2006. "Migrant Worker Activism in Singapore and Malaysia: Freedom of Association and the Role of the State." *Asian and Pacific Migration Journal* 15 (3): 359–80.

Pratt, Geraldine. 1997. "Stereotypes and Ambivalence: The Construction of Domestic Workers in Vancouver, BC." *Gender, Place, and Culture* 4 (2): 159–77.

———. 2012. *Families Apart: Migrant Mothers and the Conflicts of Labor and Love.* Minneapolis: University of Minnesota Press.

PSA (Philippine Statistics Authority). 2018. "2017 Survey on Overseas Filipinos." https://psa.gov.ph/content/2017-survey-overseas-filipinos-results-2017-survey-overseas-filipinos.

Qi, Tingting. 2010. "Transforming Sisterhood to an All-Relational Solidarity." *Race, Gender, and Class* 17 (3/4): 327–35.

Rafael, Vicente. 1997. "'Your Grief Is Our Gossip': Overseas Filipinos and Other Spectral Presences." *Public Culture* 9 (2): 267–91.

Ramirez, Judith. 1982. "Domestic Workers Organize!" *Canadian Women's Studies* 4 (2): 89–91.

Rice, James J., and Michael J. Prince. 2013. *Changing Politics of Canadian Social Policy.* 2nd edition. Toronto, ON: University of Toronto Press.

Robertson, Phil. 2021. "Philippine General Should Answer for 'Red-Tagging.'" *Human Rights Watch News.* https://www.hrw.org/news/2021/02/10/philippine-general-should-answer-red-tagging.

Rodriguez, Robyn. 2002. "Migrant Heroes: Nationalism, Citizenship, and the Politics of Filipino Migrant Labor." *Citizenship Studies* 6 (3): 341–56.

———. 2010. *Migrants for Export: How the Philippine State Brokers Labor to the World.* Minneapolis: University of Minnesota Press.

———. 2013. "Beyond Citizenship: Emergent Forms of Political Subjectivity among Migrants." *Identities* 20 (6): 738–54.

Root, Lori. 2008. "'I May Be Lost but I Know How to Find My Way': The 'Lived' Experiences of Filipina Live-In Caregivers in the Live-In Caregiver Program in Halifax." MA thesis, Mount Saint Vincent University. dc.msvu.ca:8080/xmlui/handle/10587/349.

Rosenthal, Star. 1979. "Union Maids: Organized Women Workers in Vancouver 1900–1915." *BC Studies* 41 (Spring): 36–55.

Russell, Andrew, and Brian Hill. 2017. "Inadmissible: Canada Rejects Hundreds of Immigrants Based on Incomplete Data, Global News Finds." *Global News*, July 4. https://globalnews.ca/news/3551772/inadmissible-canada-rejects-hundreds-of-immigrants-based-on-incomplete-data-global-investigation-finds/.

Sales, Joy. 2021. "Activism as Essential Work: Filipino Healthcare Workers and Human Rights in the Philippines." *Diplomatic History* 45 (3): 595–603.

Sarol, Joyce. 2011. "Thankful to Canada." *First Ontario Alliance of Caregivers in Canada Newsletter*, January 5.

Sayo, Emmanuel. 2011. "Towards Building a Movement for Social Change: Integrating the Filipino-Canadian Movement into the General Struggle for Social Change and

Transformation in Canada." The Manny Papers. https://www.themannypapers.com /towards-building-a-movement-for-social-change-integrating-the-filipino-canadian -movement-into-the-general-struggle-for-social-change-and-transformation-in -canada.

Schwartz-Shea, Peregrine, and Dvora Yanow. 2011. *Interpretive Research Design: Concepts and Processes*. London: Routledge.

Schwenken, Helen. 2005. "The Challenges of Framing Women Migrants' Rights in the European Union." *Revue Européenne des Migrations Internationales* 21 (1): 177–94.

Sealy, Antonia. 1991. "Situation of a Forgotten Group of Domestic Workers." Personal essay for the Barbados Association, box 10–001-S1-F12222, Canadian Women's Movement Archives, University of Ottawa.

Serafico, Lorina. 1993. "Employment and Immigration Announces Change to Live-In Caregiver Program." *Domestic's Info: A Monthly Newsletter of the Committee for Domestic Worker's and Caregiver's Rights*, June 1993.

Sevenhuijsen, Selma. 1998. *Citizenship and the Ethics of Care: Feminist Considerations on Justice, Morality, and Politics*. London: Routledge.

———. 2003. "The Place of Care: The Relevance of the Feminist Ethic of Care for Social Policy." *Feminist Theory* 4 (2): 179–97.

Sharma, Nandita. 2006. *Home Economics: Nationalism and the Making of Migrant Workers in Canada*. Toronto, ON: University of Toronto Press.

Sharpe, Pamela. 2001. "Gender and the Experience of Migration." In *Women, Gender, and Labor Migration: Historical and Global Perspectives*, edited by Pamela Sharpe, 1–14. London: Routledge.

Showden, Carisa R. 2011. *Choices Women Make: Agency in Domestic Violence, Assisted Reproduction, and Sex Work*. Minneapolis: University of Minnesota Press.

Sim, Amy. 2010. "Lesbianism among Indonesian Women Migrants in Hong Kong." In *Negotiating Gender and Sexuality in Mainland China and Hong Kong*, edited by Ching Yau, 37–50. Aberdeen, HK: Hong Kong University Press.

Simbulan, Grace. 2020. "Dreaming of the Future(s): An Exploration of the Dreams and Resistance of the Obo-Manobo." In *Indigenous Futures and Learnings Taking Place*, edited by Ligia Lopez Lopez and Gioconda Coello, 98–116. London: Routledge.

Su, Zachariah. 2017. "National Interests and Migrants' Rights: The Non-ratification of ICMW by Canada and Singapore." MA thesis, McGill University.

Sun, Yazhou, Kristine Servando, and Rosalie E'Silva. 2022. "Hong Kong's COVID Crackdown Hits Domestic Workers the Hardest." *Bloomberg*, February 25. https:// www.bloomberg.com/news/articles/2022-02-26/hong-kong-s-covid-crackdown -hits-domestic-helpers-the-hardest.

Ticar, Jessica. 2018. "Embodied Transnational Lives among Filipina/o/x Youth in Urban Educational Spaces." *Gender, Place, and Culture* 25 (4): 612–16.

Ticku, Alisha. 2017. "Dreamscapes of Dubai: Geographies and Genealogies of Global City Status." PhD dissertation, York University. https://yorkspace.library.yorku.ca.

Tillu, Jasmine. 2011. "Spatial Empowerment: The Appropriation of Public Spaces by Filipina Domestic Workers in Hong Kong." PhD dissertation, Massachusetts Institute of Technology. https://dspace.mit.edu.

Tiosen, Edna. 2011. "Fil-Core Support Group Presents Miss Caregiver." *Atin Ito Community Round-up*, June 6.

Triadafilopoulos, Triadafilos. 2010. "Global Norms, Domestic Institutions, and the Transformation of Immigration Policy in Canada and the US." *Review of International Studies* 36:169–94.

Tronto, Joan. 2013. *Caring Democracy: Markets, Equality and Justice*. New York: NYU Press.

Tuck, Eve. 2009. "Suspending Damage: A Letter to Communities." *Harvard Educational Review* 79 (3): 409–27.

Tungohan, Ethel. 2013. "Reconceptualizing Motherhood, Reconceptualizing Resistance: Migrant Domestic Workers, Transnational Hyper-maternalism and Activism." *International Feminist Journal of Politics* 15 (1): 39–57.

———. 2016. "Intersectionality and Social Justice: Assessing Activists' Use of Intersectionality through Grassroots Migrants' Organizations in Canada." *Politics, Groups, and Identities* 4 (3): 347–62.

———. 2017. "Advocates Criticize Liberal Government for Keeping Caregivers Apart from Their Families." http://rabble.ca/news/2017/07/advocates-criticize-liberal-government-keeping-caregivers-apart-their-families.

———. 2018. "Living with Compromised Legal Status: Irregular Temporary Foreign Workers in Alberta and the Importance of Imagining, Strategizing, and Inter-provincial Legal Consciousness." *International Migration* 56 (6): 207–20.

Tungohan, Ethel, Rupa Banerjee, Wayne Chu, Petronila Cleto, Conely de Leon, Mila Garcia, Philip Kelly, Marco Luciano, Cynthia Palmaria, and Christopher Sorio. 2015. "After the Live-In Caregiver Program: Filipina Caregivers' Experiences with Uneven and Graduated Citizenship." *Canadian Ethnic Studies* 47 (1): 87–105.

Ty, Eleanor. 2004. *The Politics of the Visible in Asian North American Narratives*. Toronto, ON: University of Toronto Press.

Tyner, James. 2019. *Dead Labour: Toward a Political Economy of Premature Death*. Minneapolis: University of Minnesota Press.

Vanyoro, Kudakwashe. 2021. "Activism for Migrant Domestic Workers in South Africa: Tensions in the Framing of Labor Rights." *Journal for Southern African Studies* 47 (4): 663–81.

Velasco, Pura. 1997. "We Can Still Fight Back: Organizing Domestic Workers in Toronto." In *Not One of the Family: Foreign Domestic Workers in Canada*, edited by Abigail Bakan and Daiva Stasiulis, 157–64. Toronto, ON: University of Toronto Press.

———. 2002. "Filipino Migrant Workers amid Globalization." *Canadian Women's Studies* 21/22 (4): 131–35.

Villarama, Baby Ruth, dir. 2016. *Sunday Beauty Queen* (documentary). Manila: Solar Entertainment Corporation.

Vilog, Ron Bridget T., and Carlos M. Piocos III. 2021. "Community of Care amid Pandemic Inequality: The Case of Filipino Migrant Domestic Workers in the UK, Italy, and Hong Kong." *Asia-Pacific Social Science Review* 21 (2): 184–201.

Walia, Harsha. 2021. *Border and Rule: Global Migration, Capitalism, and the Rise of Racist Nationalism*. Winnipeg, MB: Fernwood.

Weekley, Kathleen. 2004. "Saving Pennies for the State: A New Role for Filipino Migrant Workers?" *Journal of Contemporary Asia* 34 (3): 349–63.

West, David. 2004. "New Social Movements." In *Handbook of Political Theory*, edited by Gerald F. Gaus and Chandran Kukathas, 265–76. Thousand Oaks, CA: Sage.

WIEGO. 2018. "International Domestic Workers' Network." Women in Informal Employment: Globalizing and Organization. https://www.wiego.org/sites/default/files/resources/files/WIEGO_Domestic_Workers_0.pdf.

Wright, Sarah. 2008. "Practicing Hope: Learning from Social Movement Strategies in the Philippines." In *Fear: Critical Geopolitics and Everyday Life*, edited by Rachel Pain and Susan Smith, 223–33. Surrey, UK: Ashgate.

Wui, Ma, Glenda Lopez, and Dina Delia. 2015. "Examining the Struggles for Domestic Workers: Hong Kong and the Philippines as Interacting Sites of Activism." *Philippine Political Science Journal* 36 (2): 190–208.

Yanow, Devorah. 2006. "Thinking Interpretively: Philosophical Presuppositions and the Social Sciences." In *Interpretation and Method: Empirical Research Methods and the Interpretive Turn*, edited by Devora Yanow and Peregrine Schwartz-Shea, 5–26. Armonk, NY: M. E. Sharpe.

Zembylas, Michalinos. 2014. "Affective, Political, and Ethical Sensibilities in Cultivating Critical Hope: Exploring the Notions of 'Critical Emotional Praxis.'" In *Discerning Critical Hope in Educational Practices*, edited by Vivienne Bozalek, Brenda Leibowitz, Ronelle Carolissen, and Megan Boler, 11–25. New York: Routledge.

Zhao, Yan. 2019. "Hong Kong's Domestic Workers Caught Up in Ongoing Protest Clashes." *Hong Kong Free Press*, October 18. https://hongkongfp.com/2019/10/18/hong-kongs-domestic-workers-caught-ongoing-protest-clashes/.

Index

Pinay Quebec, 35, 43, 103, 109
Piper, Nicola, 7, 200–201
points-based immigration system, 27–28, 41
policy. *See* immigration policy
Pollack, Marion, 204
Pratt, Geraldine, 95
prodemocracy movements, 32, 89–90, 150–51
progressive organizations: Gabriela-International, 122, 126–27; in Hong Kong, 139–45; Philippine Women's Centre, 35, 42–43, 48–49, 52, 90–96, 98; structural inequities and, 83–84, 127–28, 129–30. *See also* Caregivers Action Centre (CAC); Gabriela-Ontario; Migrante-Canada network
public space, 137–39, 151, 170–71

Quebec: Association des aides familiales du Québec, 28, 43, 49, 56, 211n15; Caregiver Program and, 56, 196, 214n12; Live-In Caregiver Program bureaucracies and, 39; Pinay Quebec, 35, 43, 103, 109. *See also* Migrante-Canada network
queer communities and partnerships, 90–91, 175, 187, 190

race: COVID-19 inequities and, 204–6; devaluing of care work and, 108, 170; in intersectional advocacy approaches, 91, 93; Live-In Caregiver Program, critiques of, 42–43; within settler-colonial project, 22, 24–27, 29–30. *See also* stigmatization
Ramsaroop, Chris, 202–3
Ramsey, Russell, 34
recruitment practices, abusive, 108–9, 132–33, 168–69
red-tagging, 212n1, 213n3
religious programming: FOACC framework, 51–52, 78; Godmother Network, 68–70; Migrante-Canada programming, 88, 190–91; providing alternative forms of involvement, 53, 76, 96
remuneration, 107–8
Rodriguez, Robyn, 102, 124

Sales, Cholo, 203
Salmon, Carol, 37
Salonga, Bernie, 48
Salvador, Joms, 129
Sana, Ellene, 131–32

Santayo, Edwina Antonio, 136
Sarmiento, Letitia, 85
Saudi Arabia, 154, 172
Sayo, Emanuel, 43, 48–49, 89–90, 94–95
Schwenken, Helen, 6
Sealy, Antonia, 25–26
settlement services, shortcomings of, 66–67
"seven Jamaican mothers" campaign, 29–30, 61
Sharma, Nandita, 27
SIKLAB-BC, 82
Singapore: COVID-19 impacts on workers, 162–63; Flor Contemplacion case, 43–44; geopolitical context, 123–24; informal groups and allies, 155–61; restrictive migrant worker policies, 152–54, 161; traditional organizations, 154–55, 159
soft violence, 152–53
Sol Pajadura, Maria, 87
Somavia, Juan, 103
Sorio, Christopher, 44, 50, 82
Sorio, Connio, 47
South Cotabato Overseas Workers Association (SCOWA), 147
Stasiulis, Daiva, 24, 37, 169
stigmatization: within Caribbean community, 26; of Filipino community, 43, 171; impeding future job prospects, 38–39, 66–67. *See also* race
storytelling, 87
structural inequities: cyclical migration and dependency, 86, 104, 114–16, 118, 129–30, 207; progressive advocacy approaches and, 83–84, 127–28, 129–30
Sunday Beauty Queen, 187

Tacuboy, Alma, 79
Tan, Bridget, 153
Tejada, Juana, 44, 45–47, 61
Temporary Employment Authorization Program, 28
Temporary Foreign Workers Program (TFWP), 53, 200
Tessa (migrant care worker), 173, 179, 180
Tessalona, Tess, 40
theatrical productions, 95, 189
Ticku, Alisha, 167, 186
Tieba, Shiela, 121, 137, 138, 141, 142
Tijuan, Antonio, Jr., 130

ETHEL TUNGOHAN is an assistant professor of politics and social science at York University.

NATIONAL WOMEN'S STUDIES ASSOCIATION /
UNIVERSITY OF ILLINOIS PRESS FIRST BOOK PRIZE

Sex Tourism in Bahia: Ambiguous Entanglements   *Erica Lorraine Williams*
Ecological Borderlands: Body, Nature, and Spirit in Chicana Feminism   *Christina Holmes*
Women's Political Activism in Palestine: Peacebuilding, Resistance,
    and Survival   *Sophie Richter-Devroe*
The Sexual Politics of Empire: Postcolonial Homophobia in Haiti   *Erin L. Durban*
Women's Activist Theatre in Jamaica and South Africa: Gender, Race,
    and Performance Space   *Nicosia M. Shakes*
Care Activism: Migrant Domestic Workers, Movement-Building,
    and Communities of Care   *Ethel Tungohan*

The University of Illinois Press
is a founding member of the
Association of University Presses.

———————————————

University of Illinois Press
1325 South Oak Street
Champaign, IL 61820-6903
www.press.uillinois.edu